NATCHEZ TRACE: TRACKS IN TIME

PHOTOGRAPHS AND TEXT BY

ANDRA WATKINS

WORD HERMIT PRESS LLC
wordhermitpress.com

Natchez Trace: Tracks in Time is a photographic memoir. It chronicles the author's actual experiences with real places along the 444-miles of the Natchez Trace. All photographs were taken by the author and remain under her sole ownership.

ISBN-13: 978-0-9908593-2-1

LIBRARY OF CONGRESS CATALOG NUMBER APPLIED FOR

DEDICATION

For my mother
Linda Ward Watkins

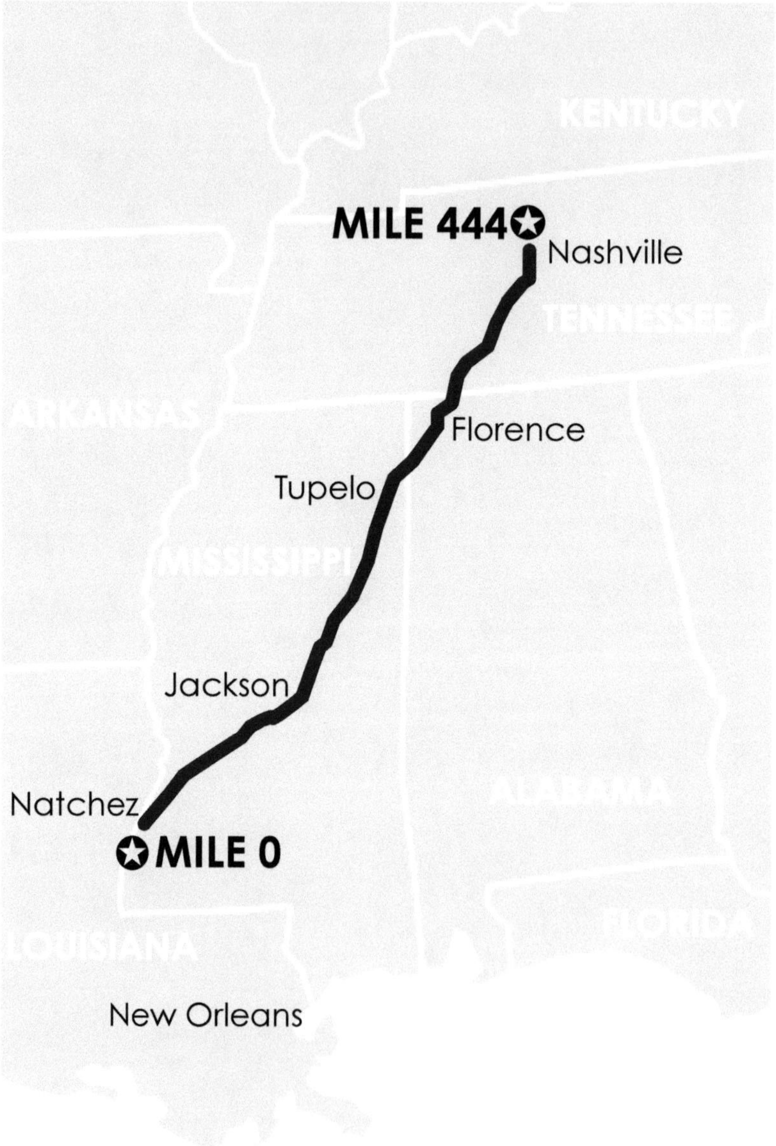

KENTUCKY

MILE 444

Nashville

TENNESSEE

ARKANSAS

Florence

Tupelo

MISSISSIPPI

Jackson

ALABAMA

Natchez

MILE 0

FLORIDA

LOUISIANA

New Orleans

How does a person fill the time when she decides to walk fifteen miles a day for thirty-four days? Five daily hours. Sometimes more. Tottering alongside a highway.

The Natchez Trace is a 10,000-year-old road. It runs from Natchez, Mississippi to Nashville, Tennessee. Its natural ridge line made the perfect migratory route for ancient animals. Every spring and fall, they formed the Natchez Trace as they wove from the Ohio River Valley to the salts licks of Mississippi. When the Native Americans arrived, it was natural for them to build their ceremonial mounds along the Trace and follow their migrating food supply.

In the 1700's and early 1800's, the Natchez Trace was the busiest highway in North America. Boatmen from the Ohio River Valley floated their goods down the Ohio and Mississippi and sold everything in New Orleans or Natchez. To get home, they walked for a month along the 450-mile Natchez Trace. For many, it was only the first leg of a longer journey.

Steam power killed the Natchez Trace. By the twentieth century, its prehistoric pathways were clogged by brambles and consumed by forest. In the 1930's, the federal government reclaimed the Trace, a Depression-era make work project that would cover the primordial dirt with a line of pavement. The historic footpath gave way to cars, trucks and camper vans.

But I wondered what it was like for millennia. Before the paved highway. Pre-car.

From March 1 to April 3, 2014, I walked the Natchez Trace in fifteen-mile-daily increments. Because no provision was made for walkers, I kept to the roadway. To stave off boredom and deflect pain, I took pictures. Of highway and sky. Of garbage. Of spring flowers. Of migrating birds. Of trees and fields and signs.

Wheels grease the path for the traveller. Speed blurs the details of a landscape. On my walk of the Natchez Trace, I documented the minutiae of forgotten Time, when Life moved at the speed of footsteps over hallowed ground. Whether one drives or cycles the Trace today, I hope these images ease the viewer into a slower pace.

To the world beyond the windshield. The motor. Pedals and gears. These pictures are for you.

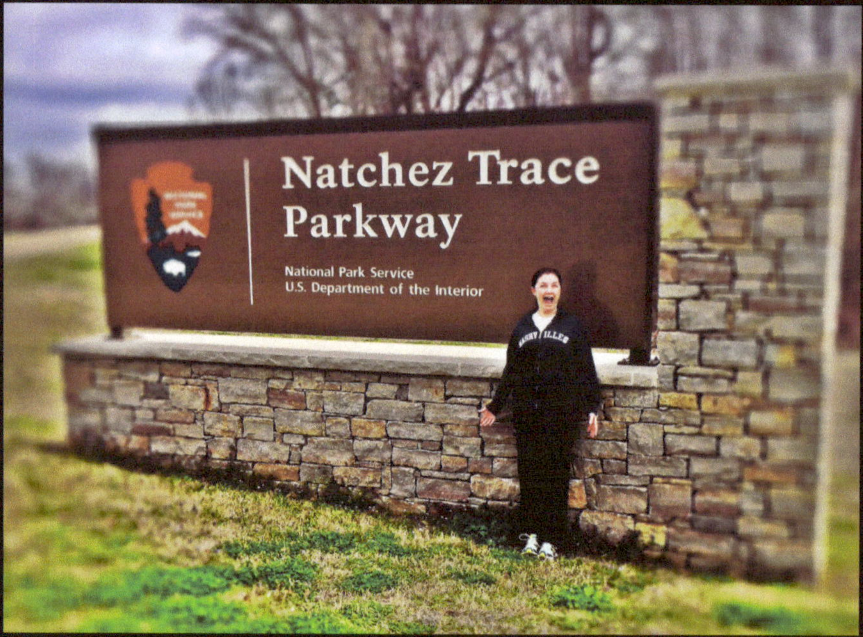

I unfolded a map of the Natchez Trace Parkway. Its twelve sections reached the windshield when I opened it flat. Air from the vent mimicked ripples in the landscape. A bold line of highway snaked north, with eastward turns south of Jackson and near the Alabama state line. Meriwether Lewis stared at me, near the fold at the top of the third section, acknowledging my pilgrimage to his grave.

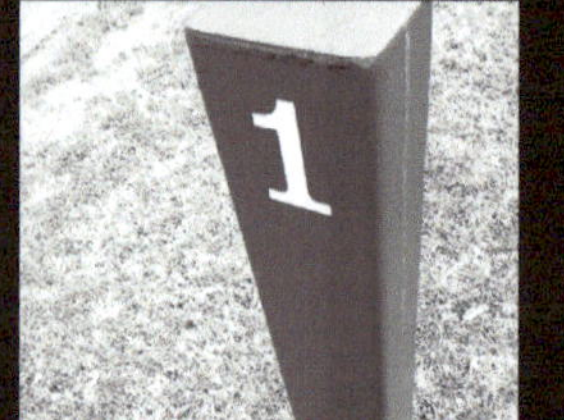

Eternity yawned before me.

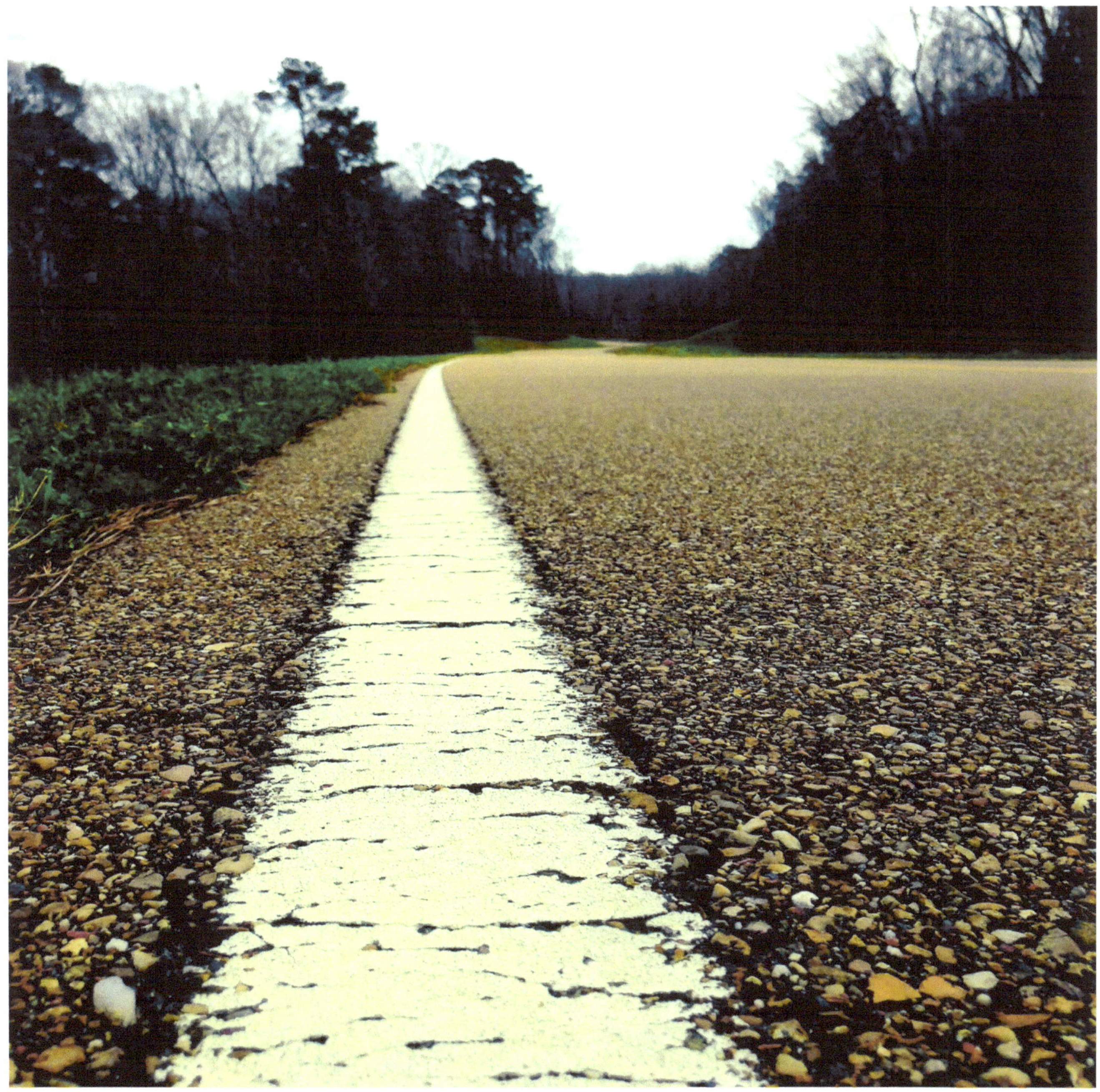

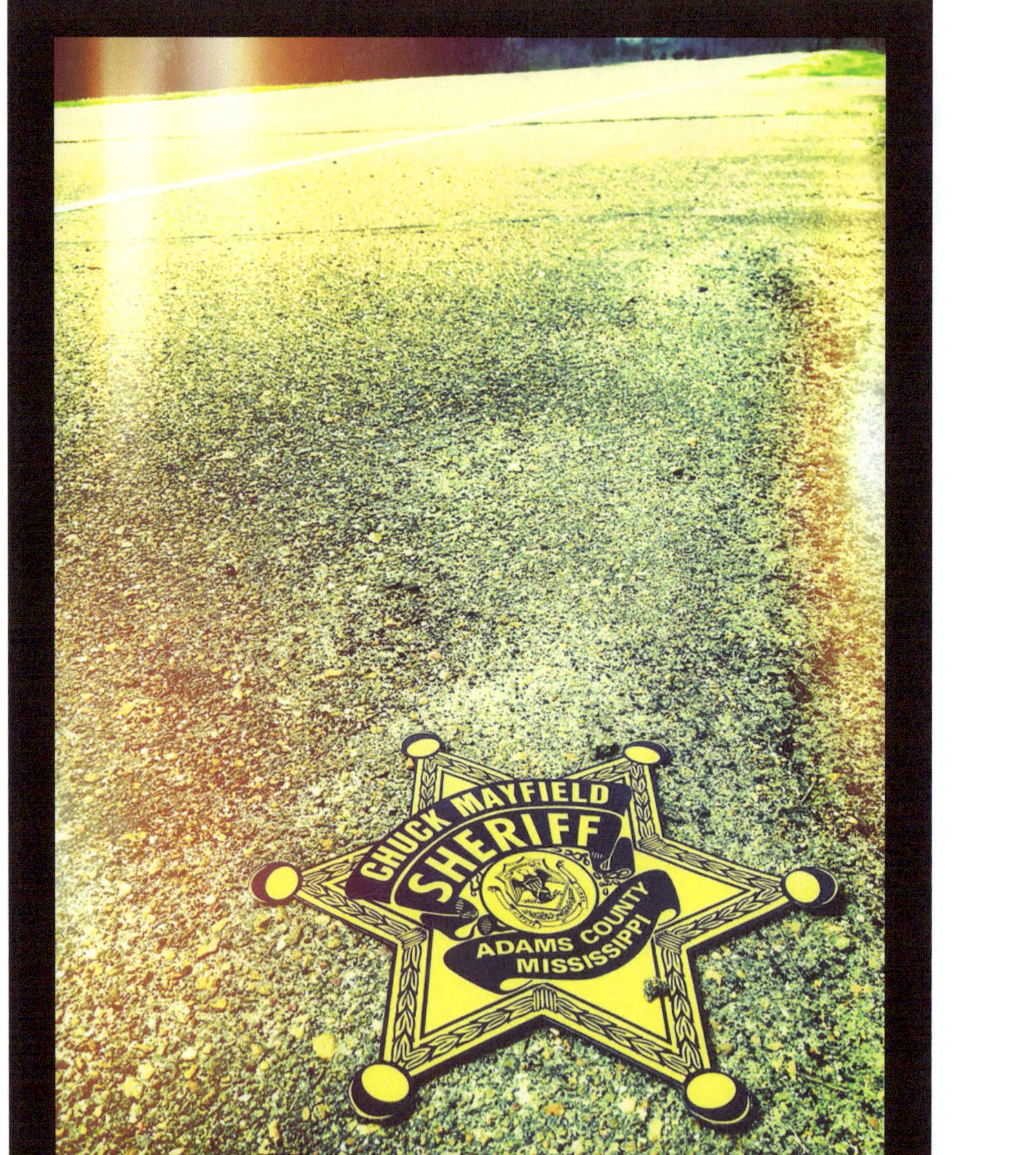
CHUCK MAYFIELD
SHERIFF
ADAMS COUNTY
MISSISSIPPI

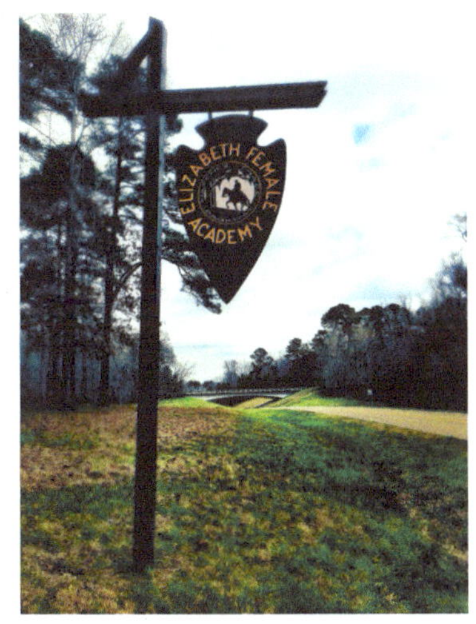
ELIZABETH FEMALE
ACADEMY

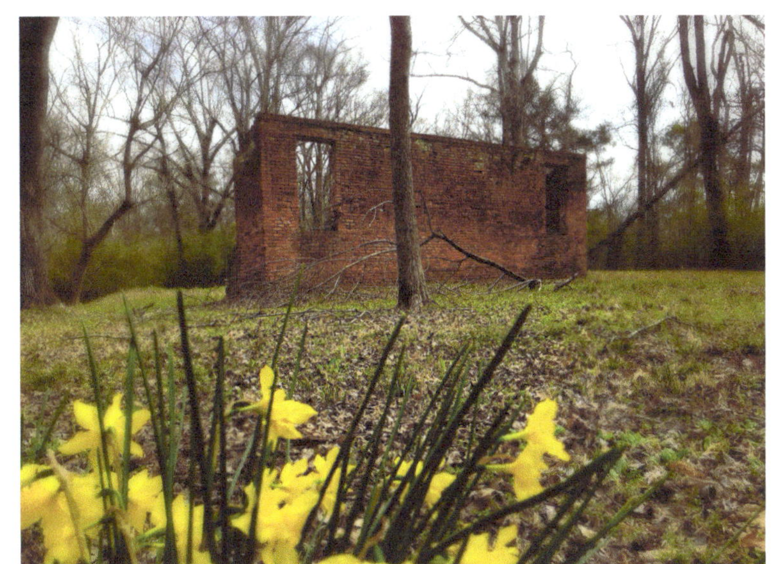

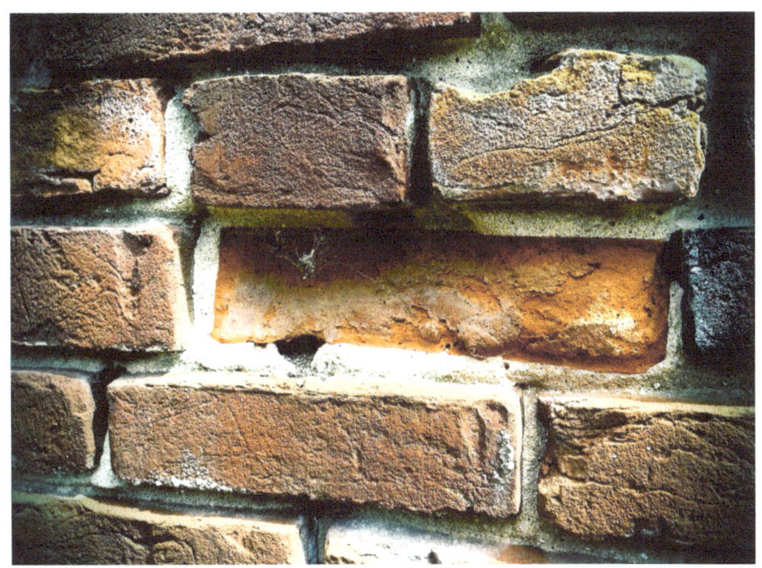

Stands were places along the Natchez Trace that provided a bed and a meal for weary travelers passing through a dangerous and desolate wilderness. They were spaced a day's walk apart, every fifteen to twenty miles all along the 444-miles of the Trace. Although modest and remote, they were a safe refuge and a comfort to the Kaintucks making their way home.

When the Trace died, most of the stands did, too. Grinder's Stand, the infamous place Meriwether Lewis was staying when he mysteriously perished, burned to the ground years ago. All that remains is a stone step.

Mount Locust, located just north of Natchez, Mississippi, is one of two original stands that remain.

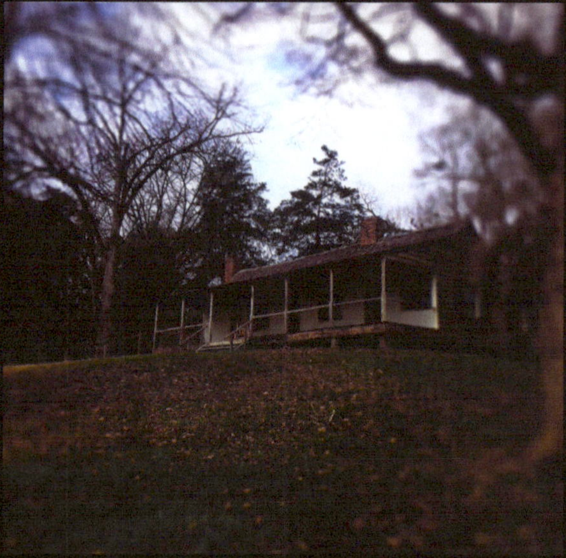

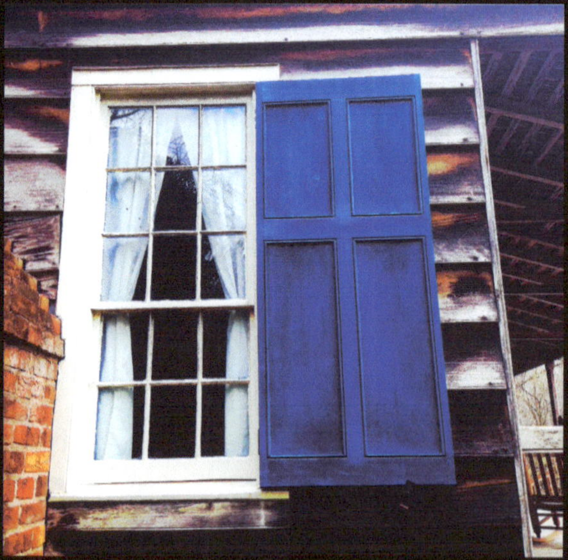

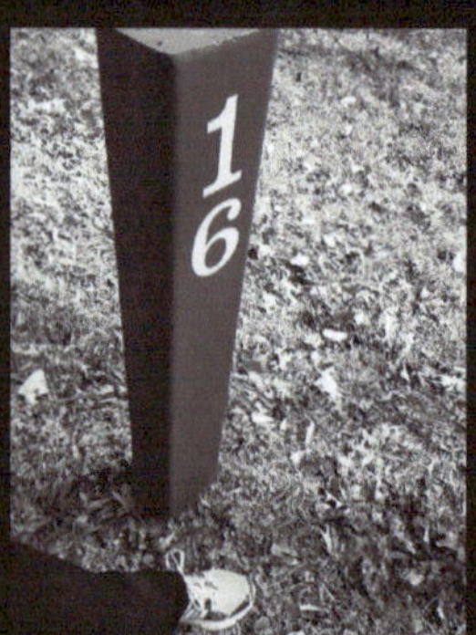

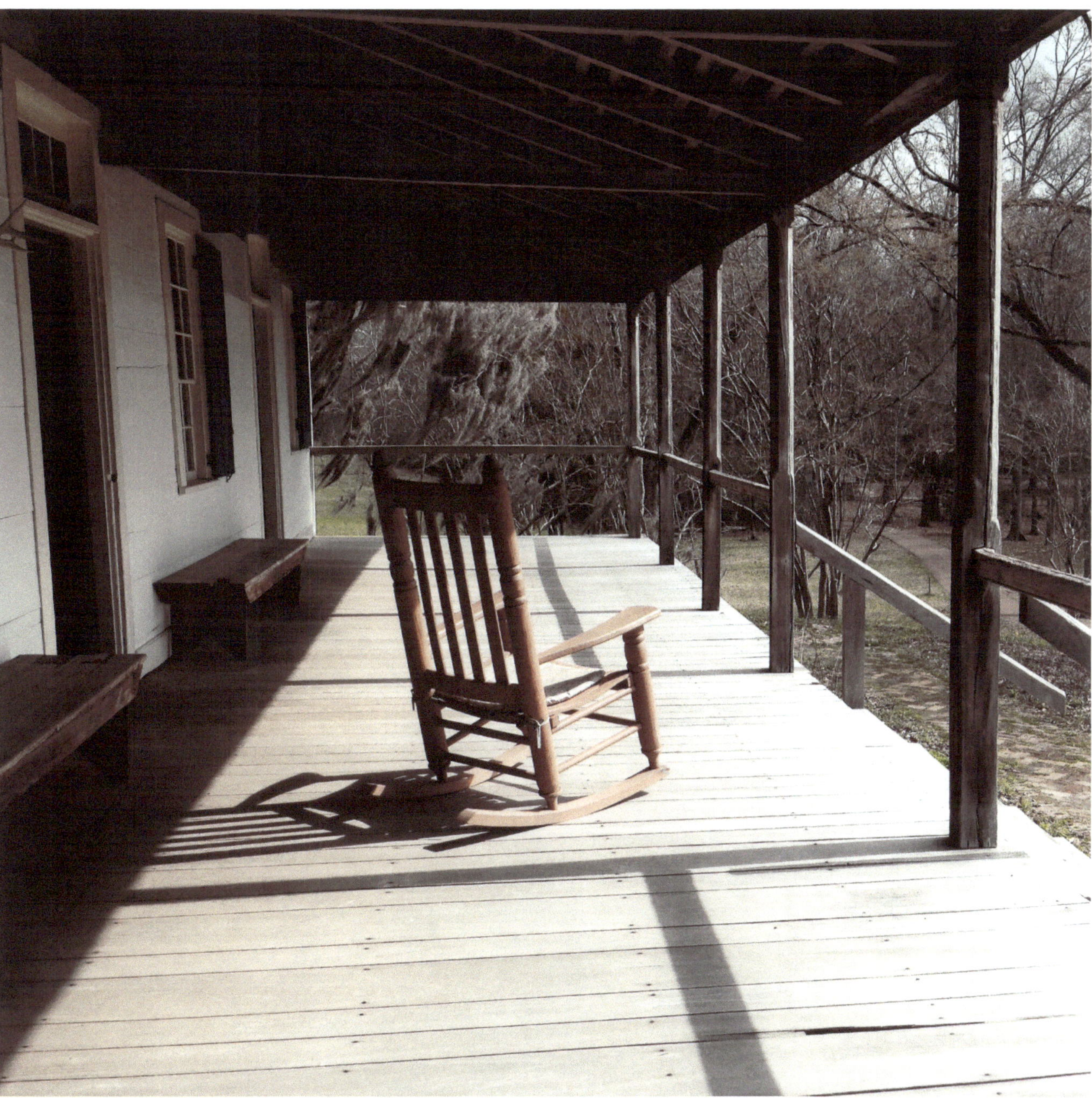

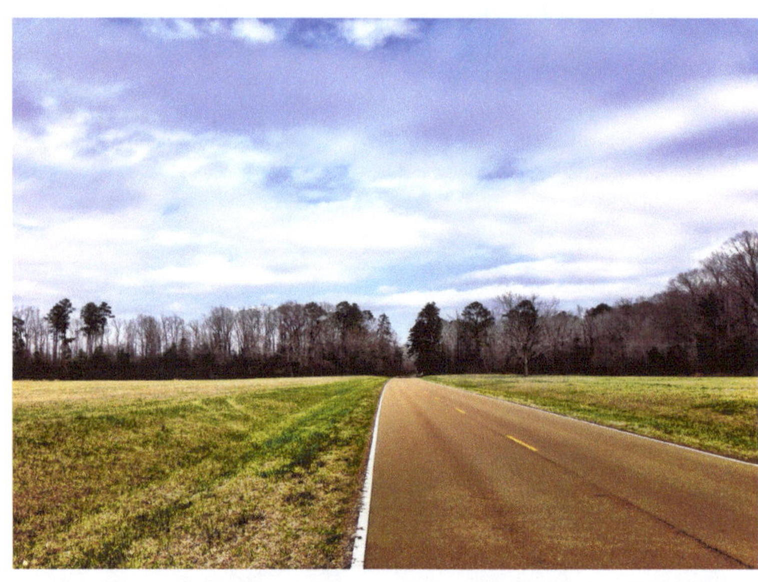

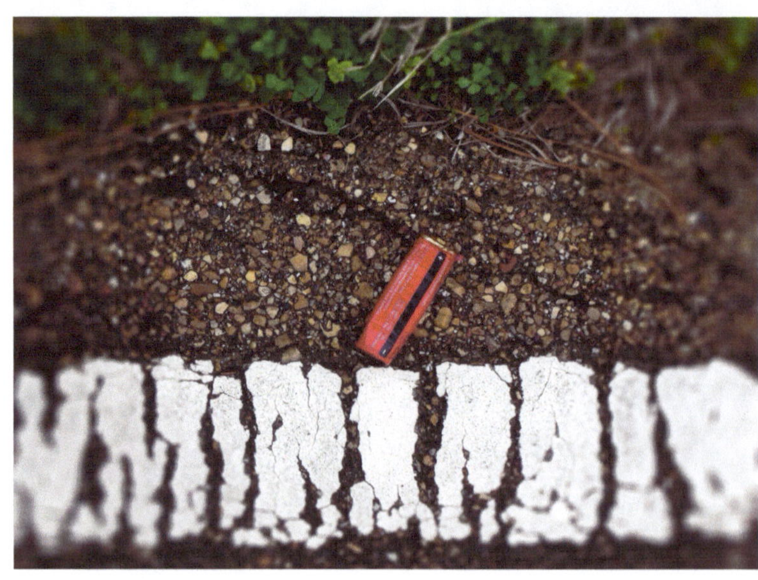

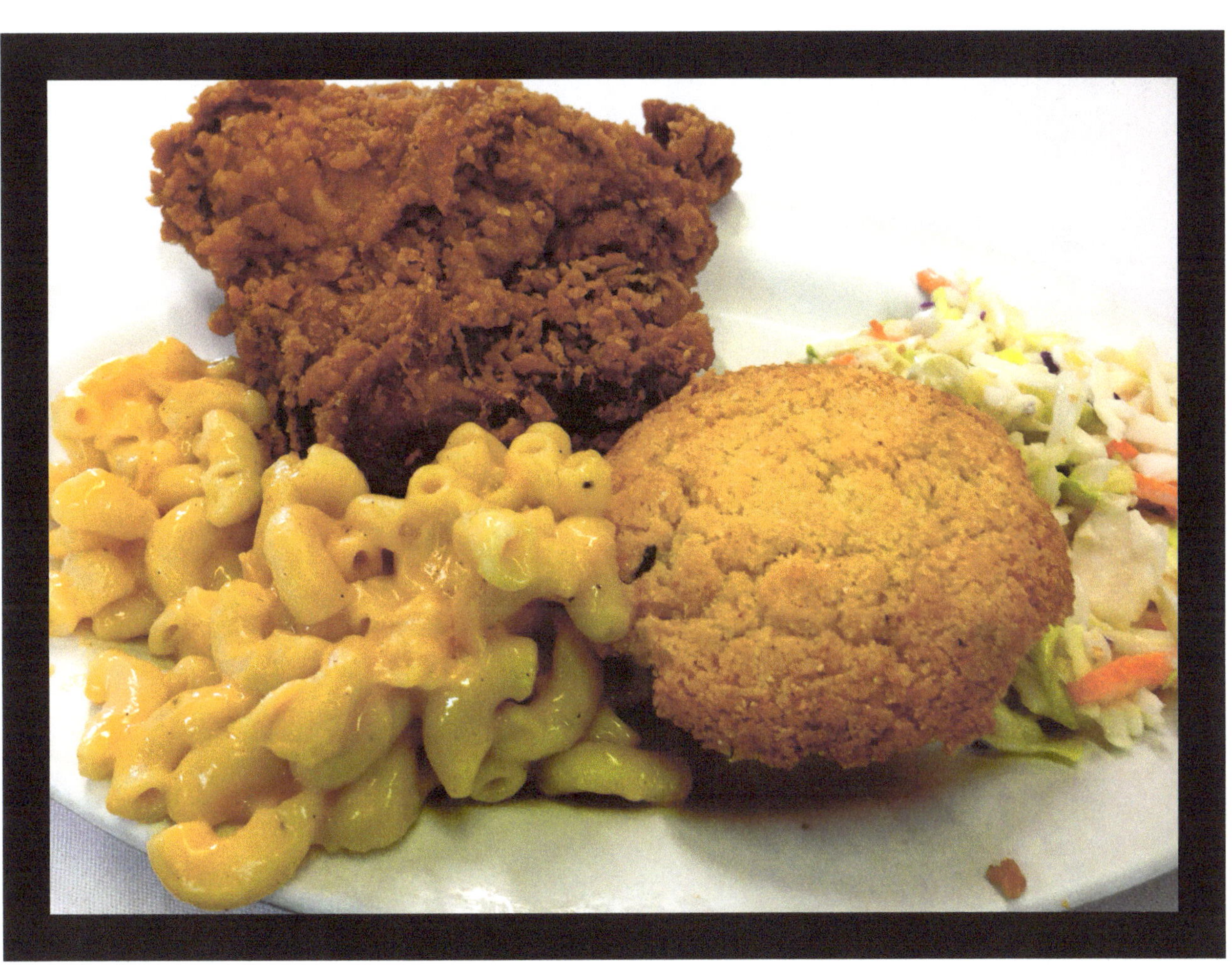

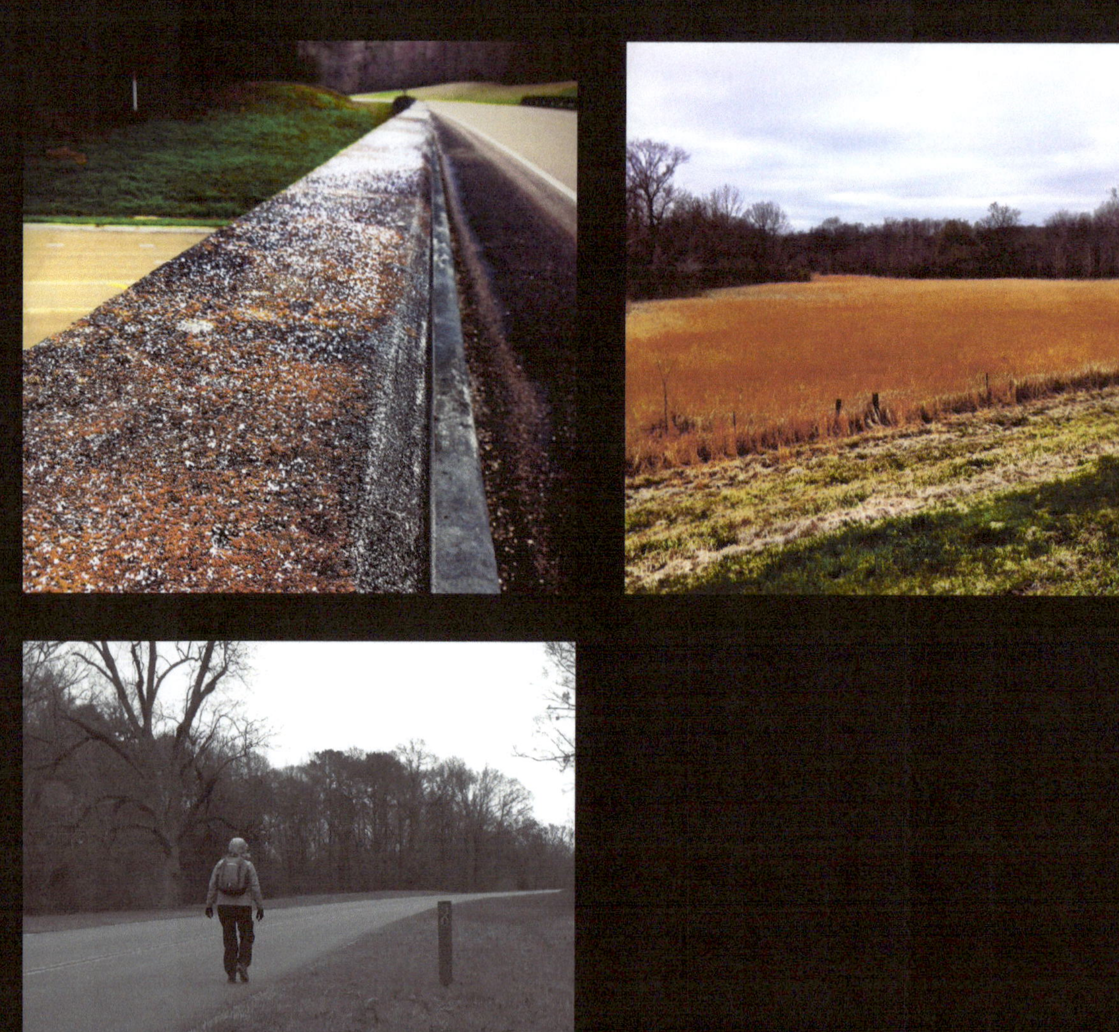

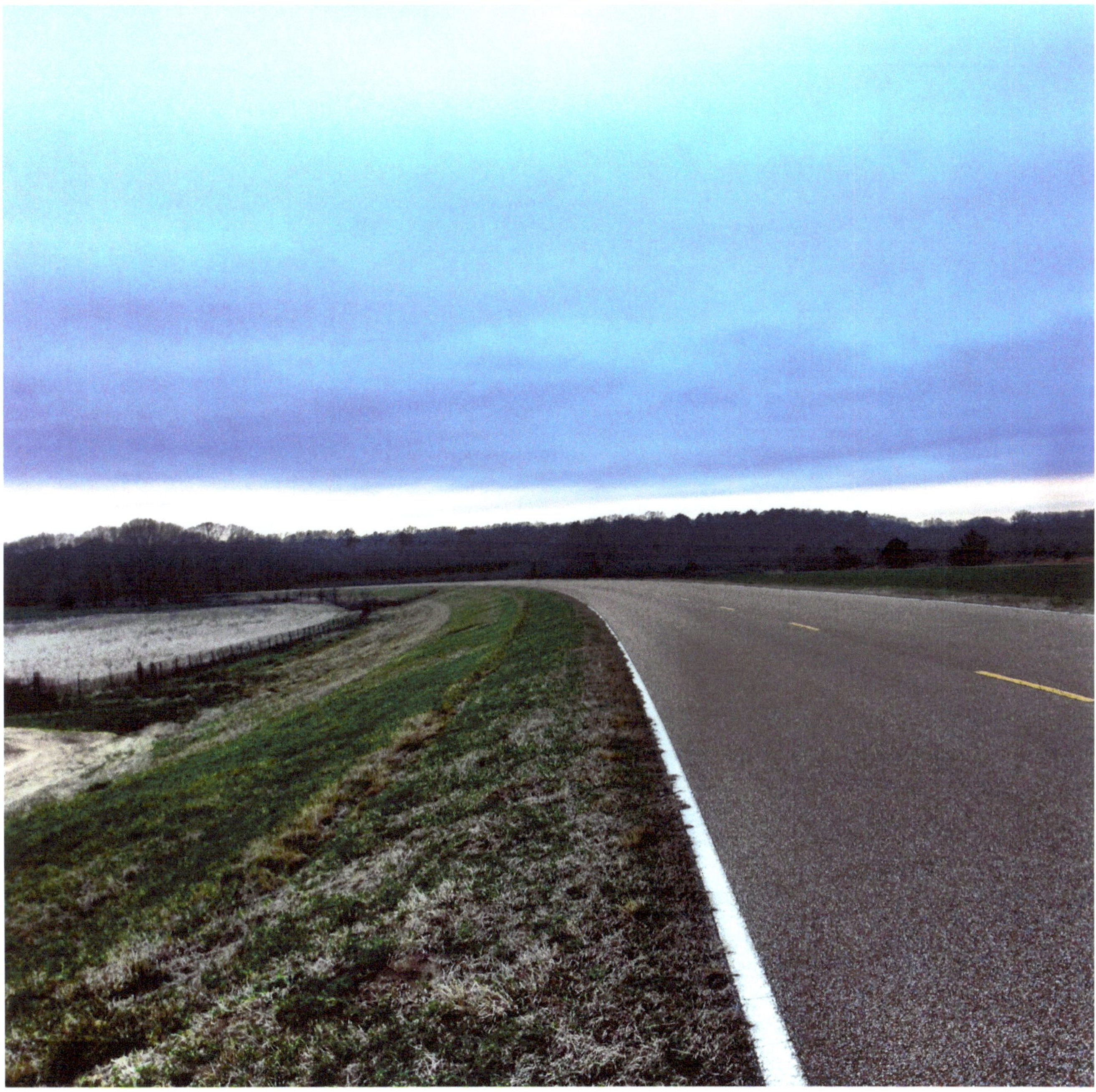

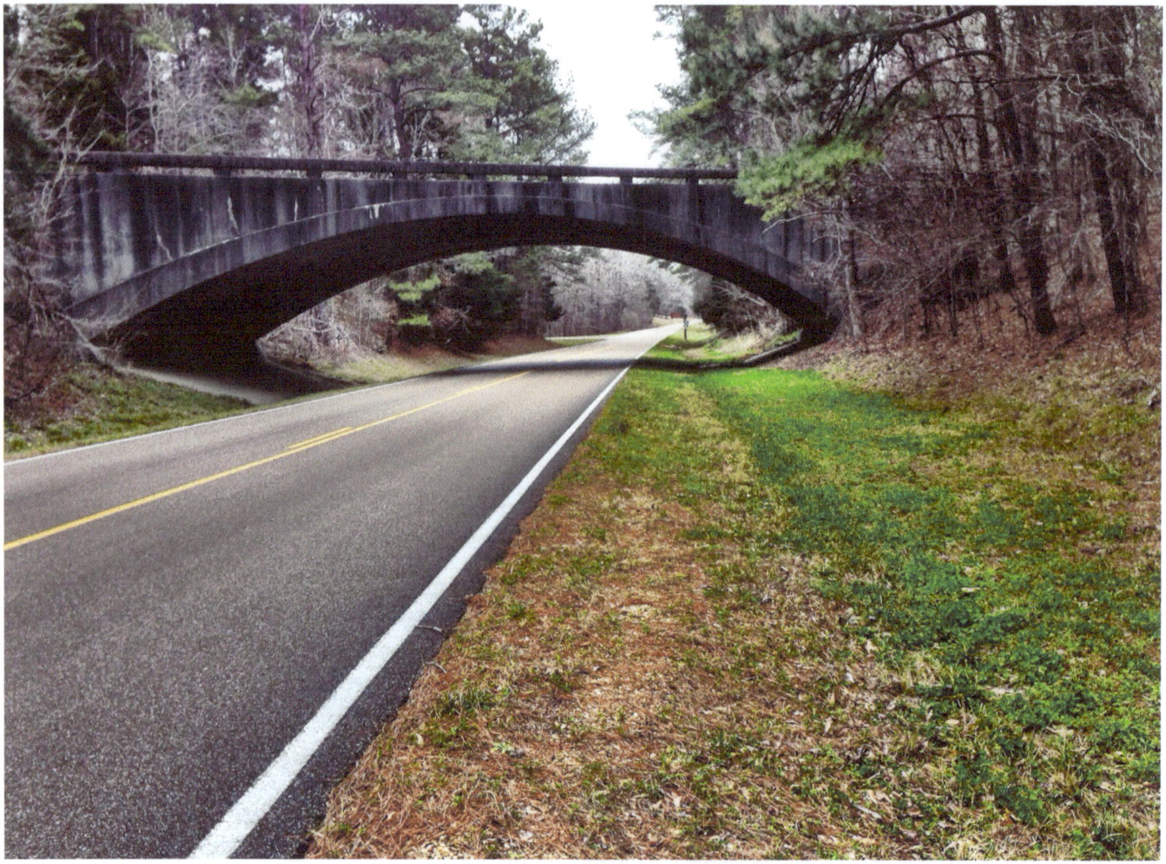

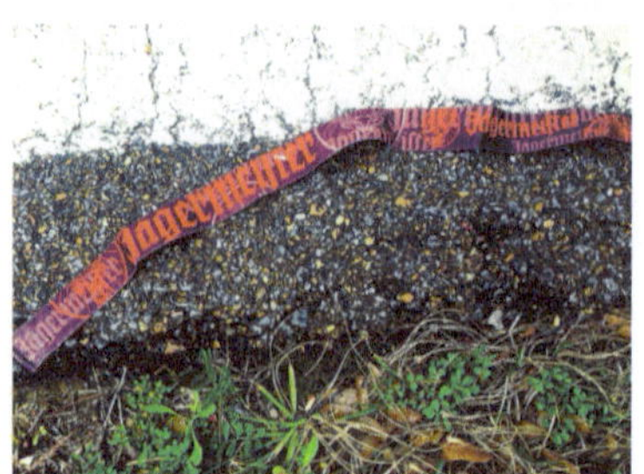

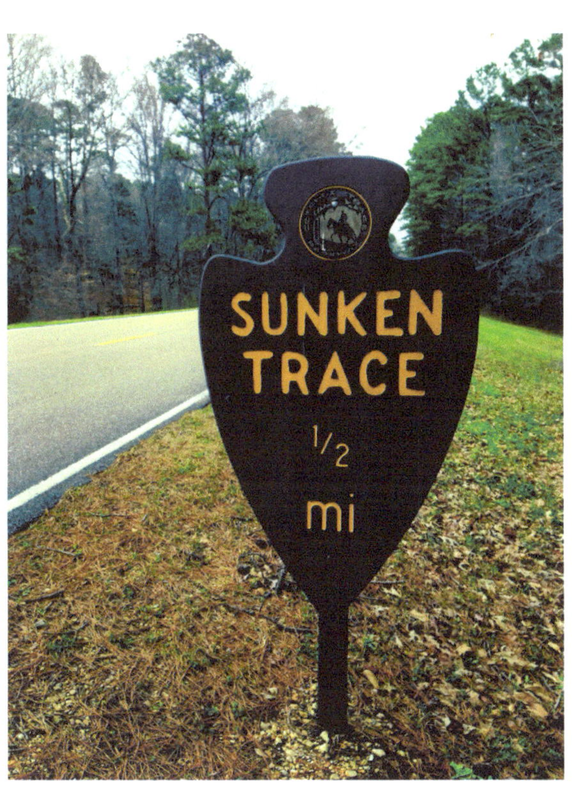
SUNKEN
TRACE
1/2
mi

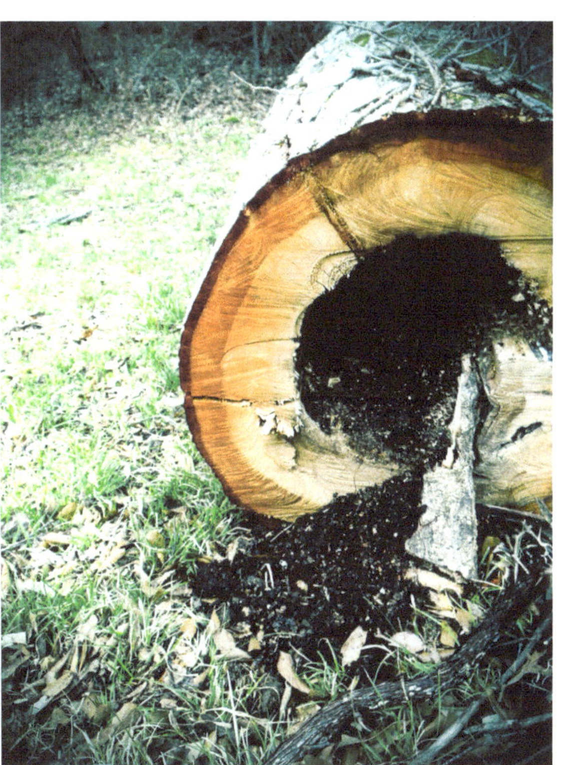

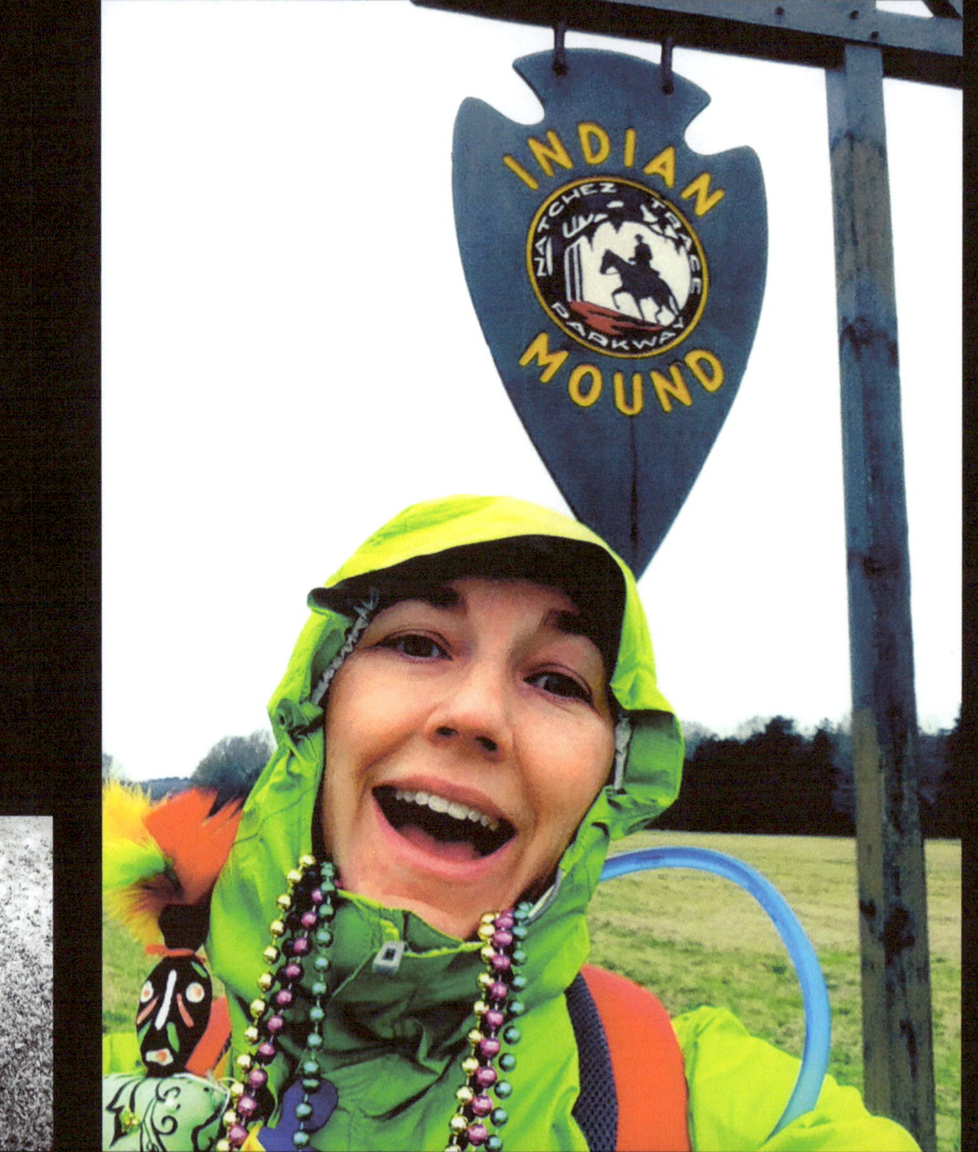
INDIAN
NATCHEZ TRACE
PARKWAY
MOUND

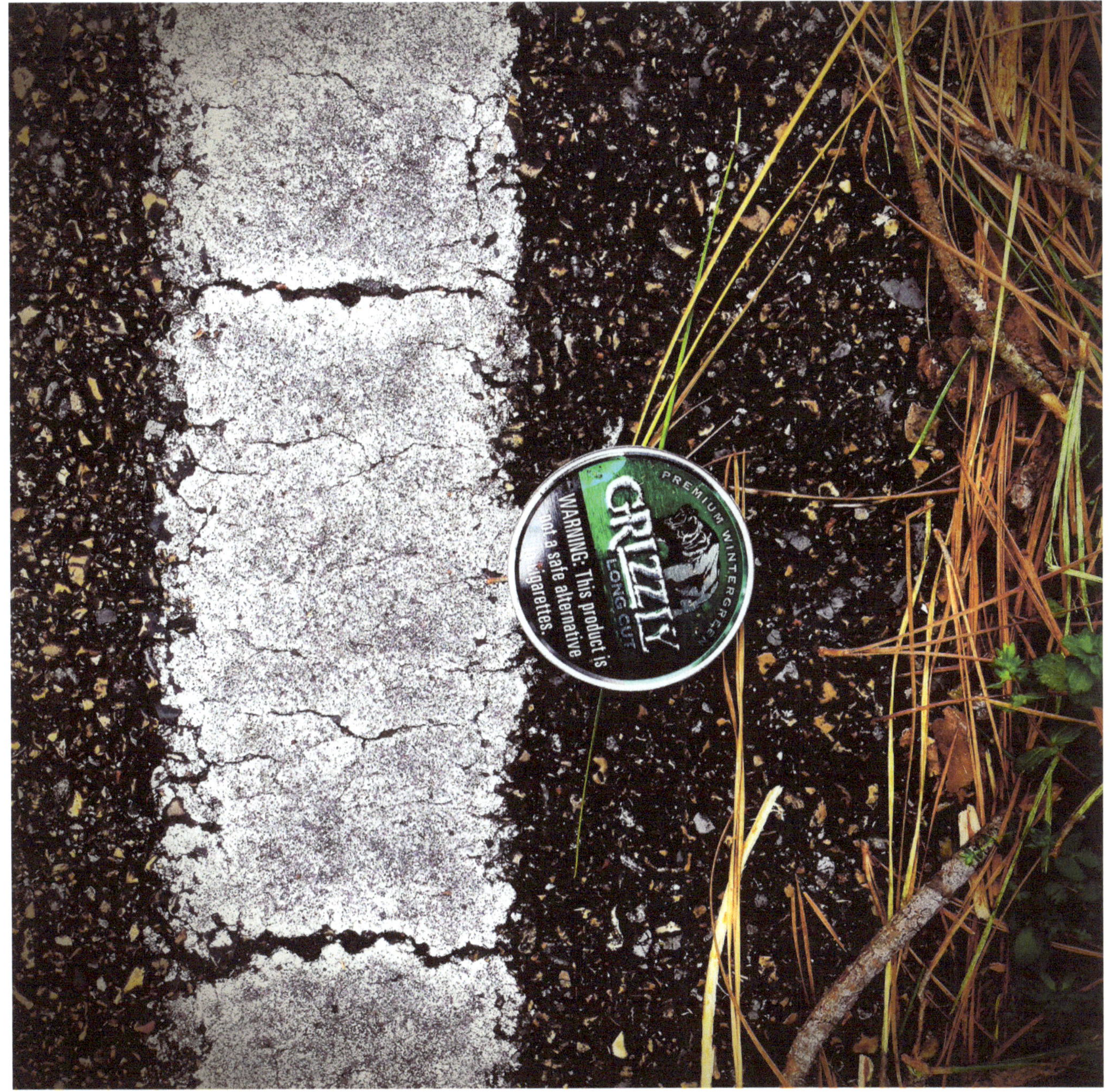
PREMIUM WINTERGRE
GRIZZLY
LONG CUT
WARNING: This product is
a safe alternative

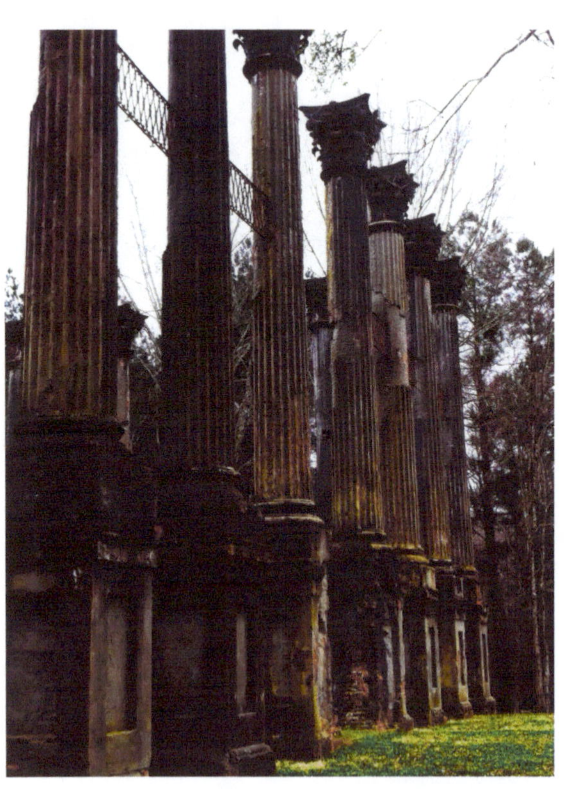

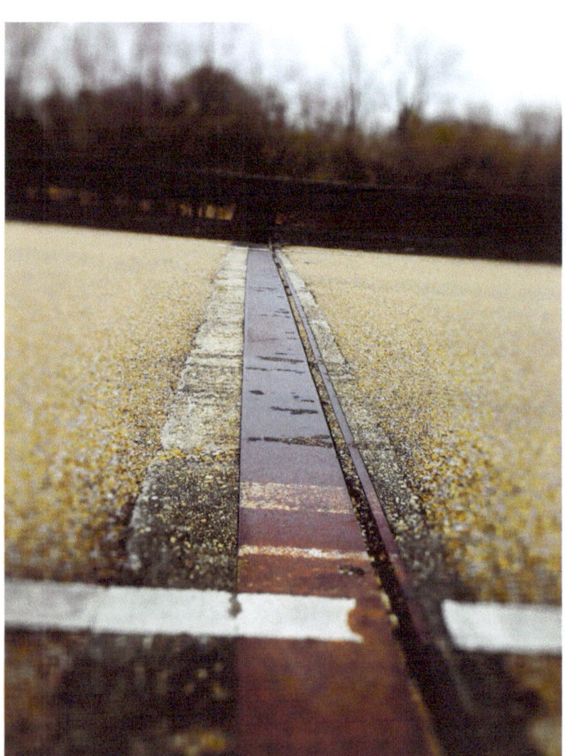

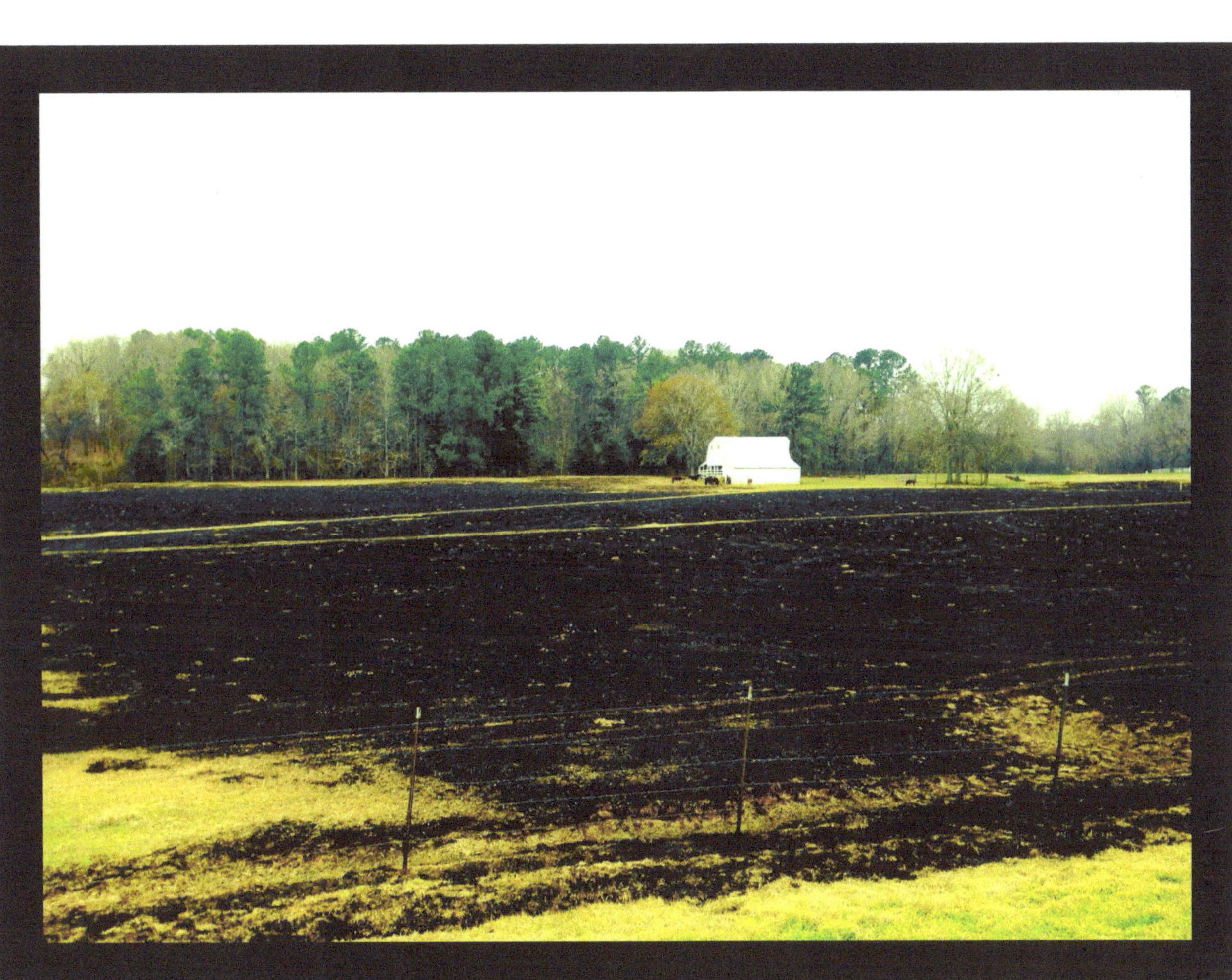

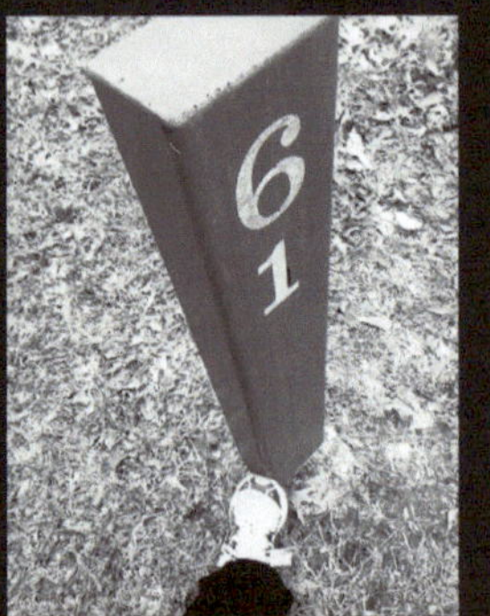
61

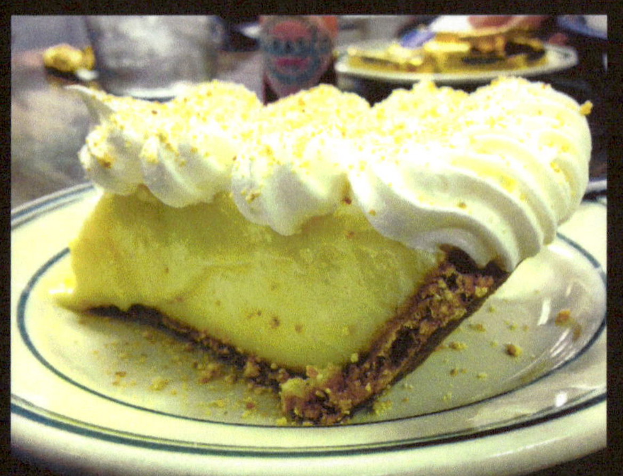

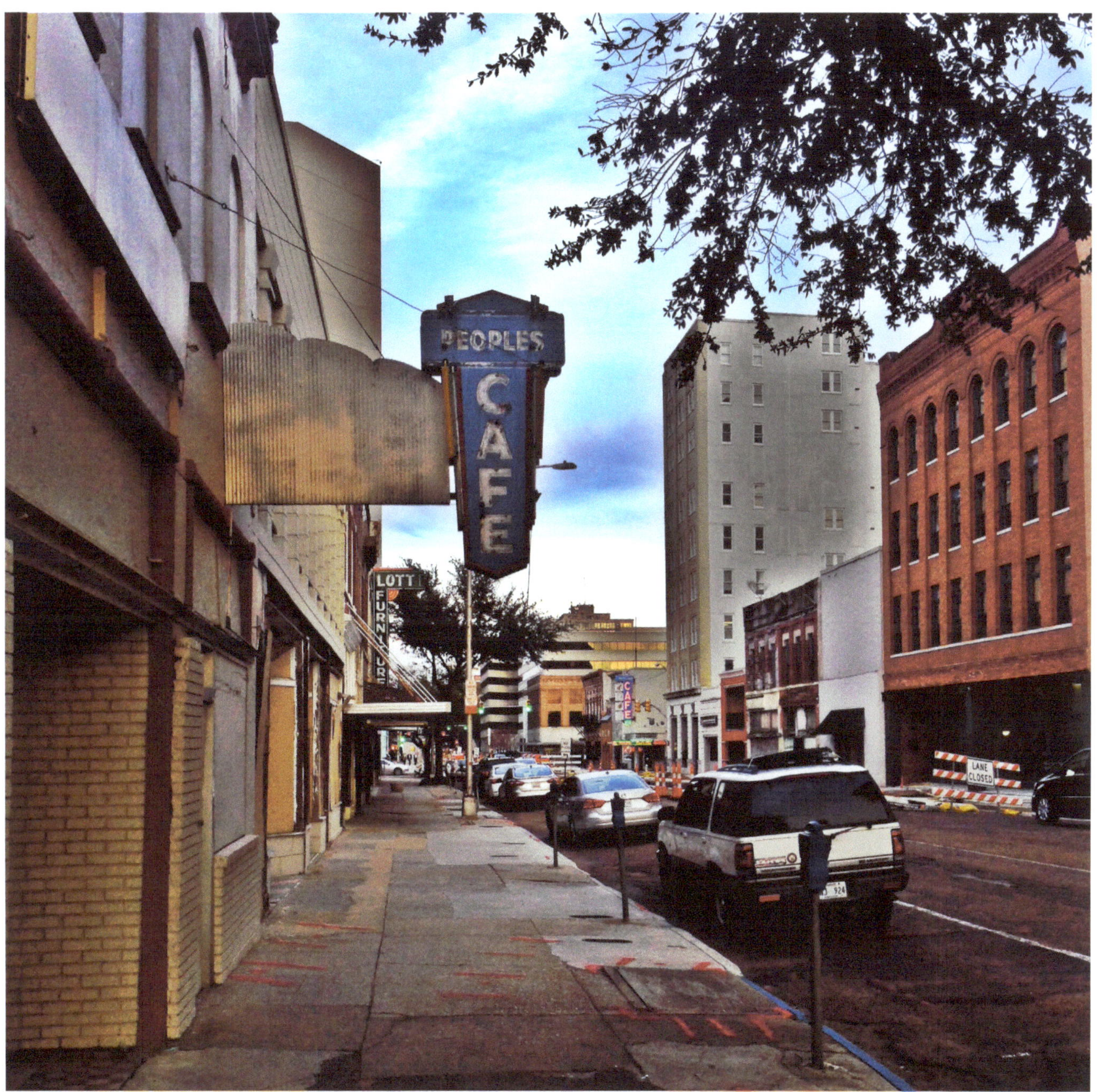
PEOPLES
CAFE
LOTT
FURNITURE
LANE
CLOSED

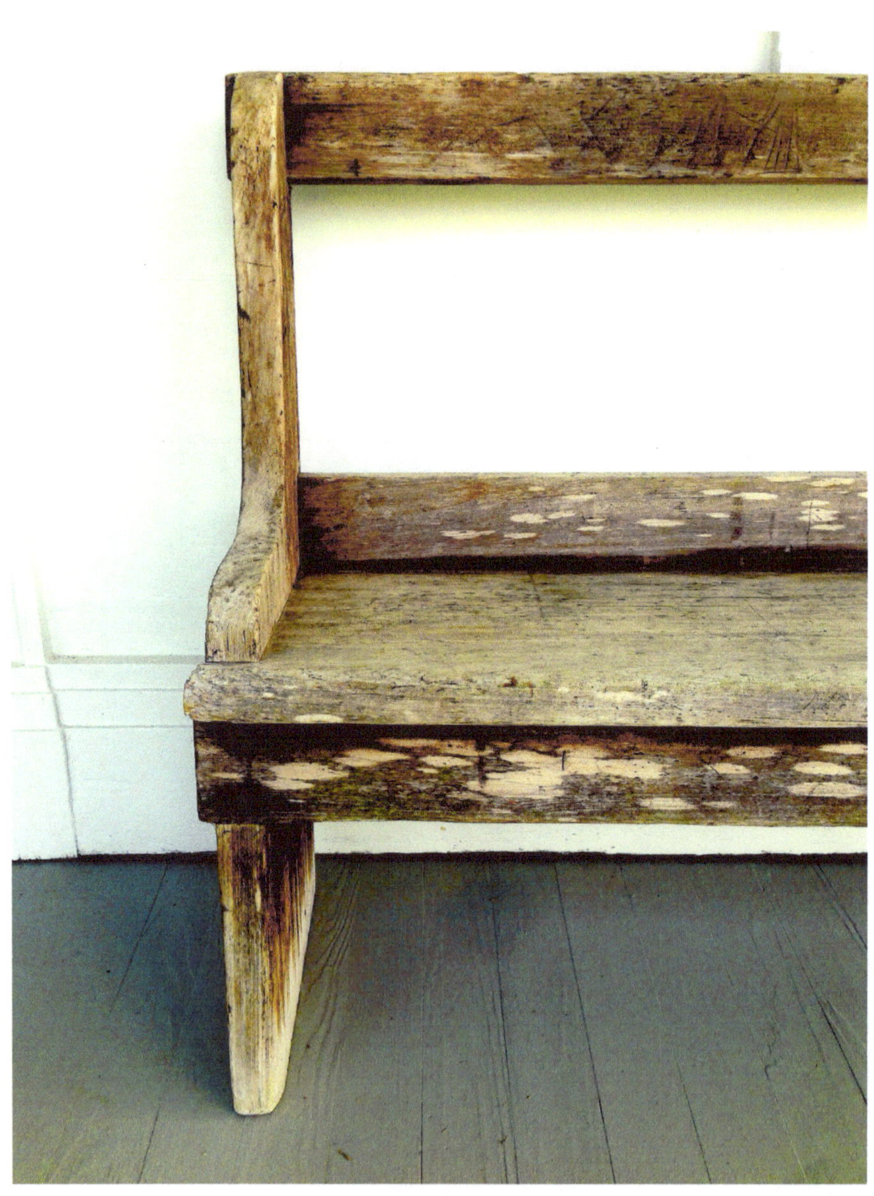

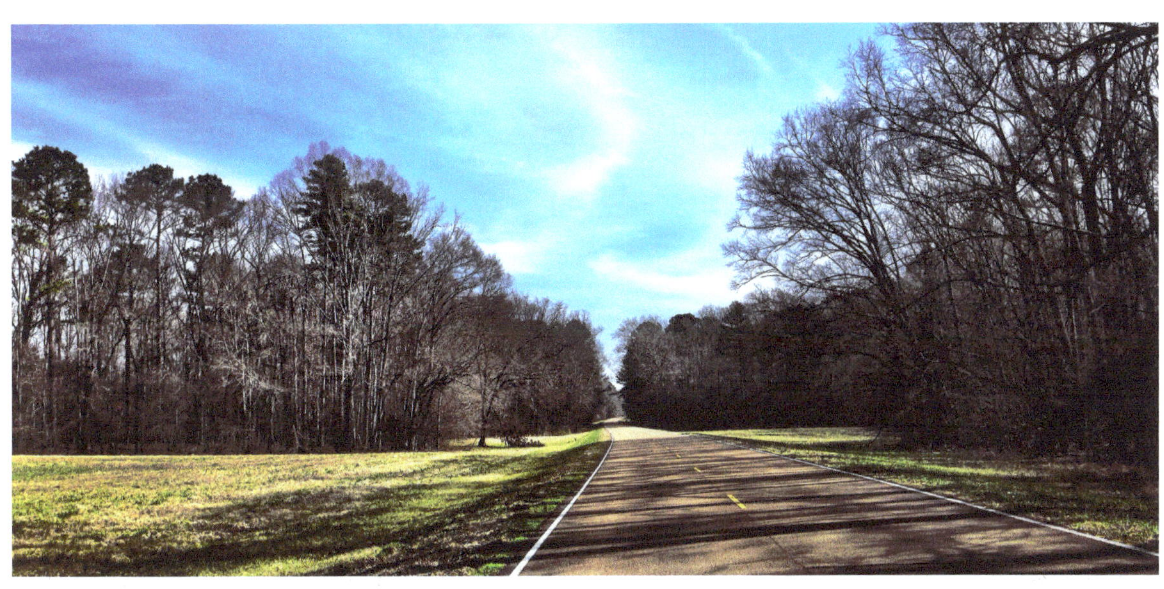

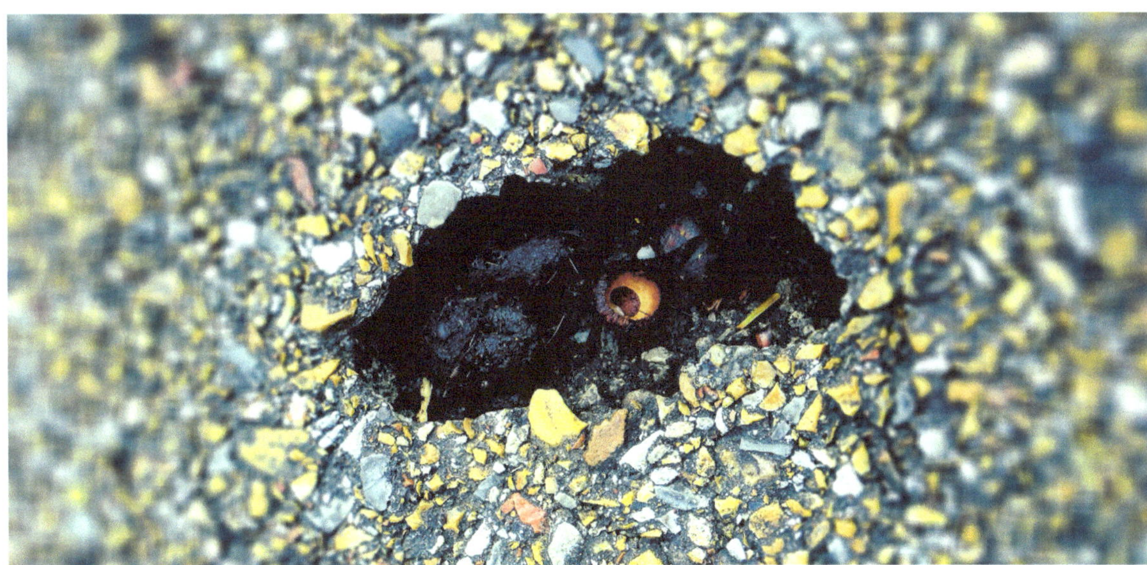

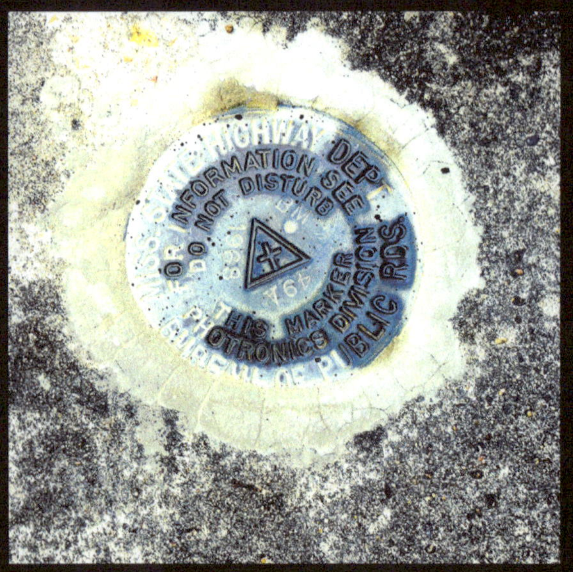
HIGHWAY DEPT
INFORMATION SEE
DO NOT DISTURB
THIS MARKER
PHOTRONICS DIVISION

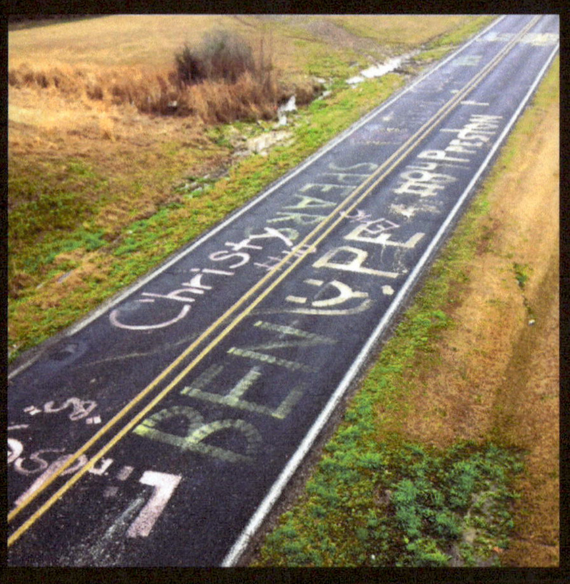
Christy
BEN

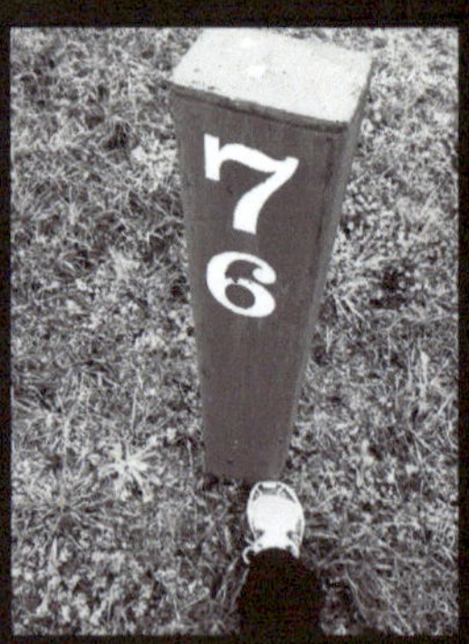
7
6

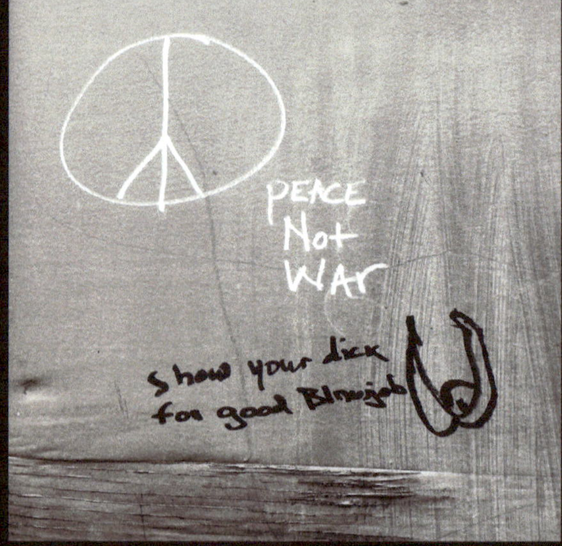
PEACE
Not
WAR
show your dick
for good Blowjob

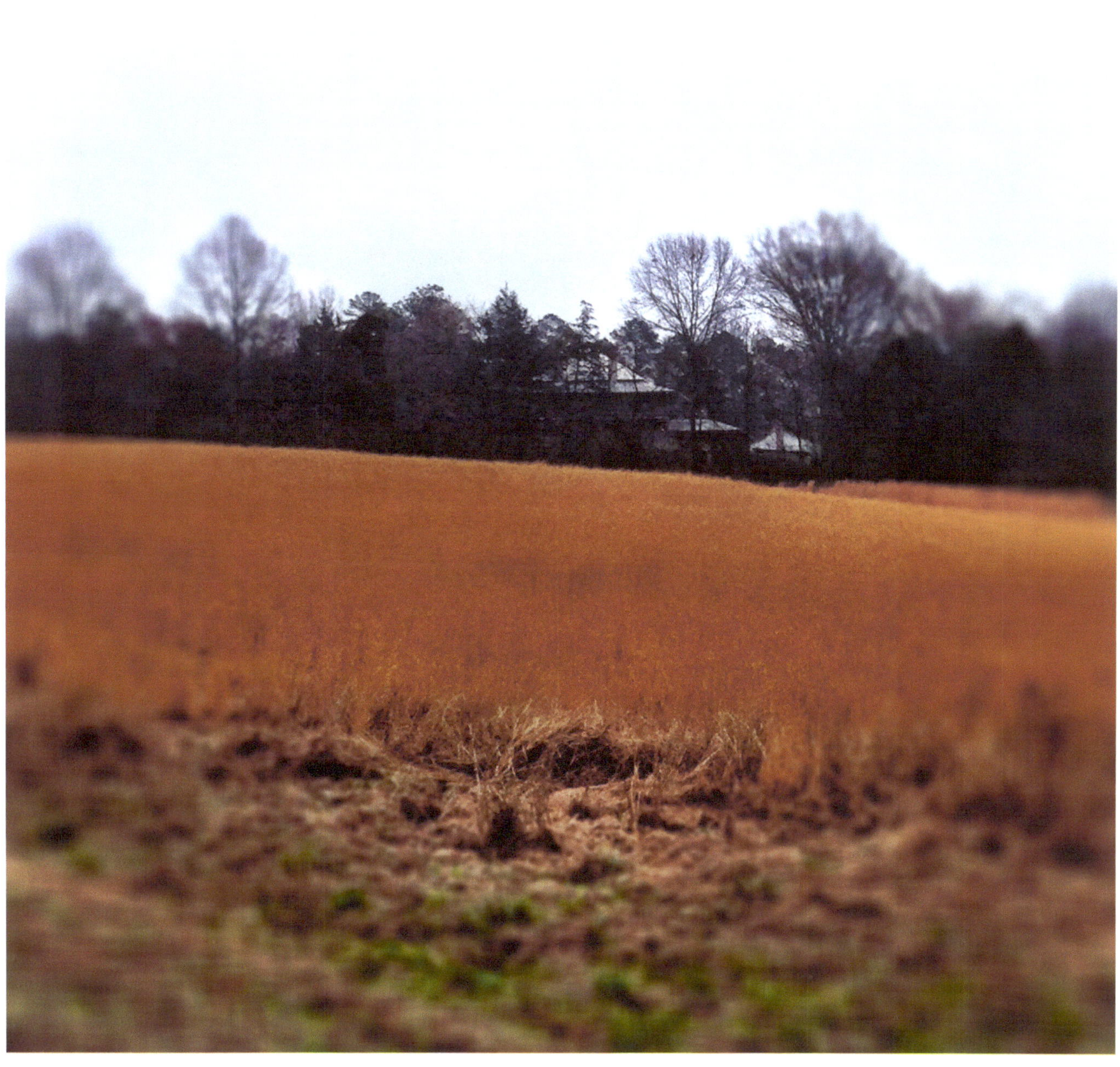

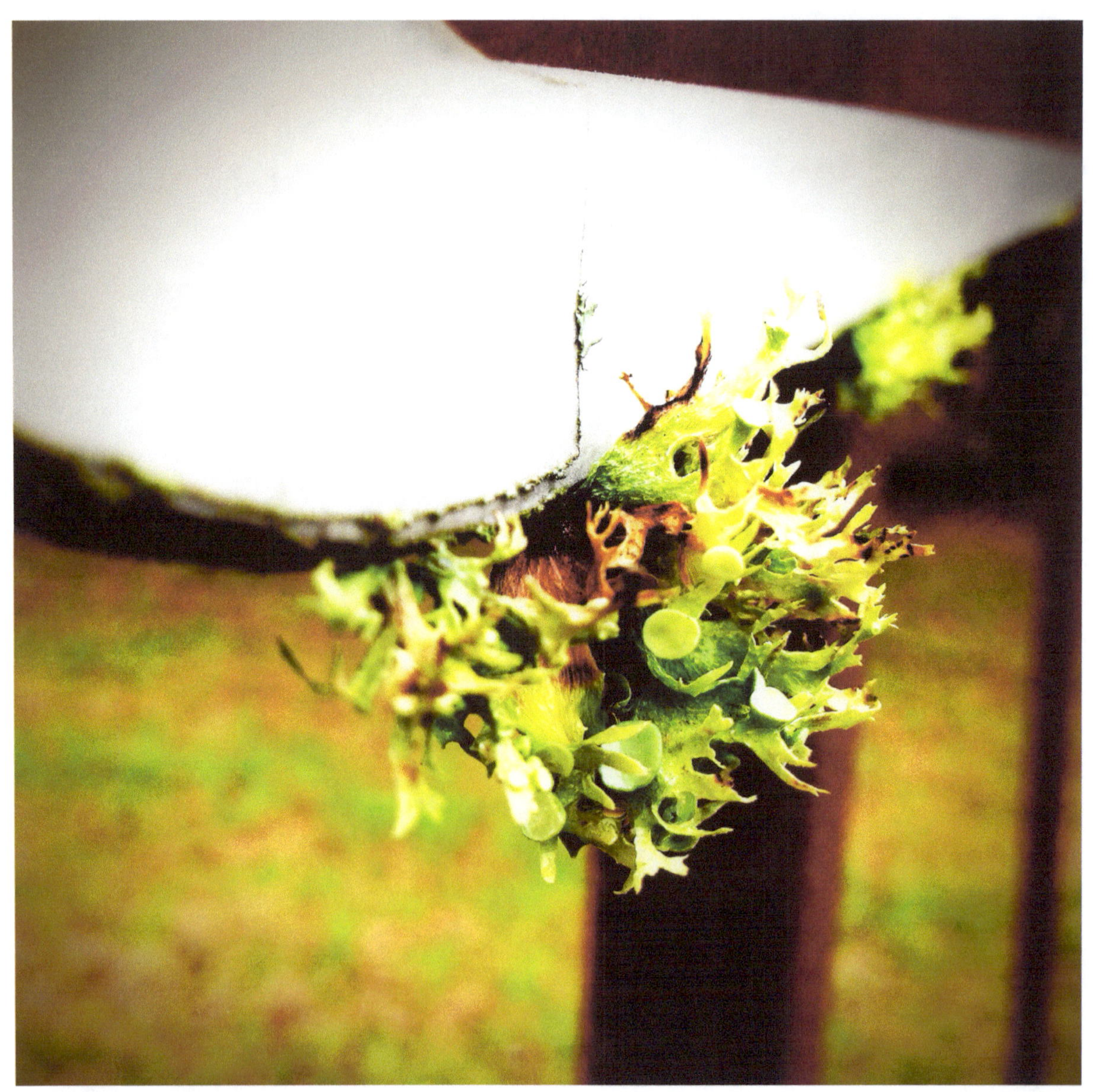

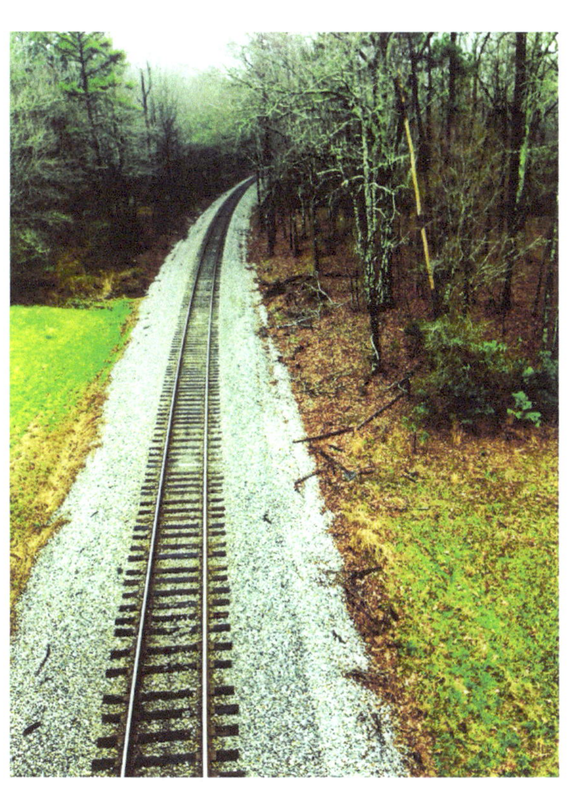

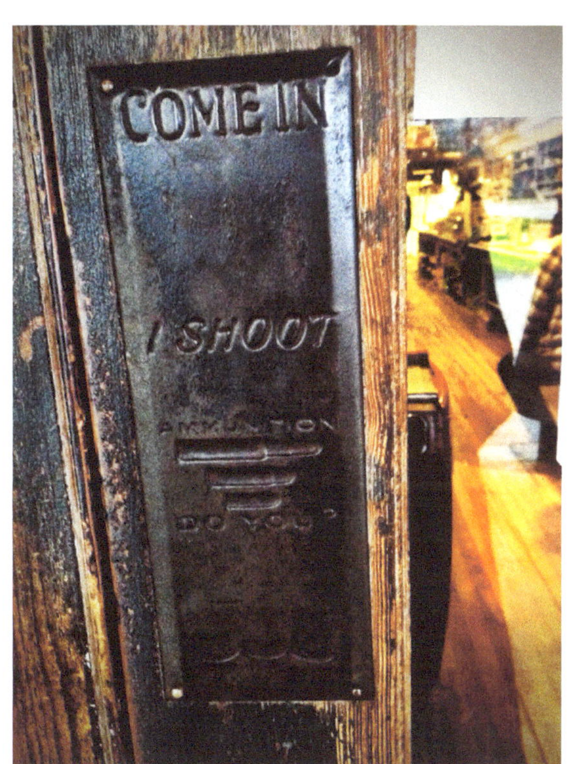
COME IN
I SHOOT

At milepost 93, I whipped out my phone and snapped another picture. "Fireball Whiskey. A big bottle this time." I made a game of photographing things along the side of the road. Five hours of monotony captured in pictures. At the end of each day, I scrolled through them and remembered. The ethereal quality of light. Brushes of bird wings. The primordial stench of swamp water. But by Jackson, my photographs developed a troubling theme. Beer bottles, crushed beer cans, empty mini bottles and Costco-sized liquor containers accounted for a third of the garbage I encountered. In one mile, I found fifteen remnants of booze.

Which meant one in every three drivers could be driving under the influence, inches from me. I needed protection.

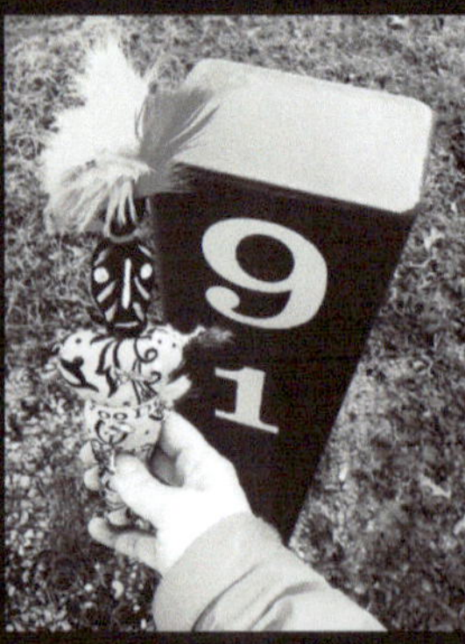

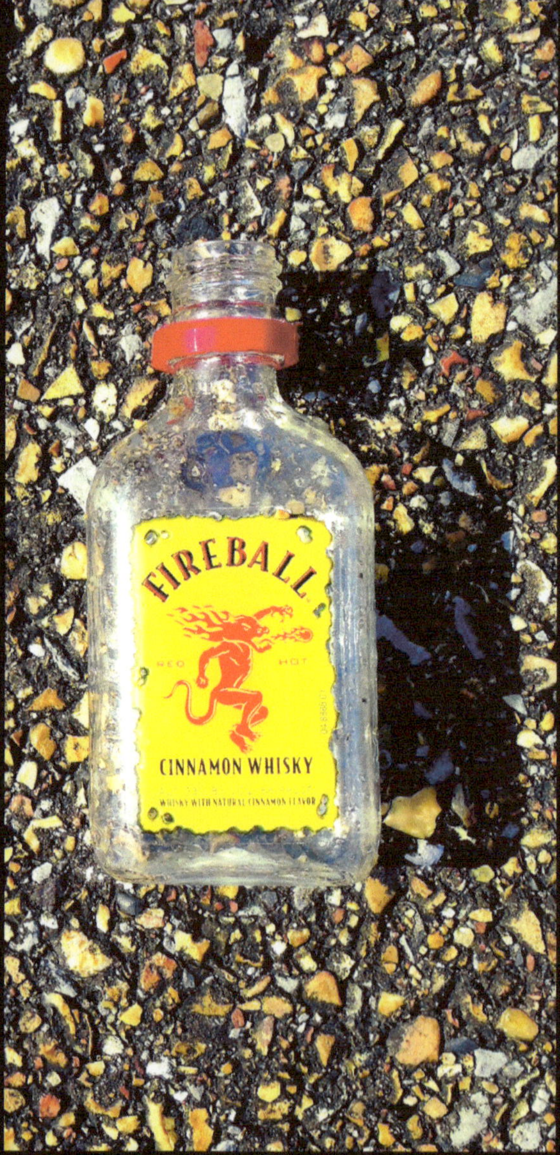

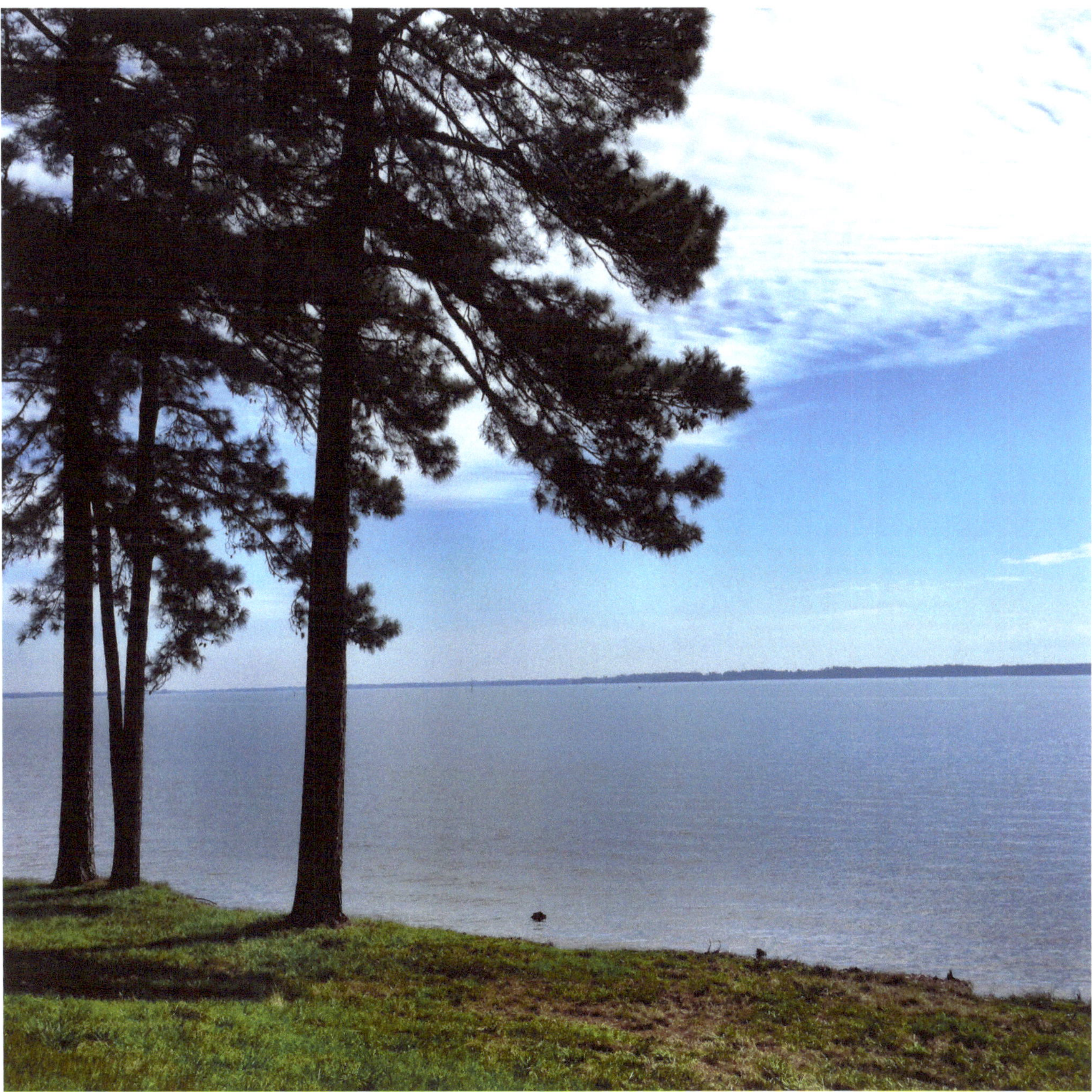

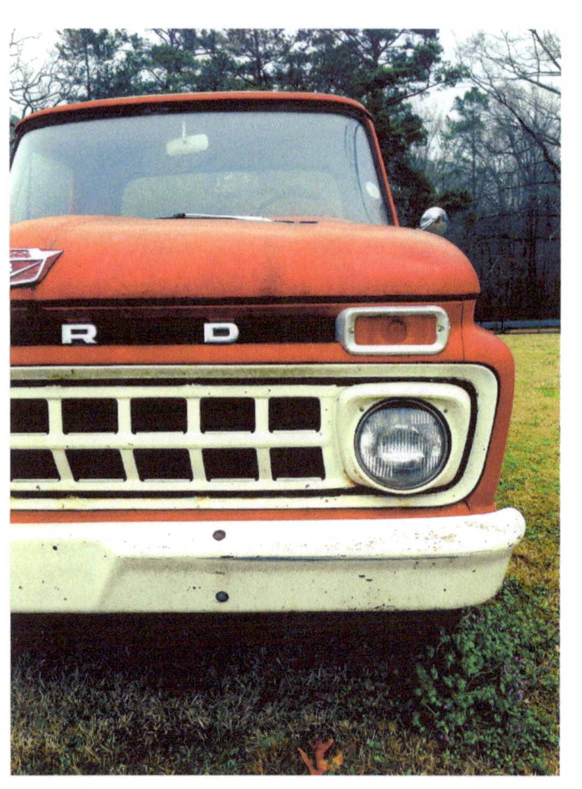
R D

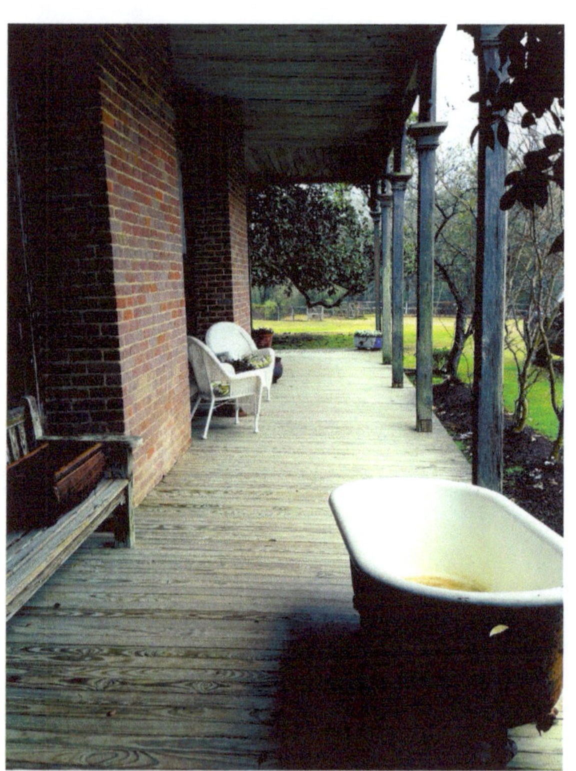

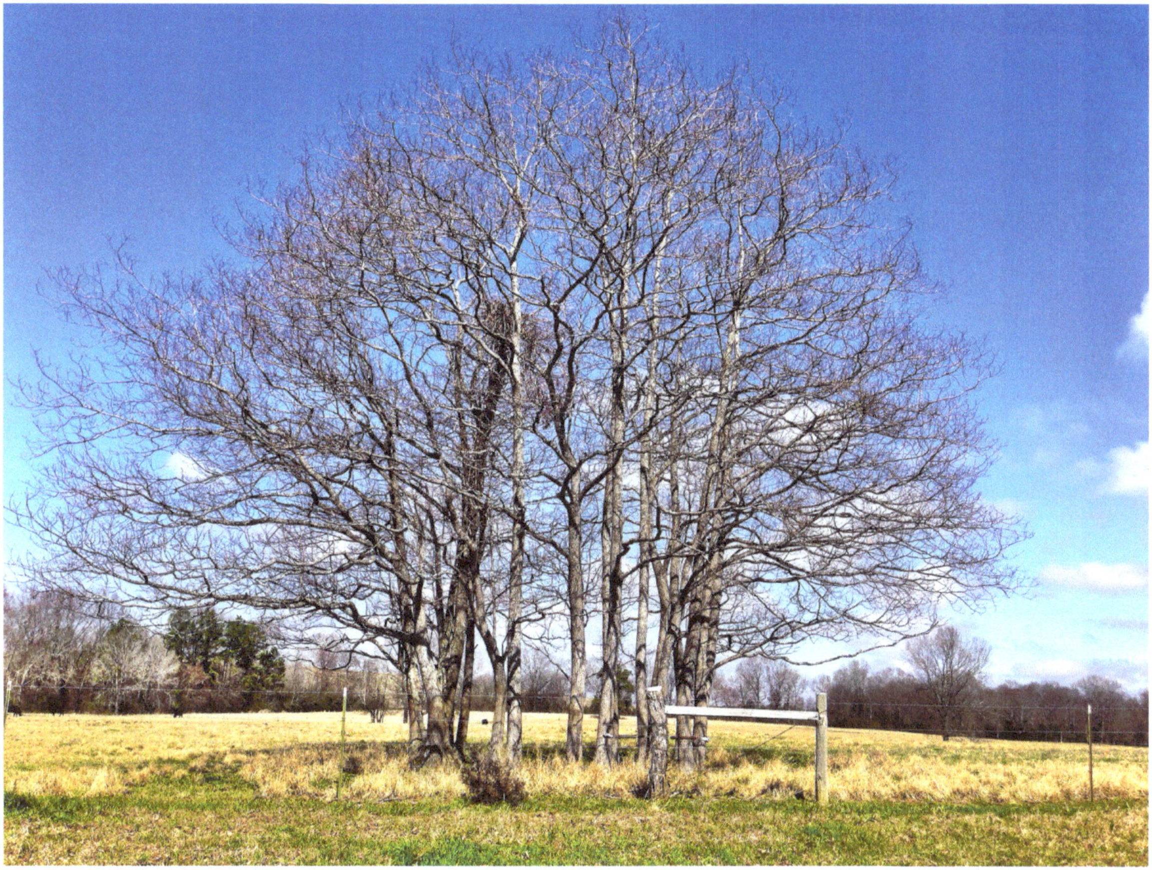

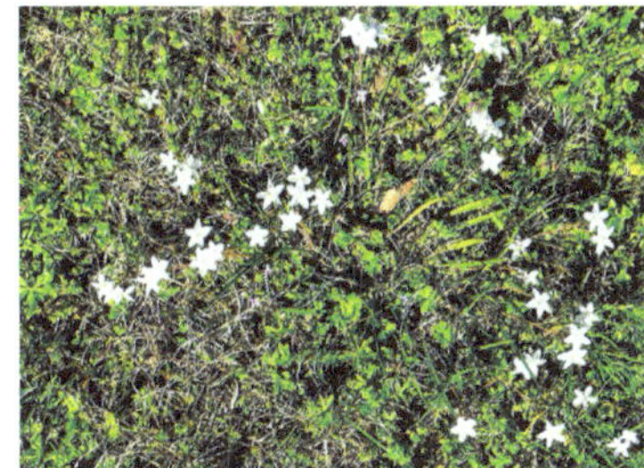

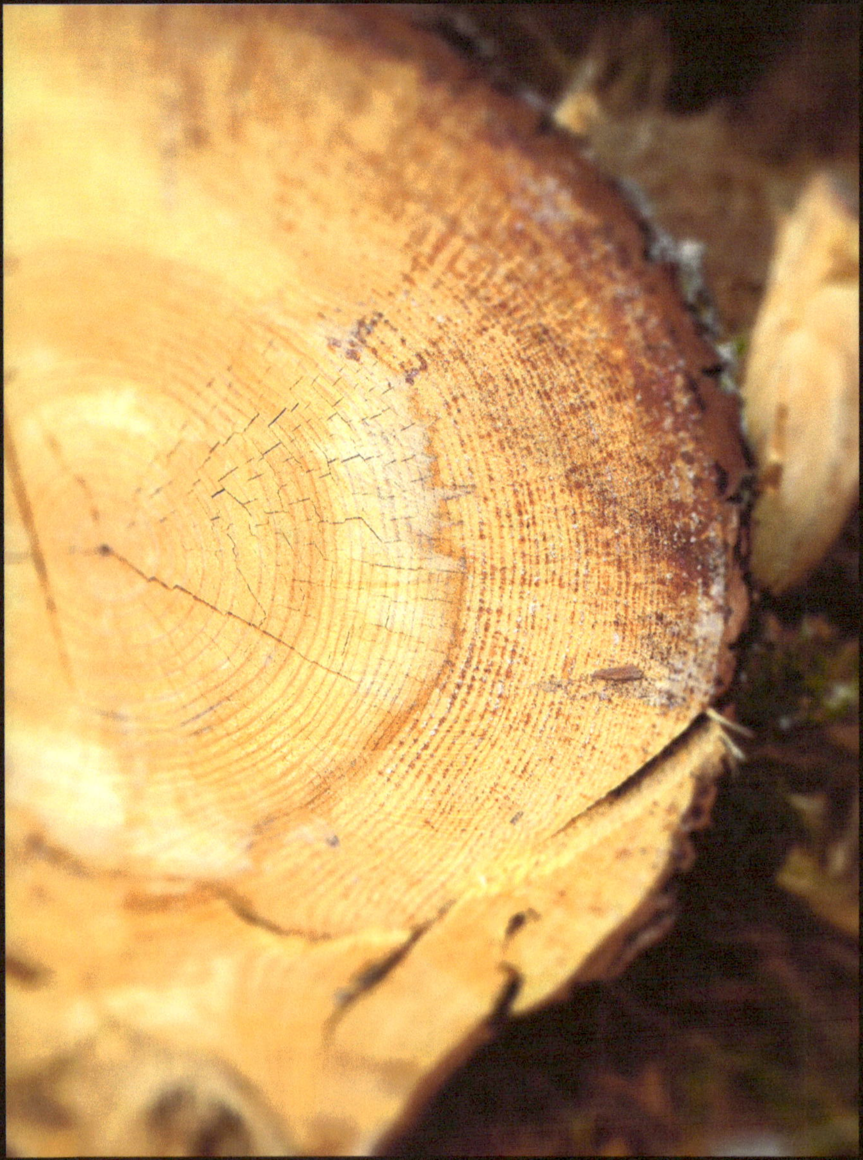

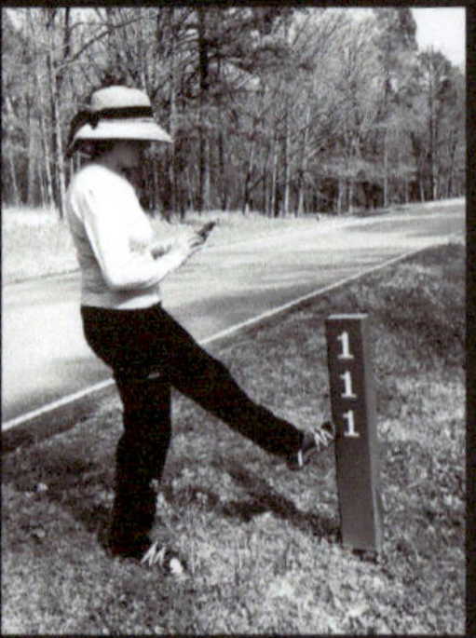
111

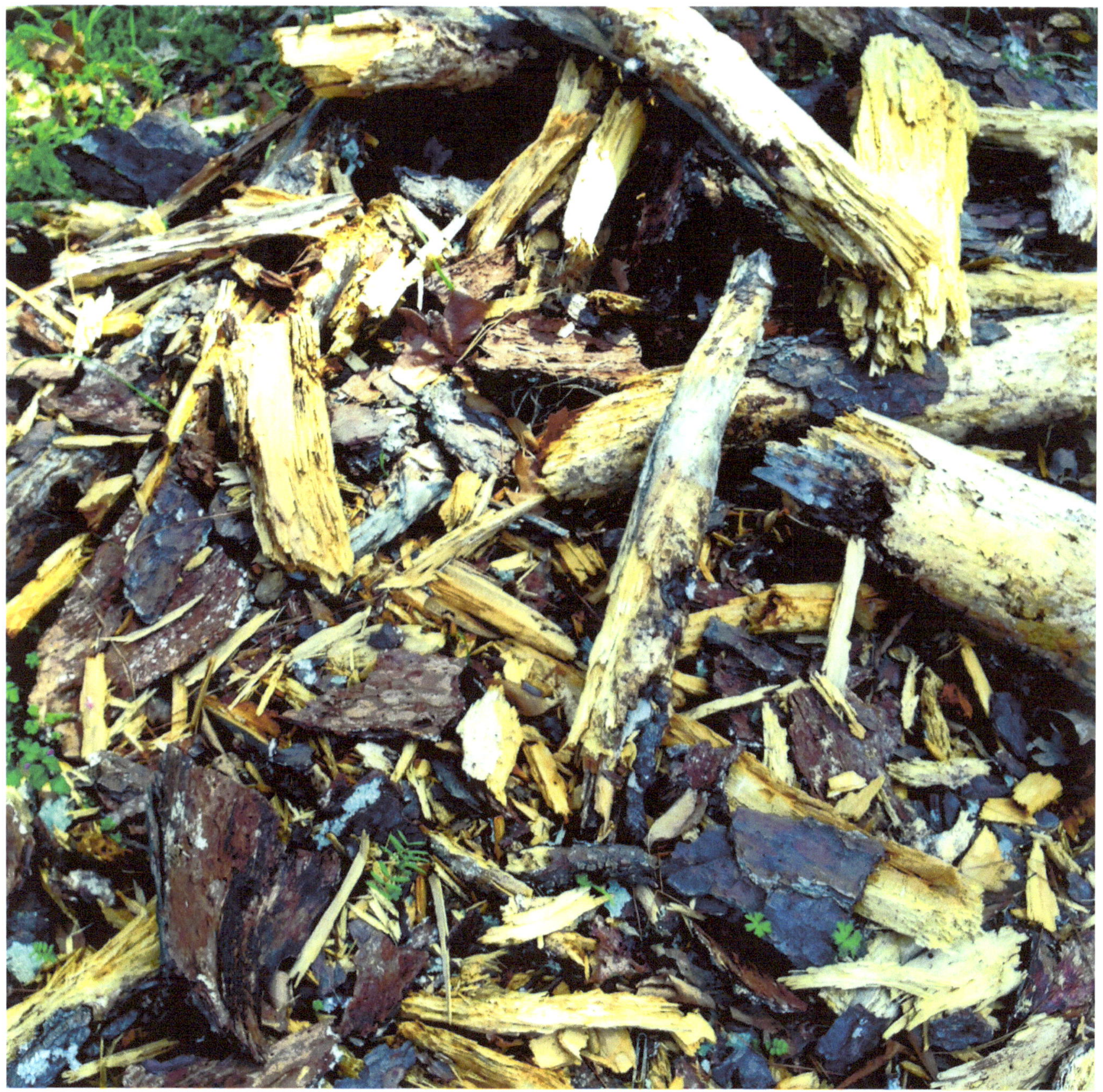

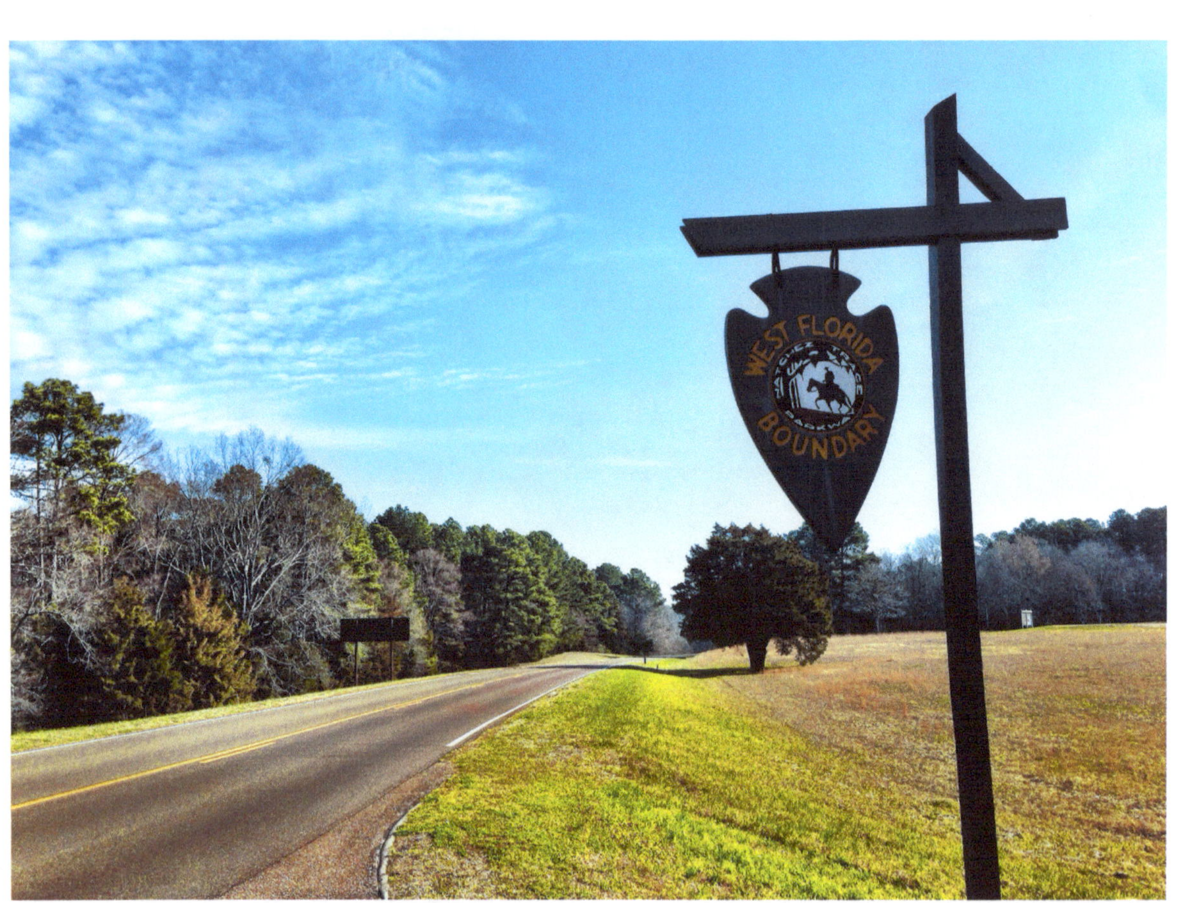
WEST FLORIDA
BOUNDARY

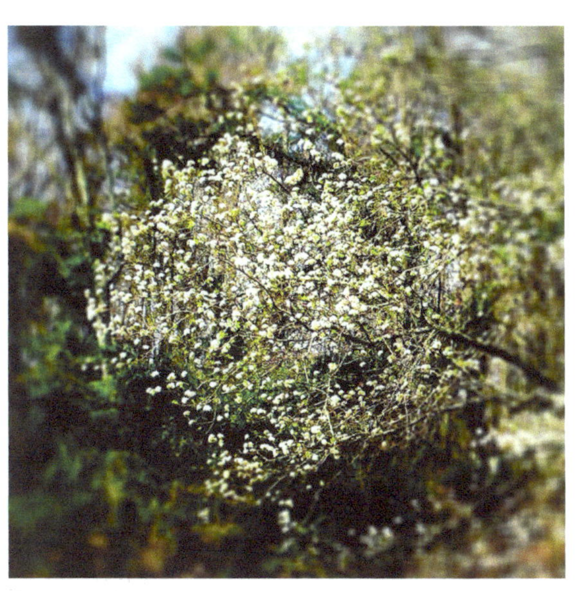

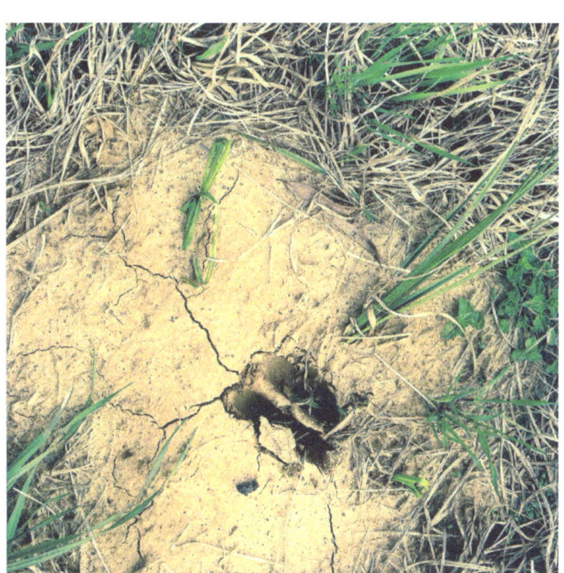

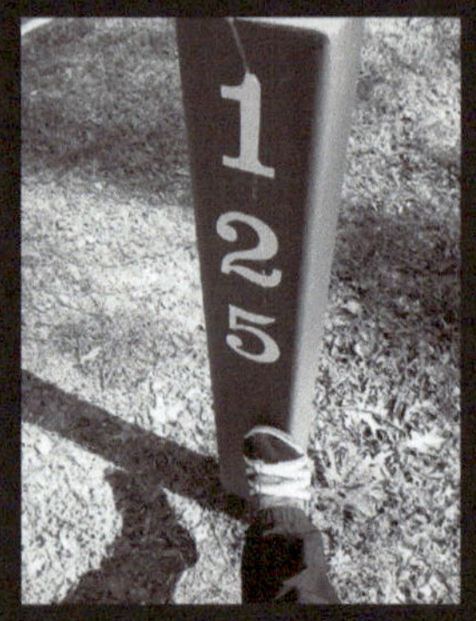
125

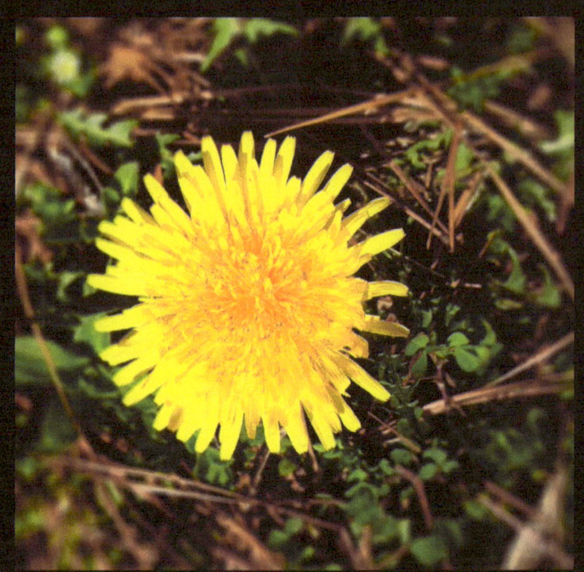

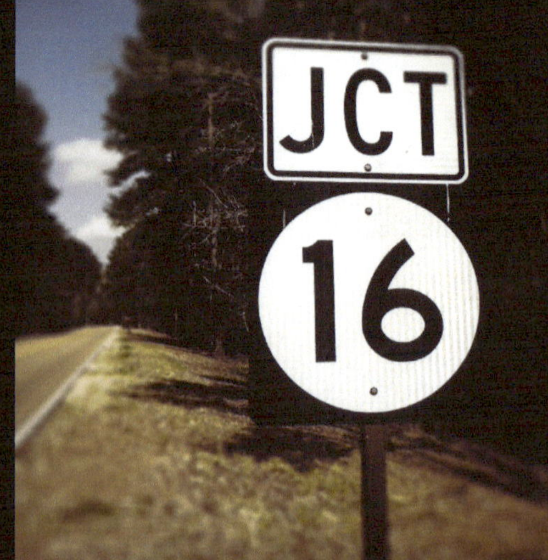
JCT
16

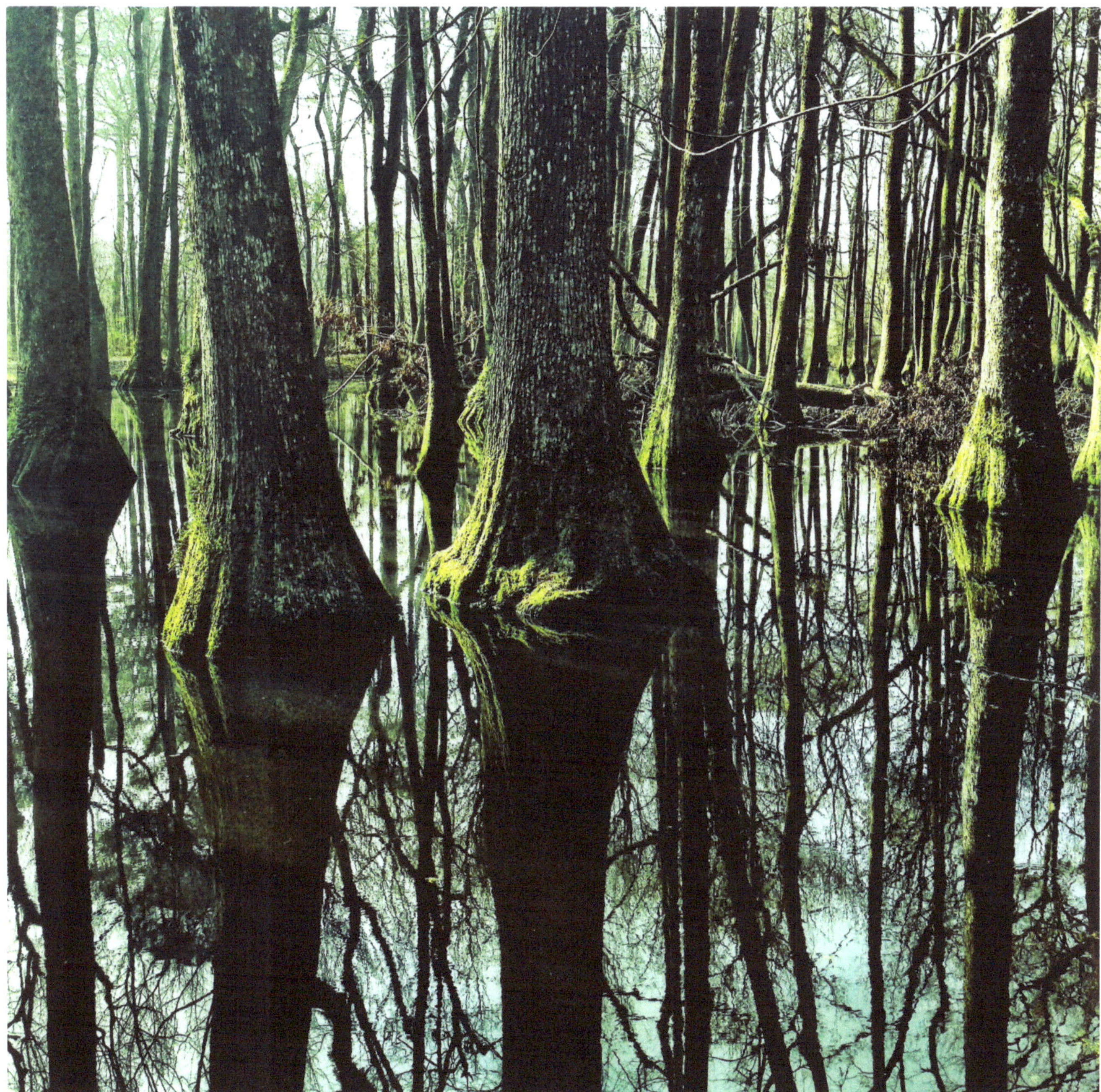

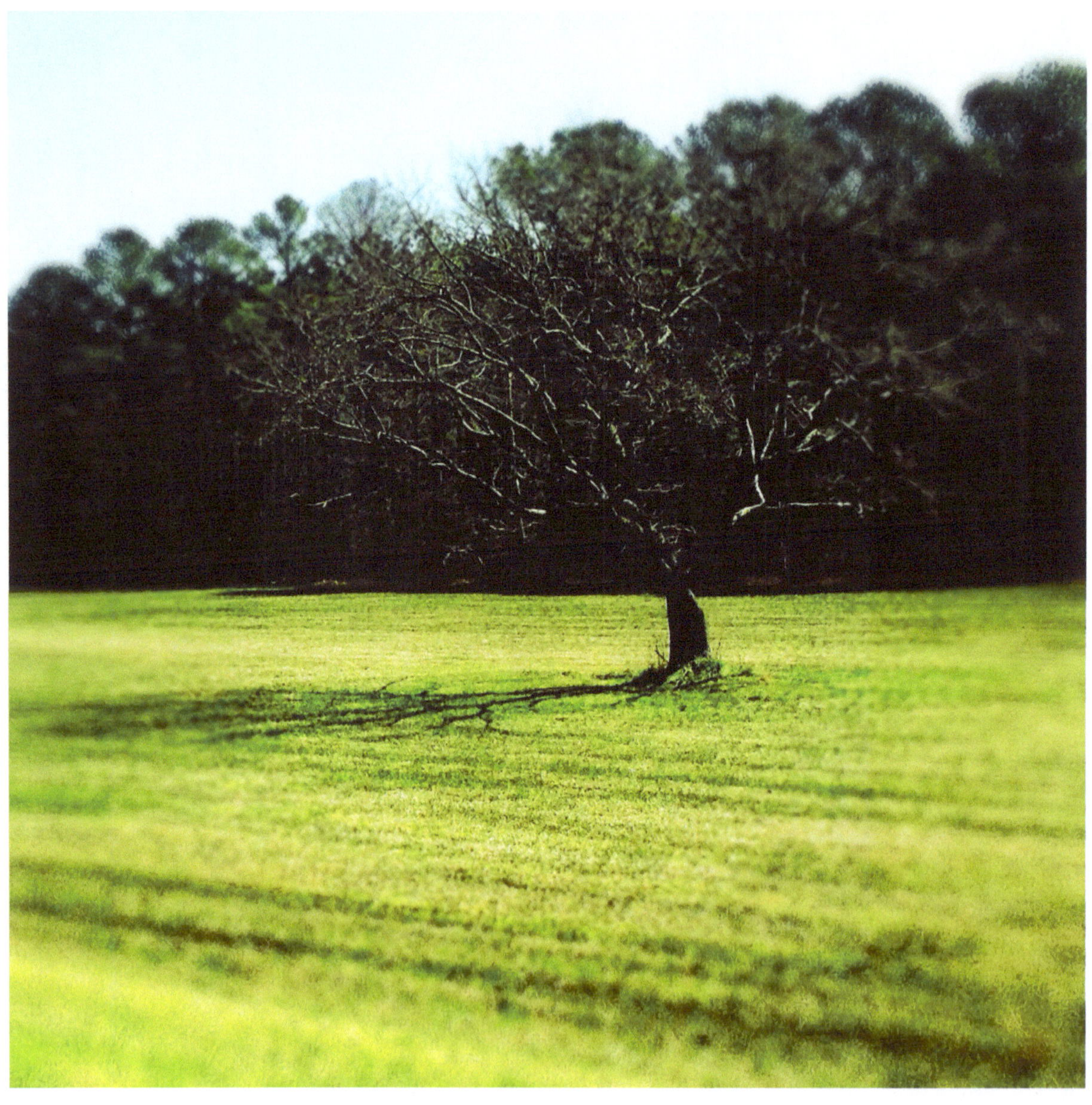

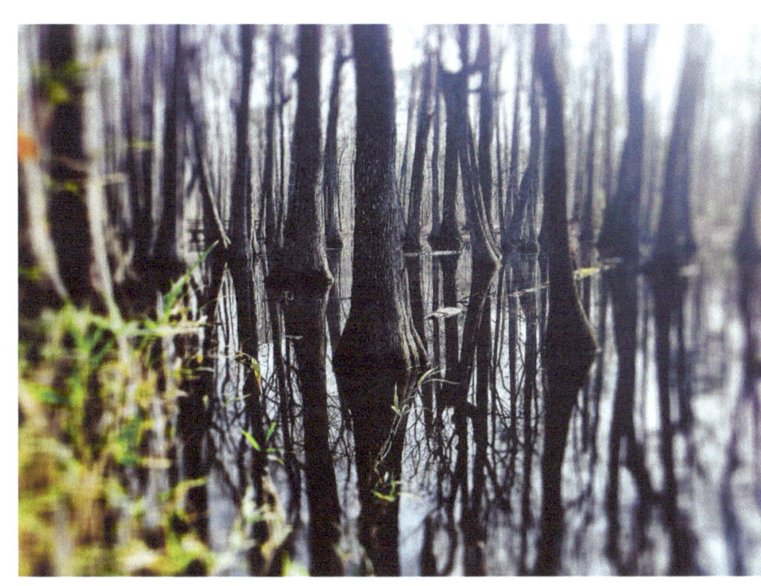

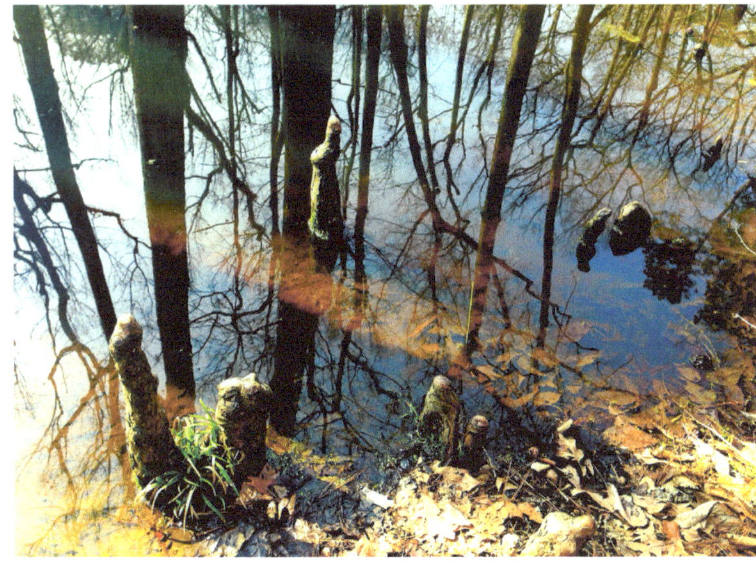

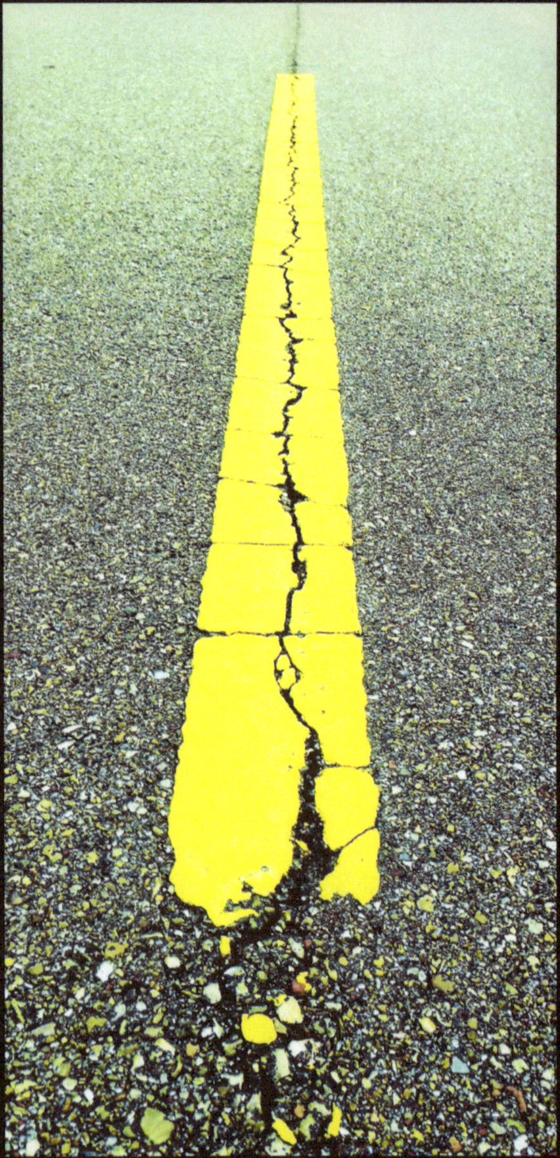

It winks at me. On the horizon. Is that what I think it is? No.

It's a blasted tree limb.

A survey stake.

Reflectors to mark an overpass. Or a culvert.

It's everything but the next rust-colored mile marker. My mind tricks my eyes into seeing things. And for the last five miles of the day, the thing I most want to see is the mile marker that announces

THE END.

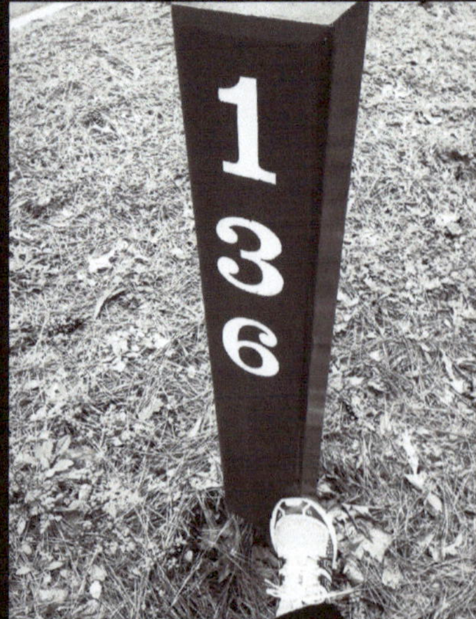

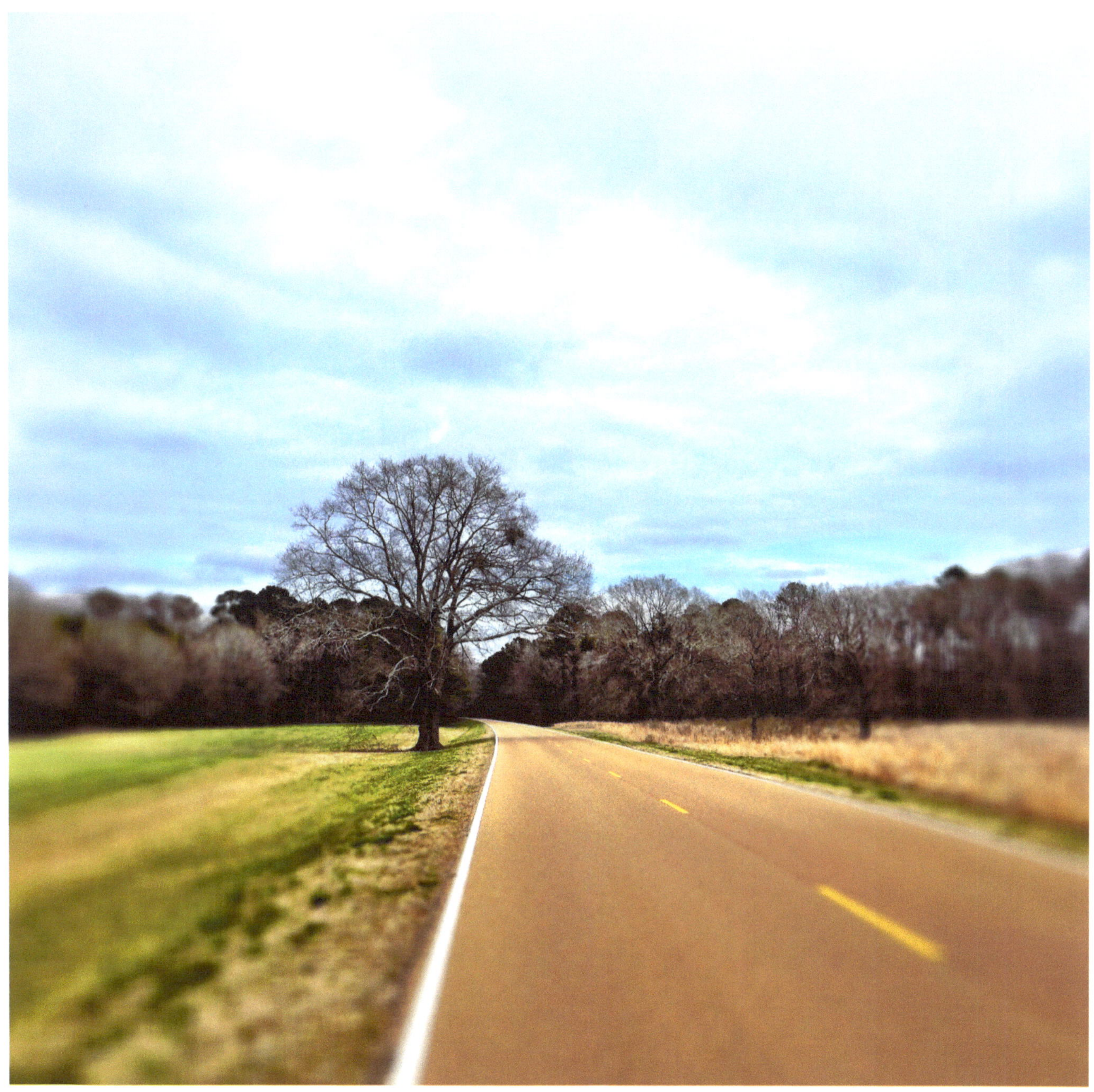

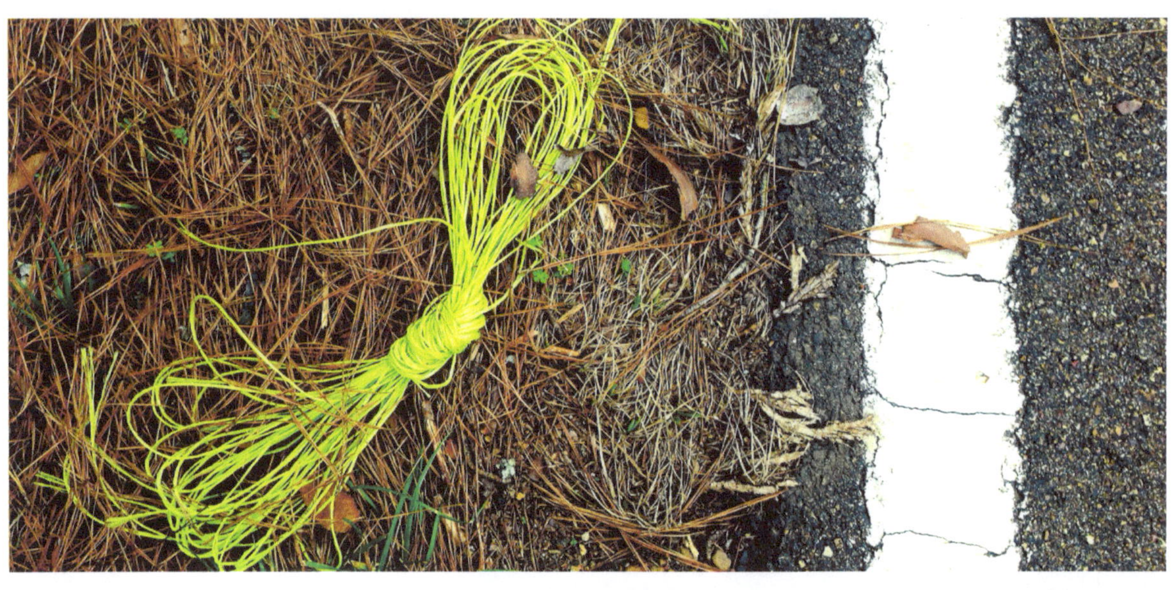

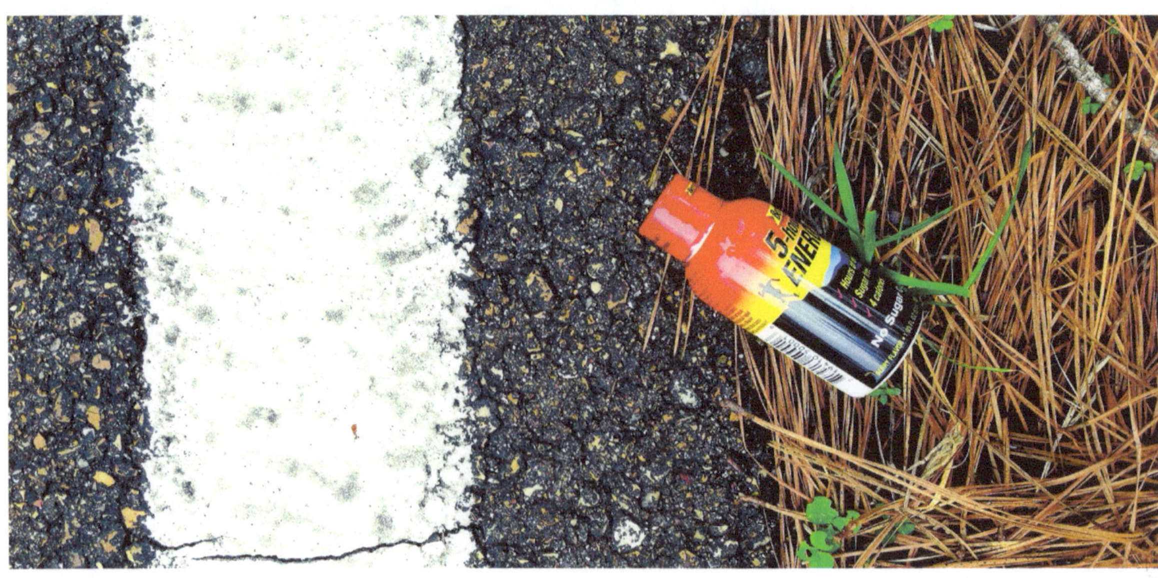

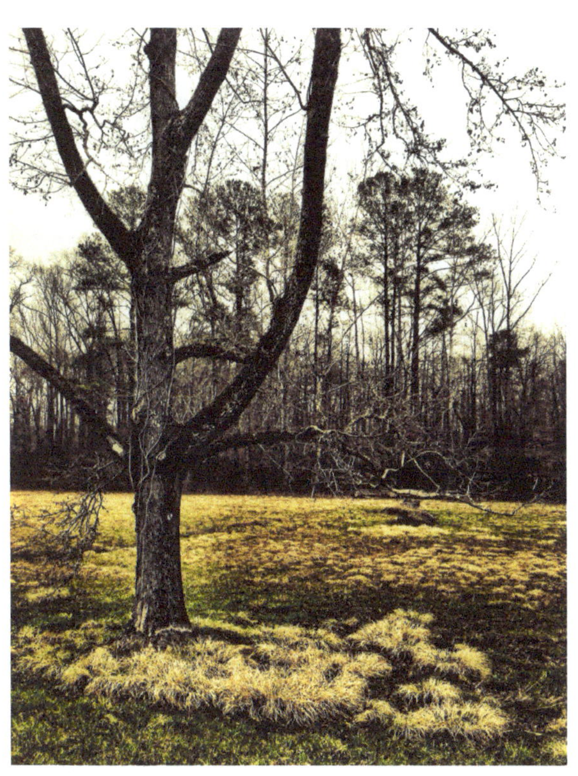

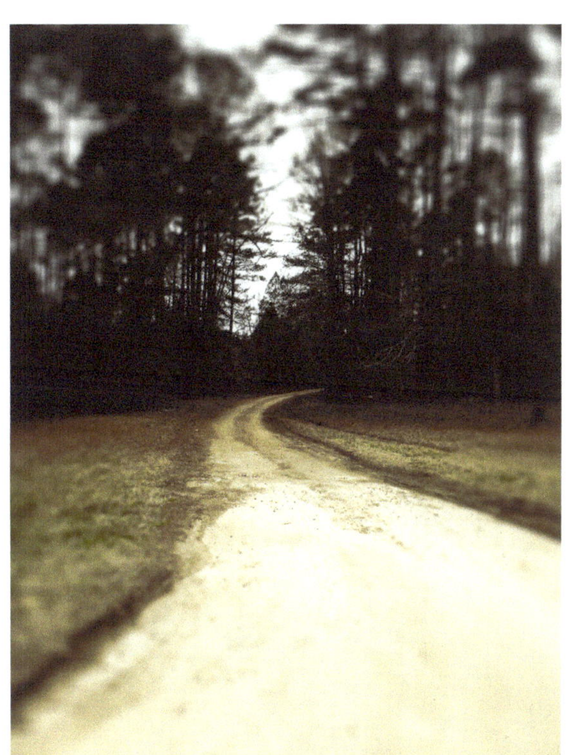

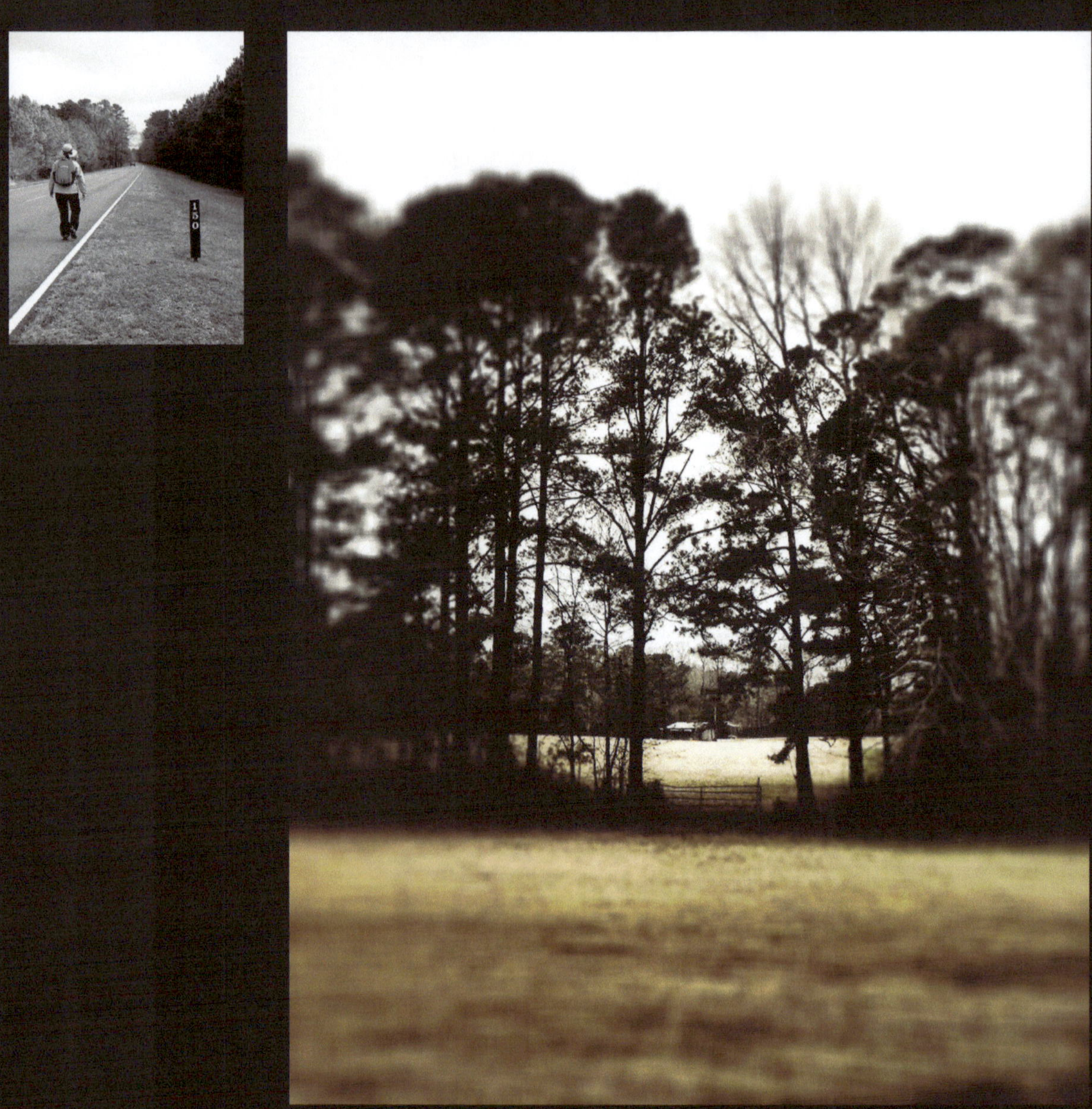
150

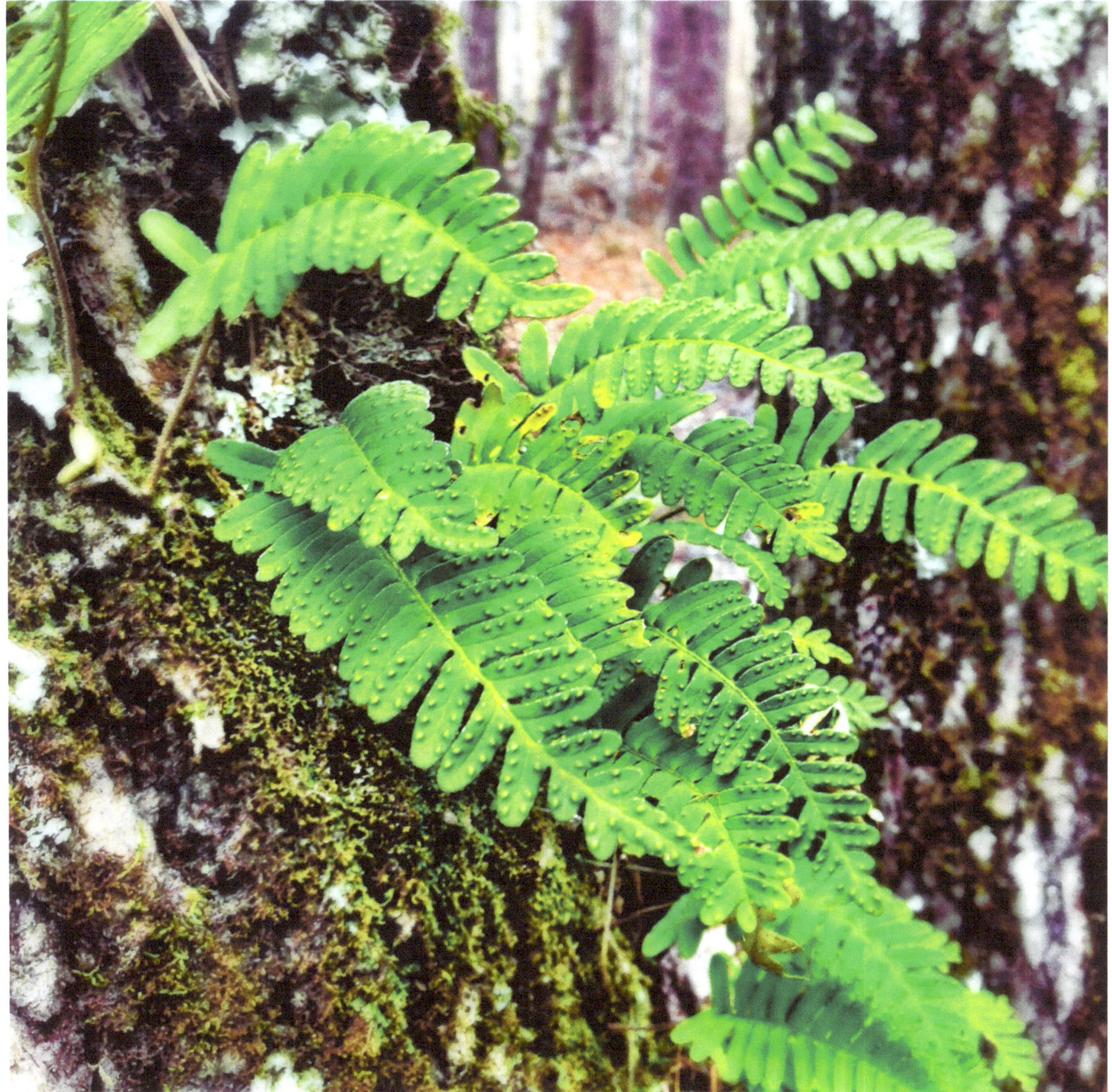

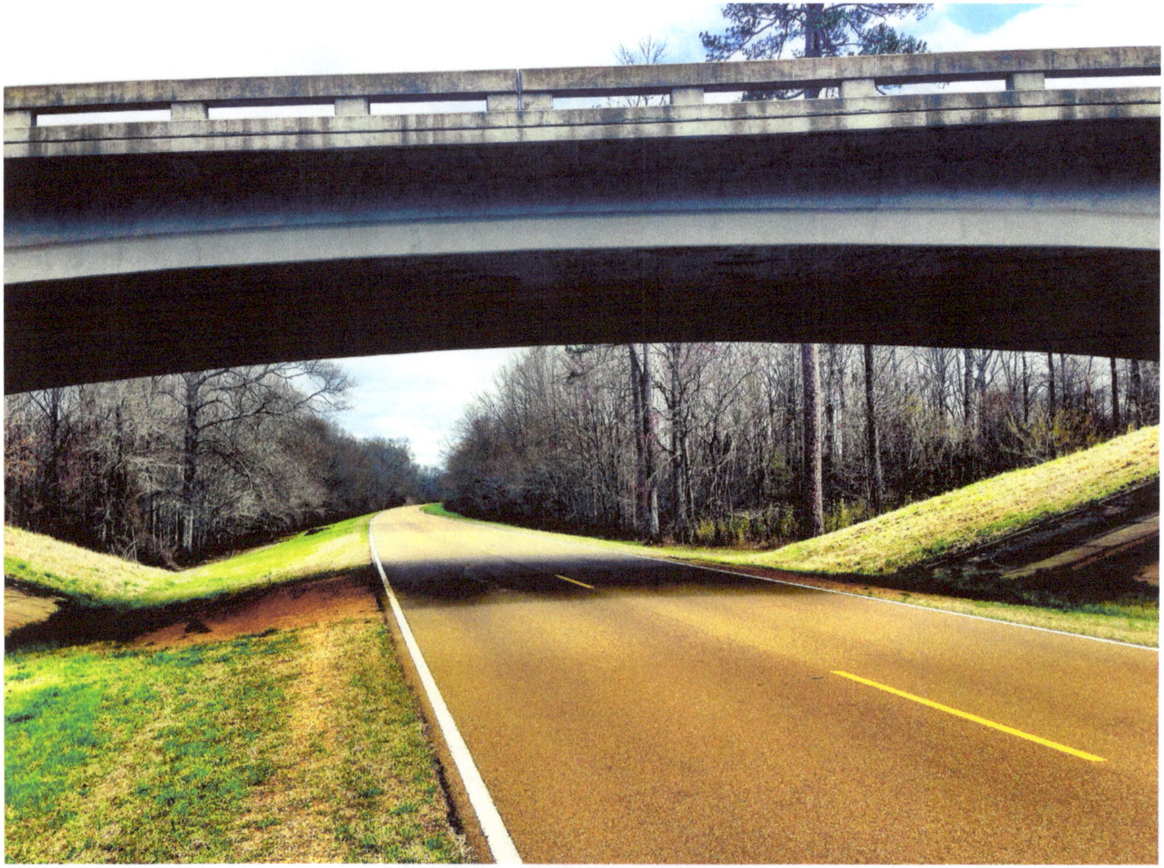

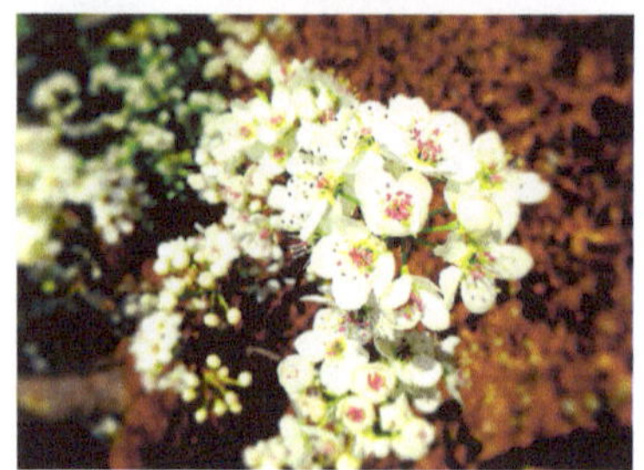

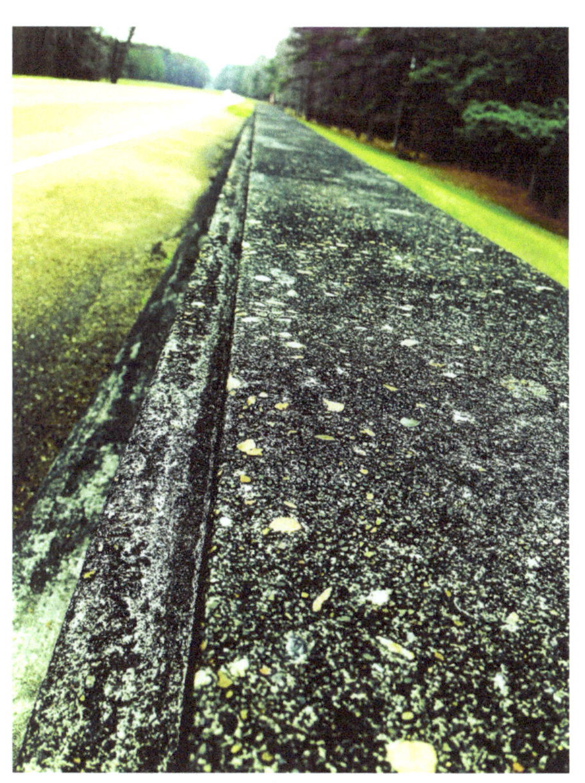

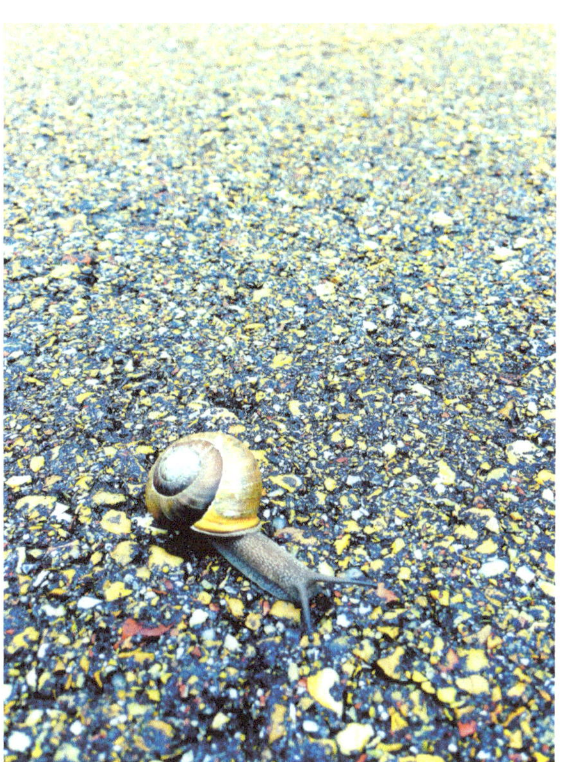

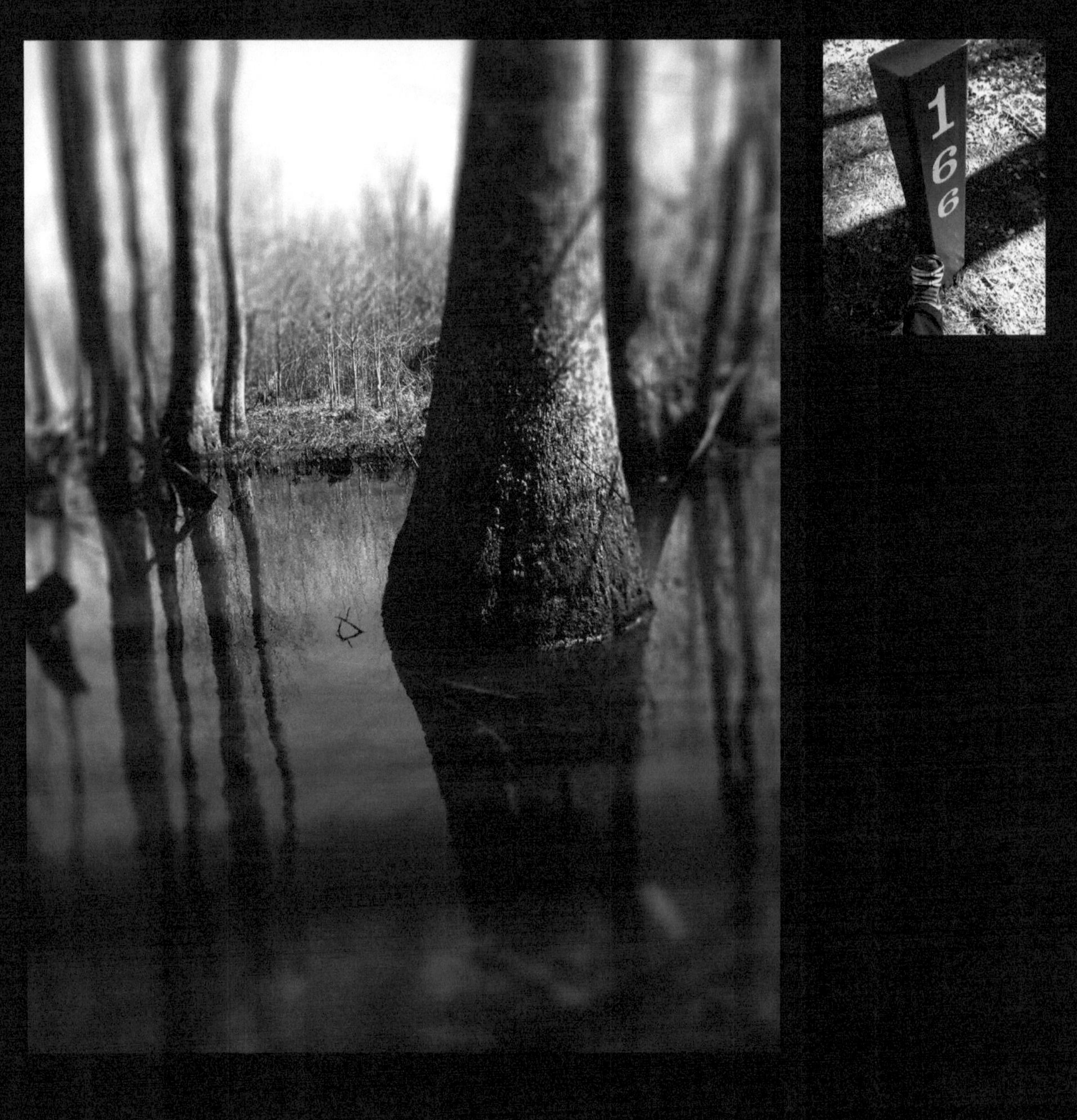
166

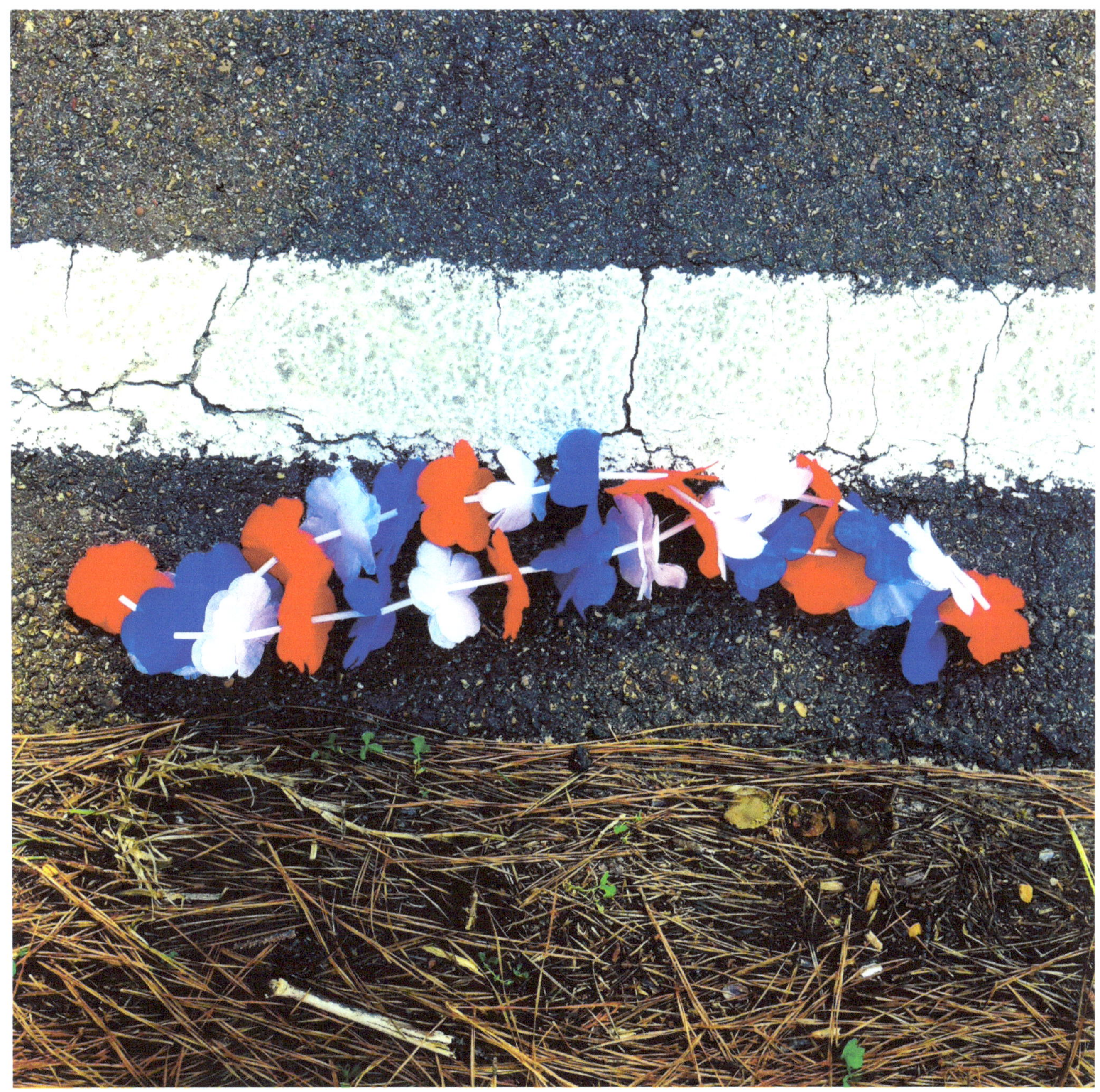

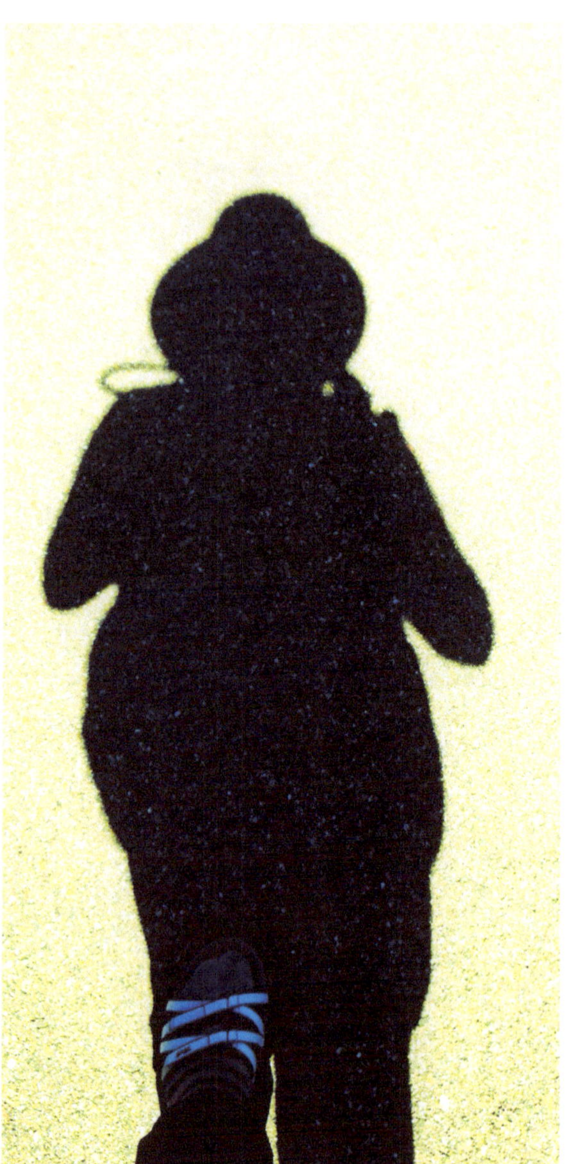

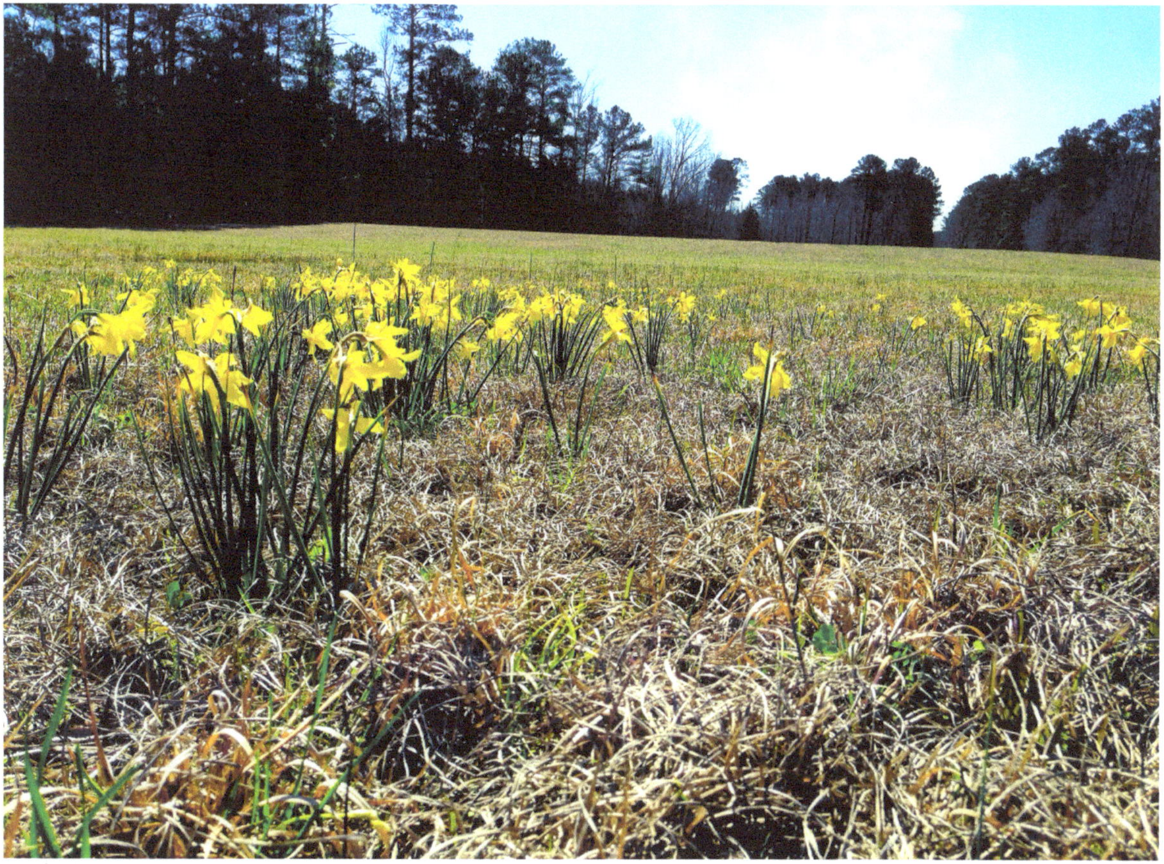

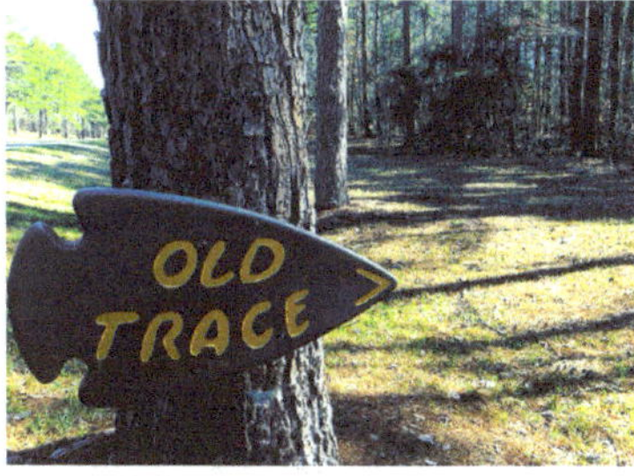
OLD
TRACE

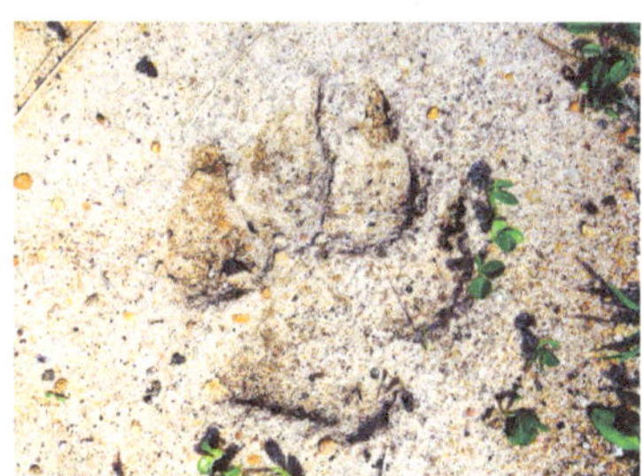

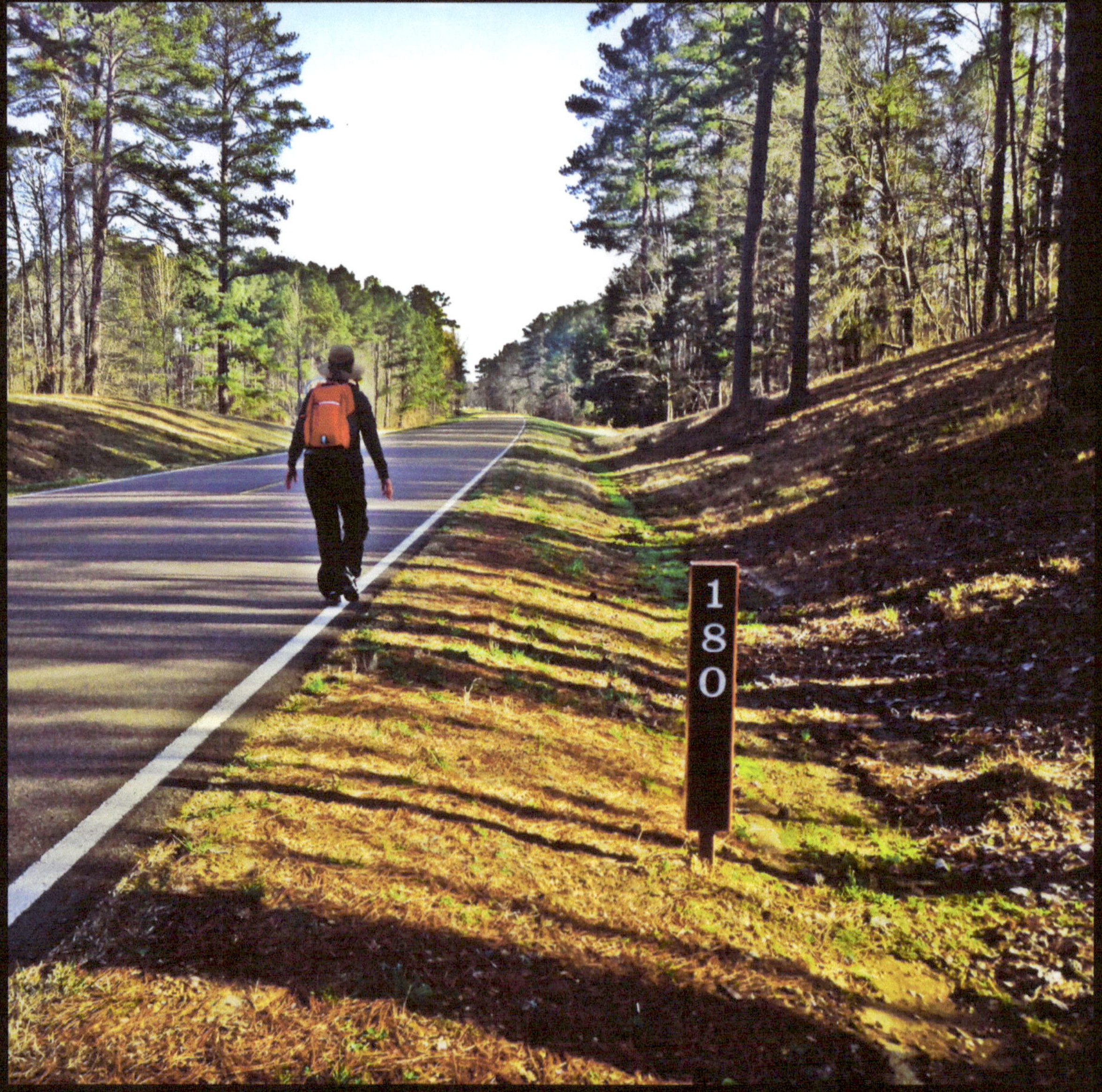
180

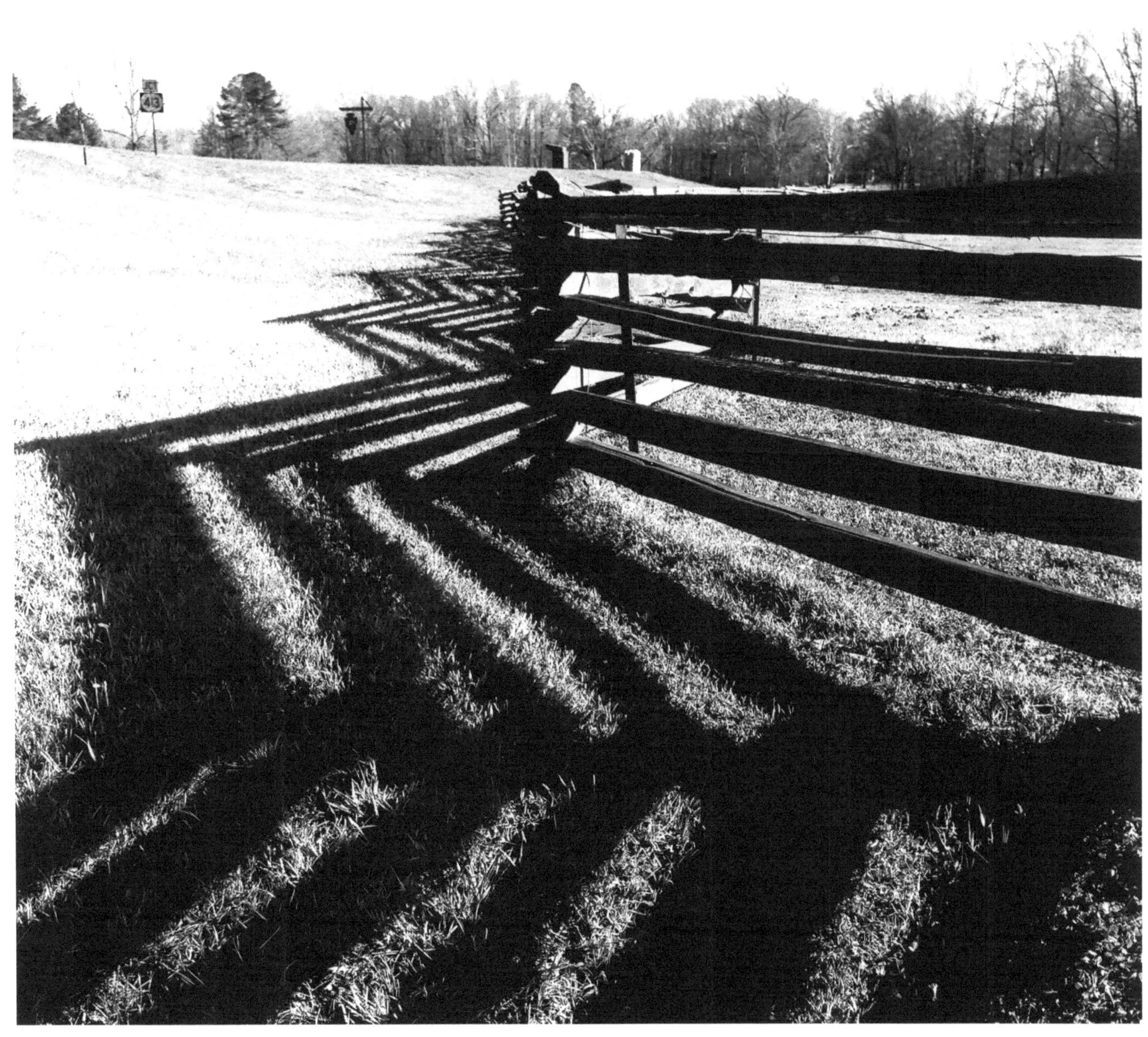
43

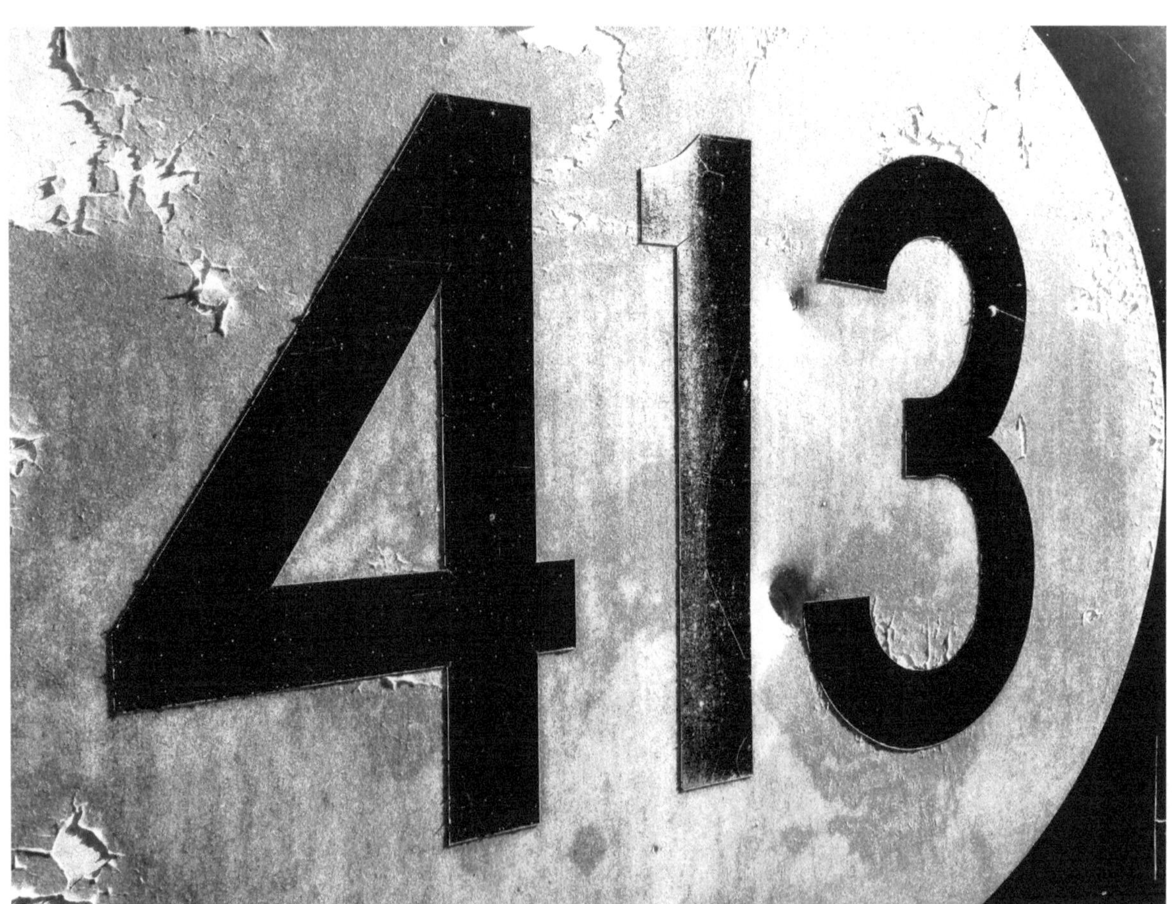
413

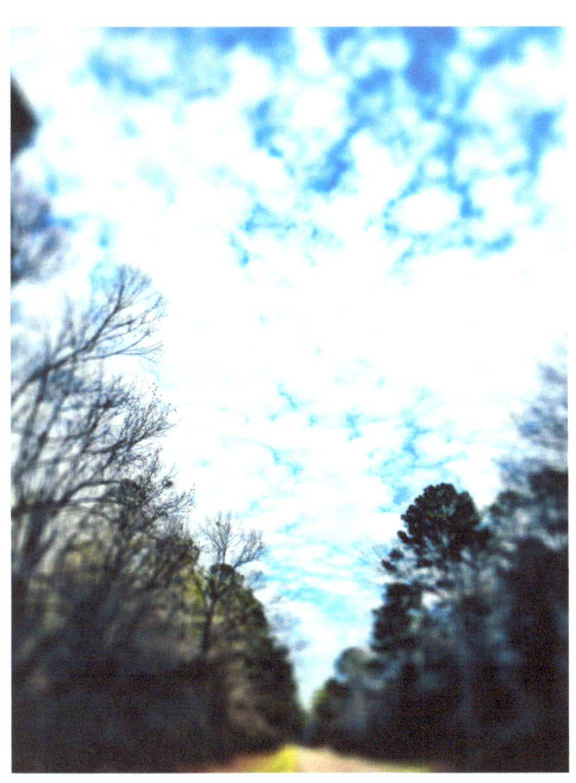

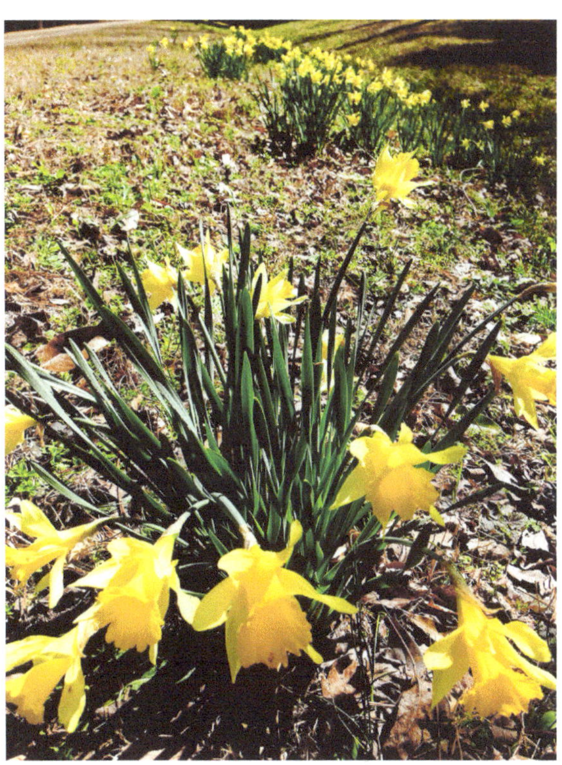

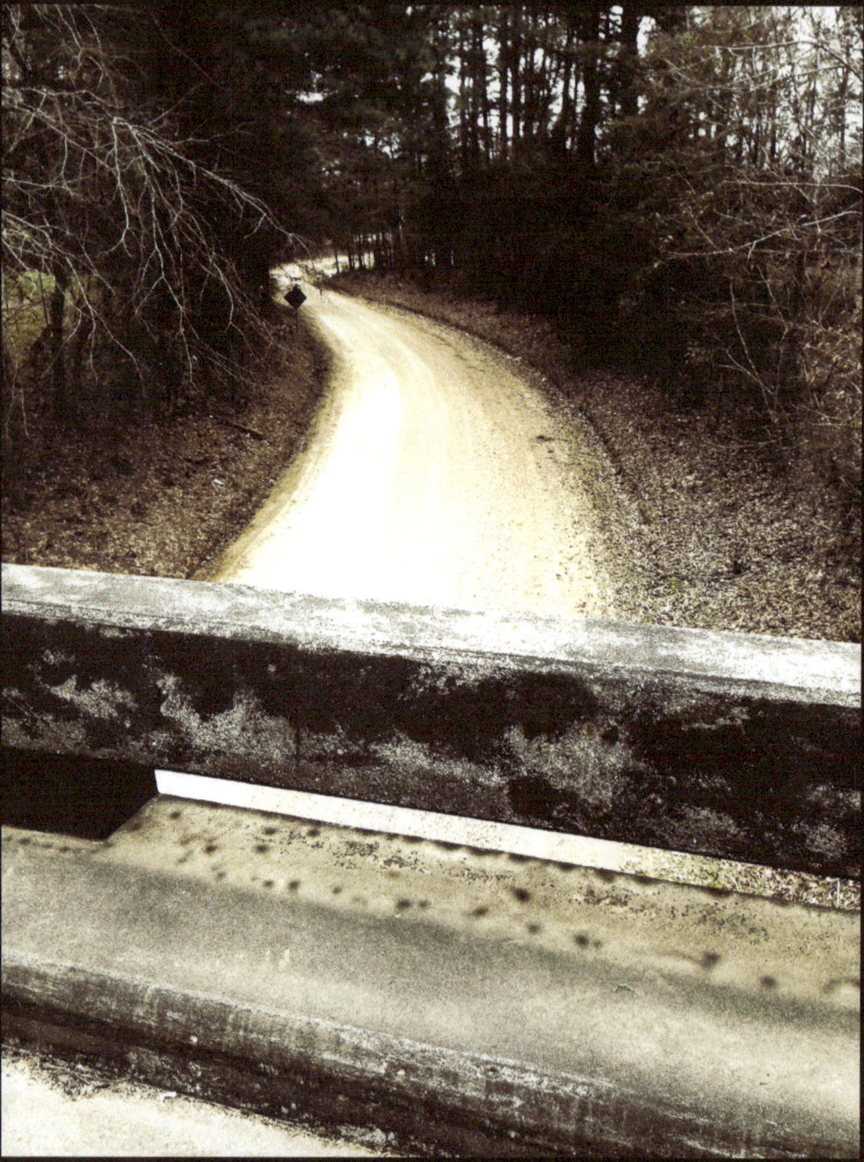

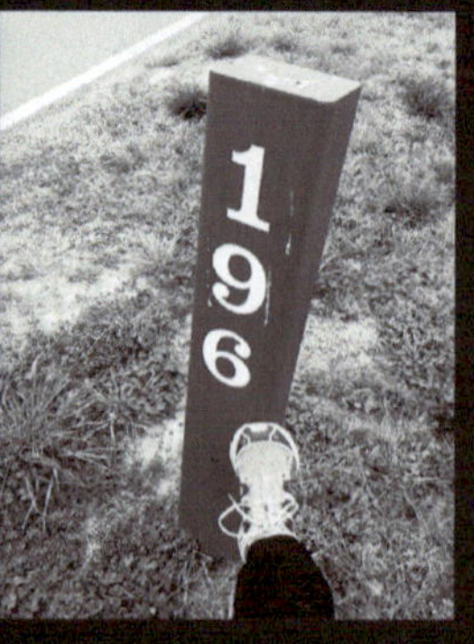
196

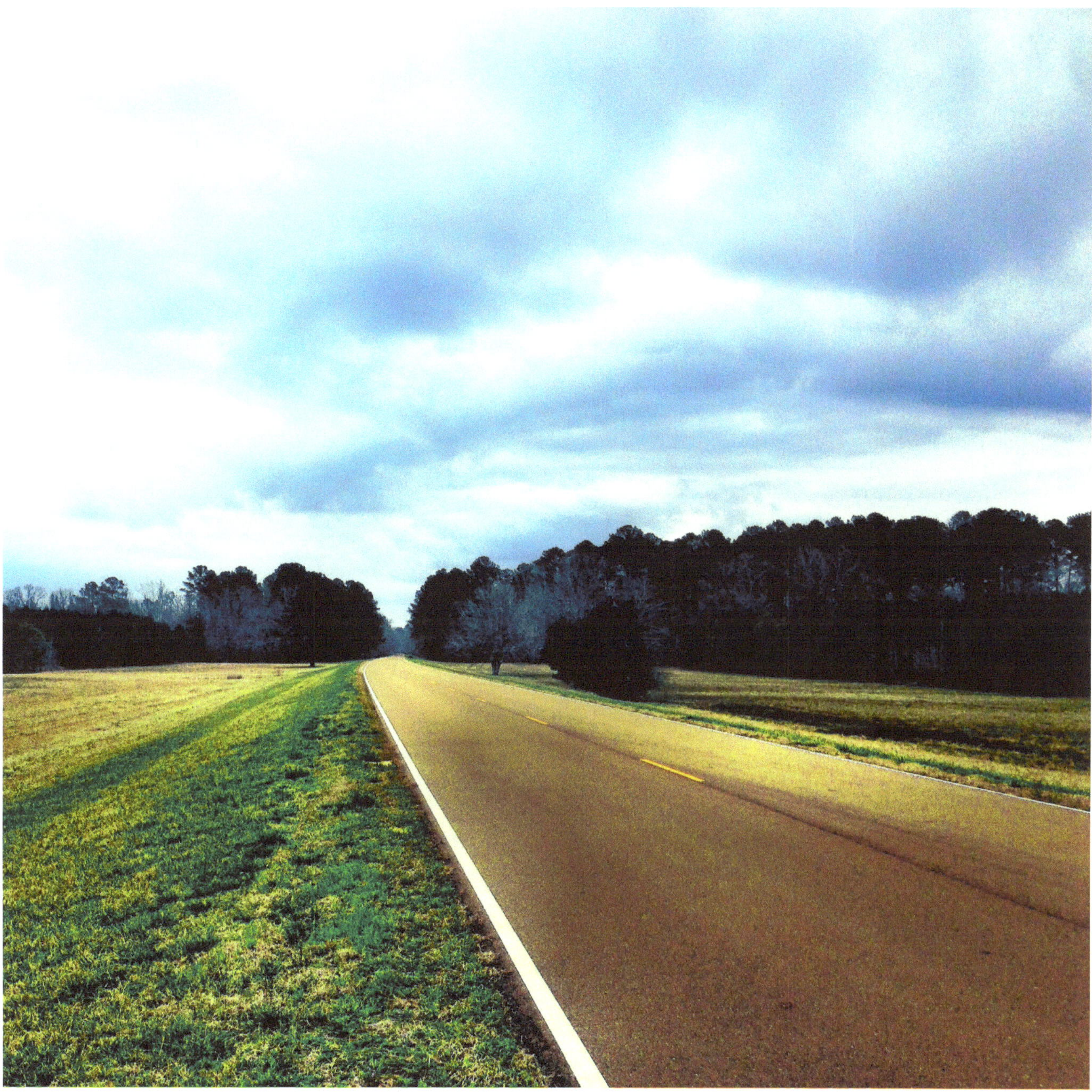

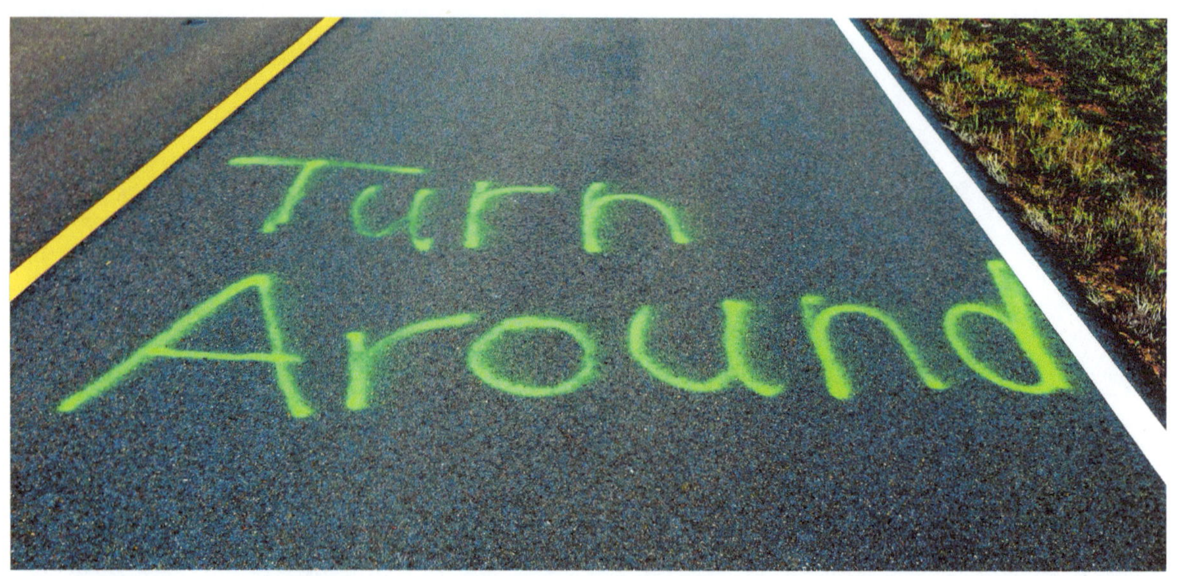
Turn
Around

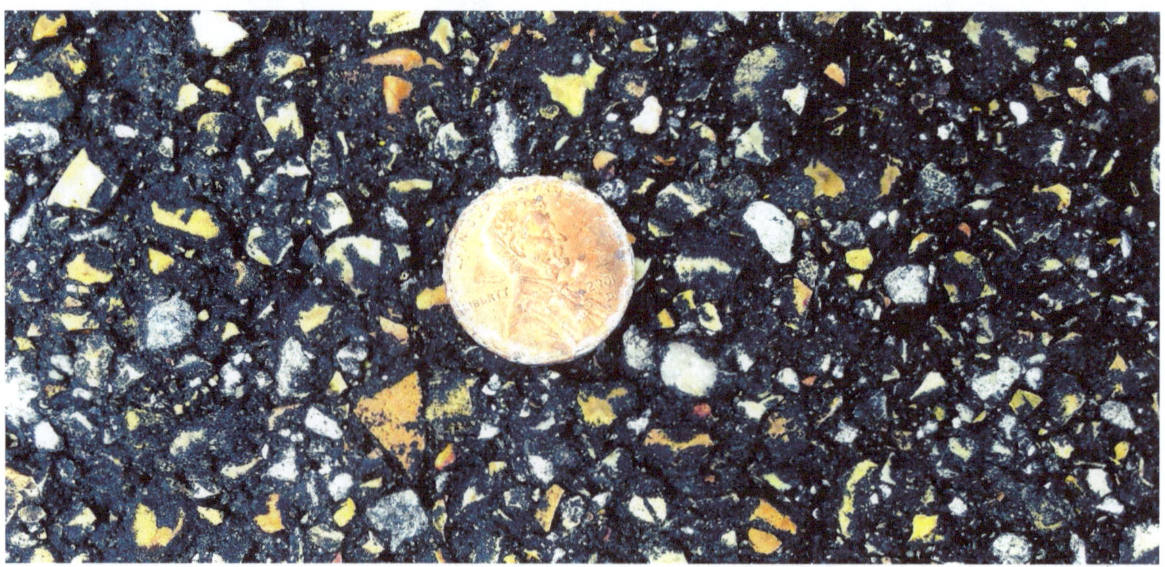

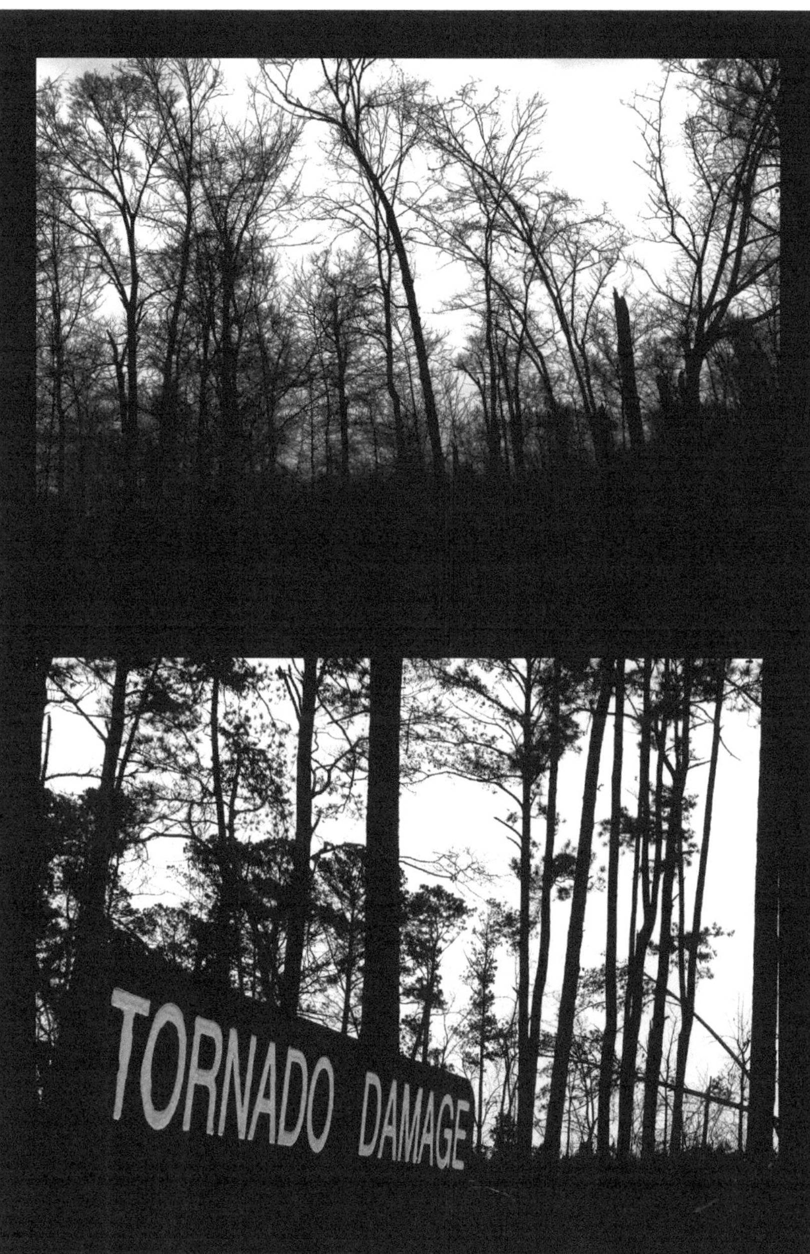
TORNADO DAMAGE

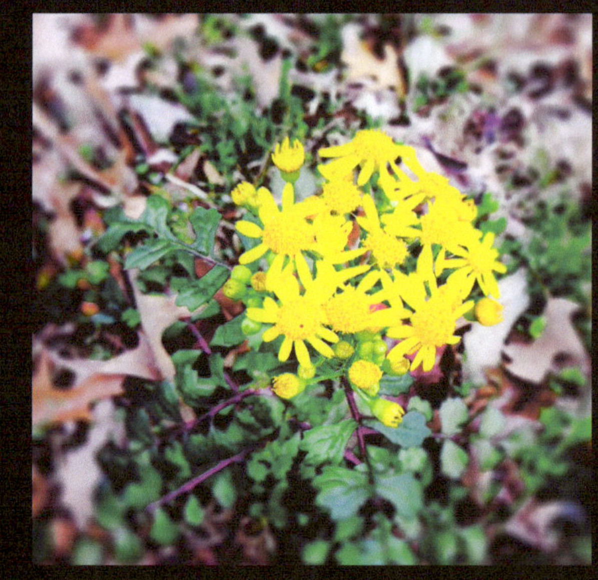

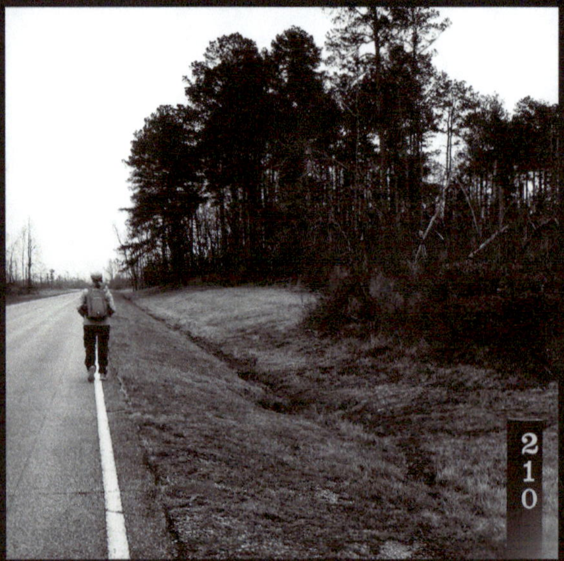
210

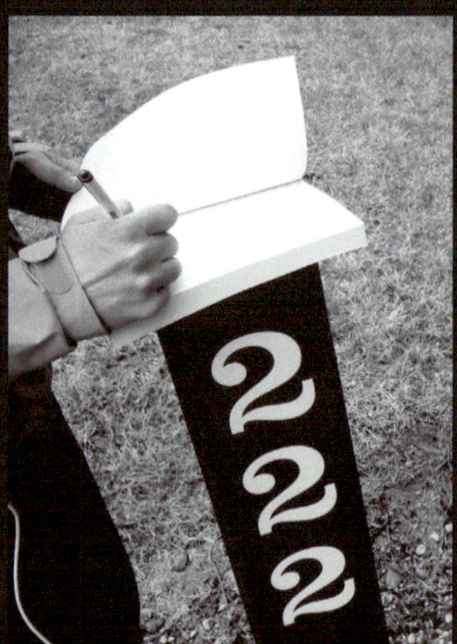
222

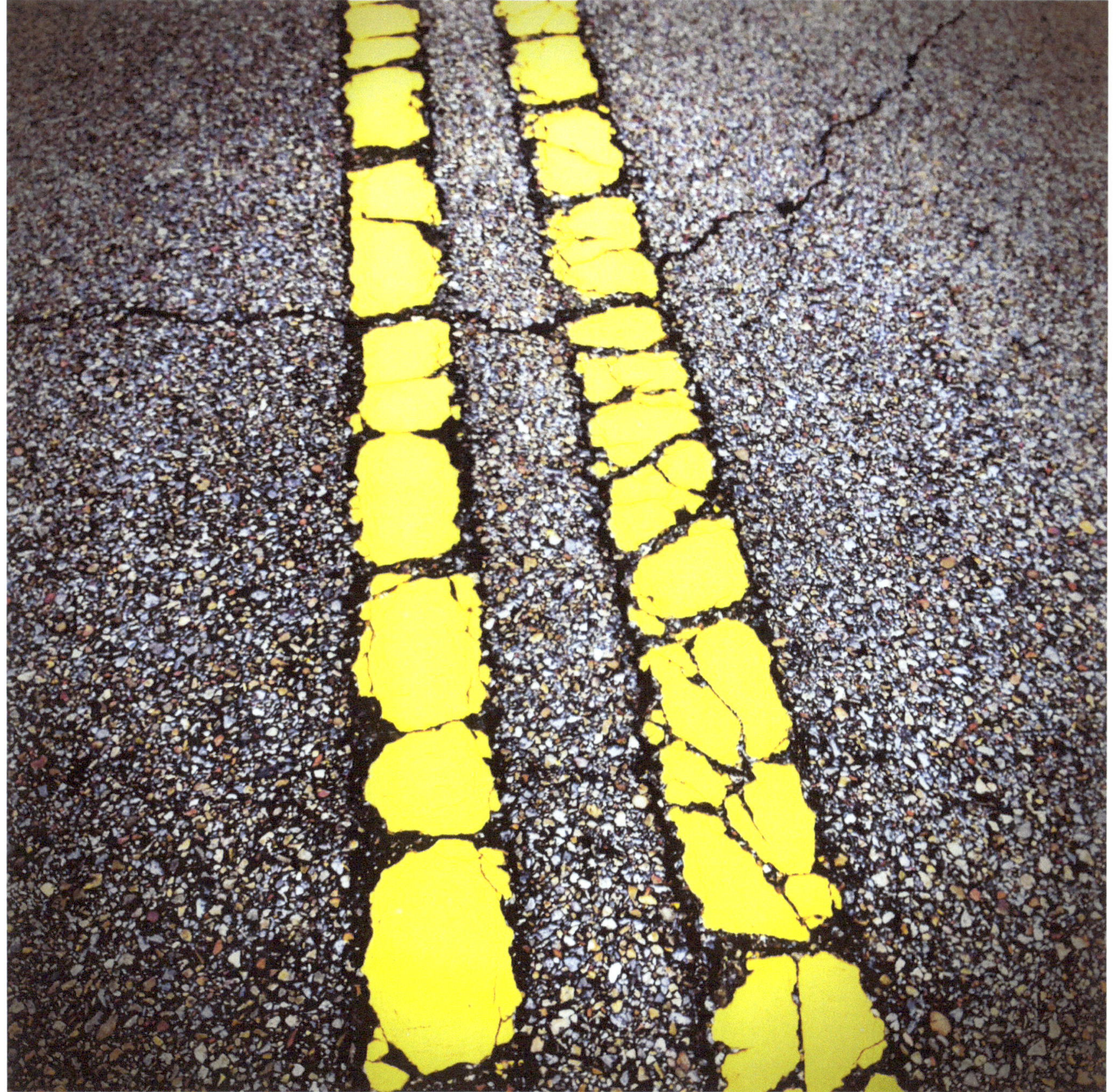

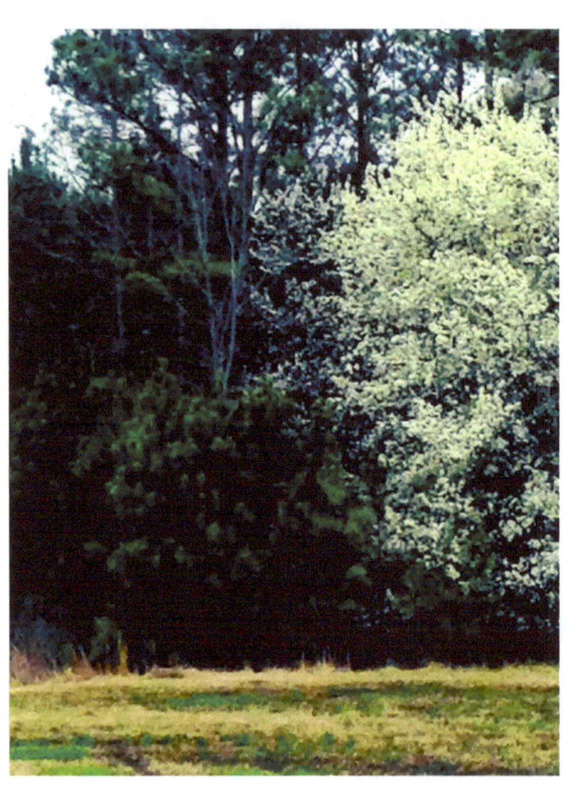

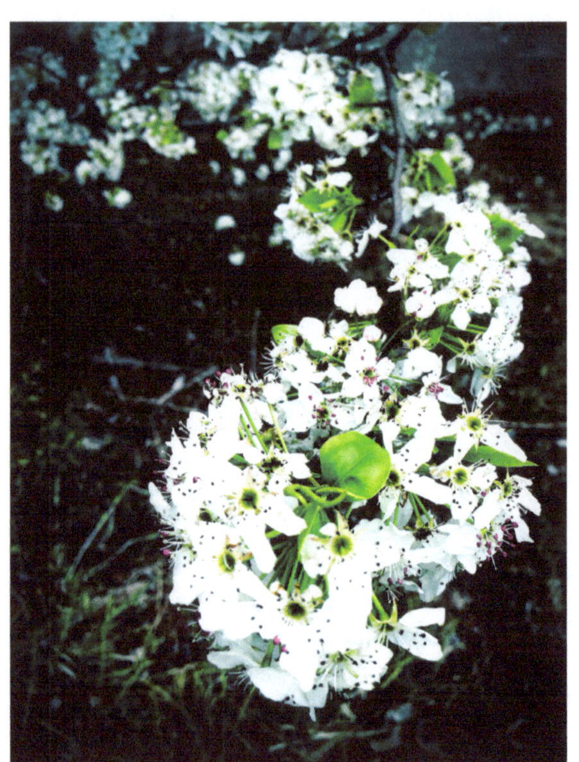

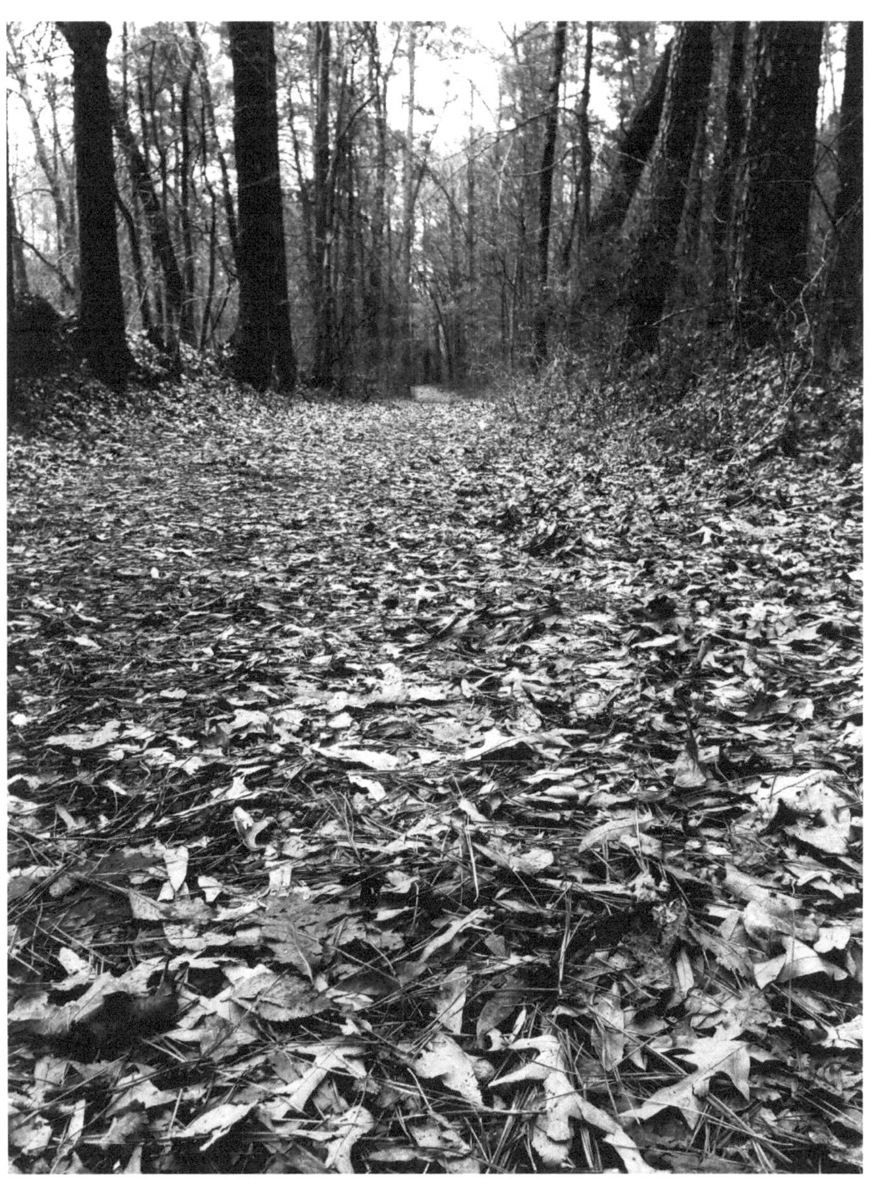

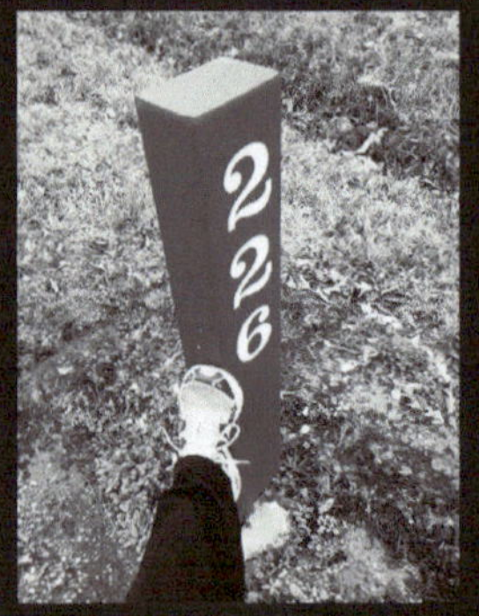
226

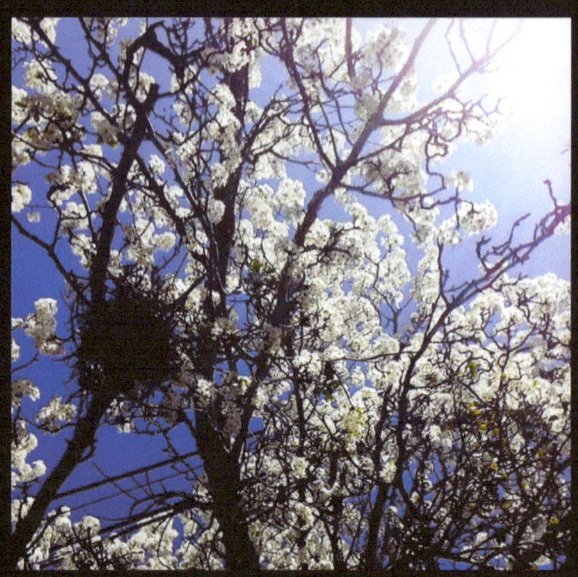

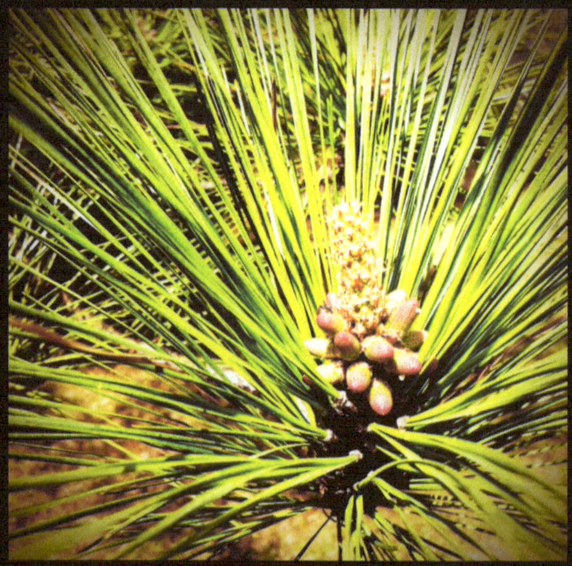

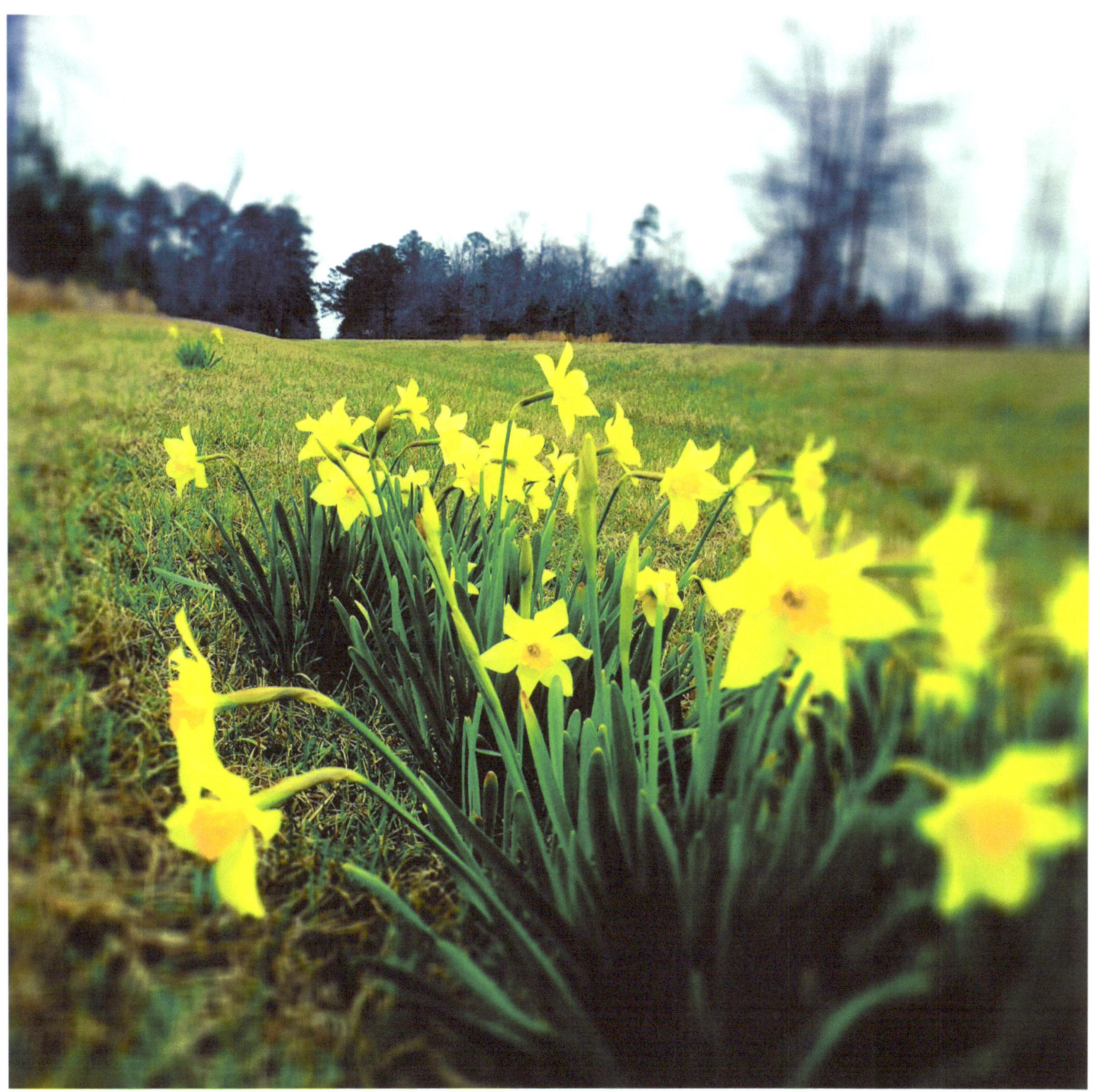

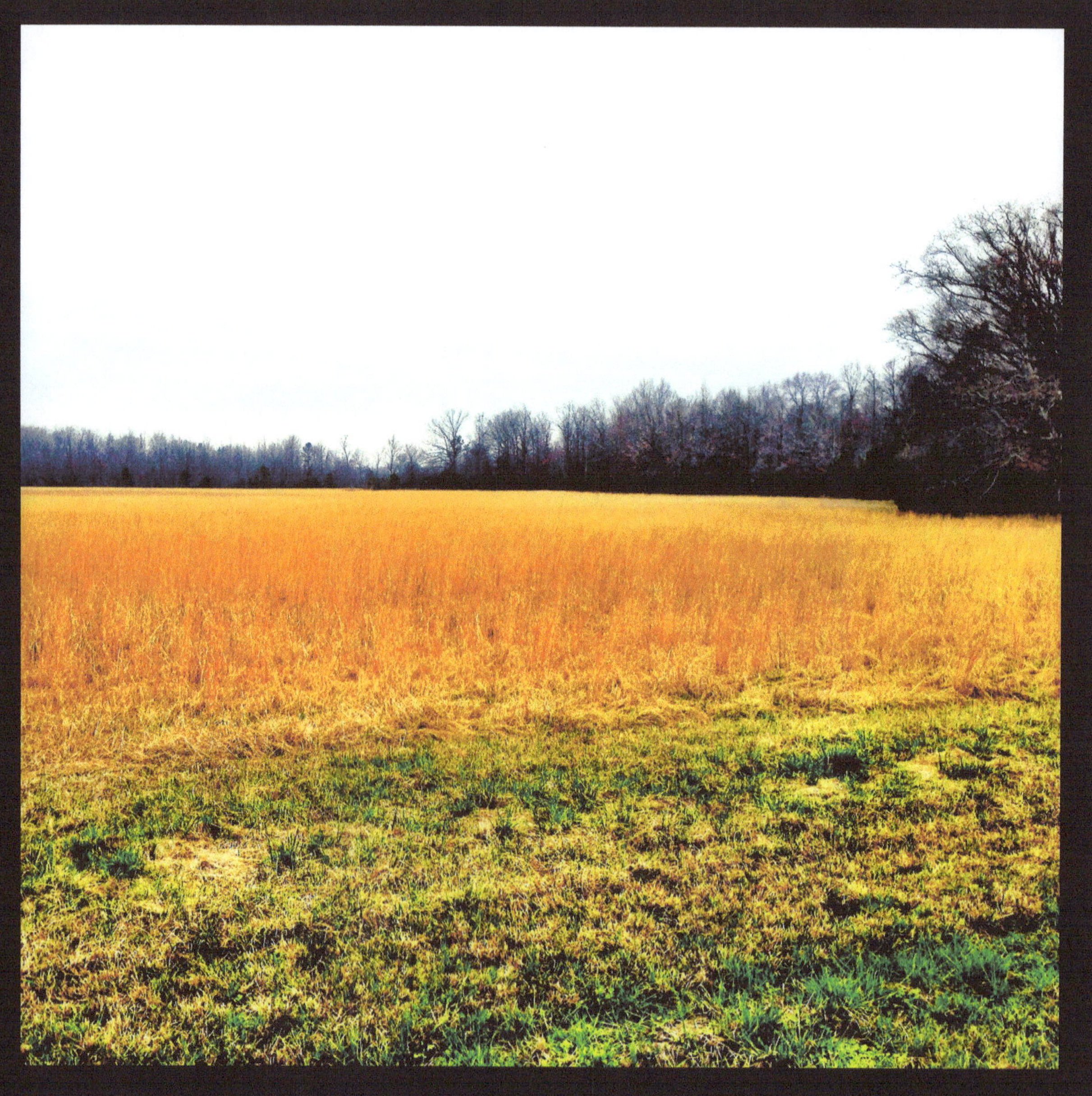

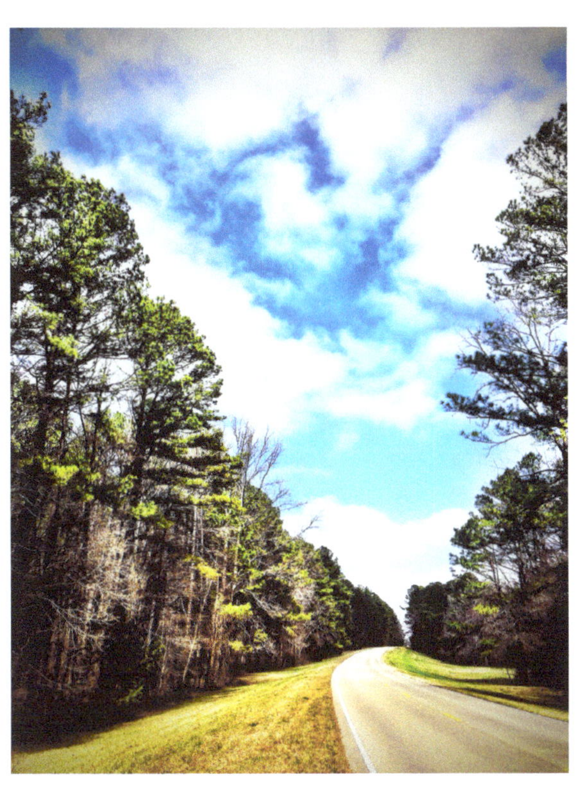

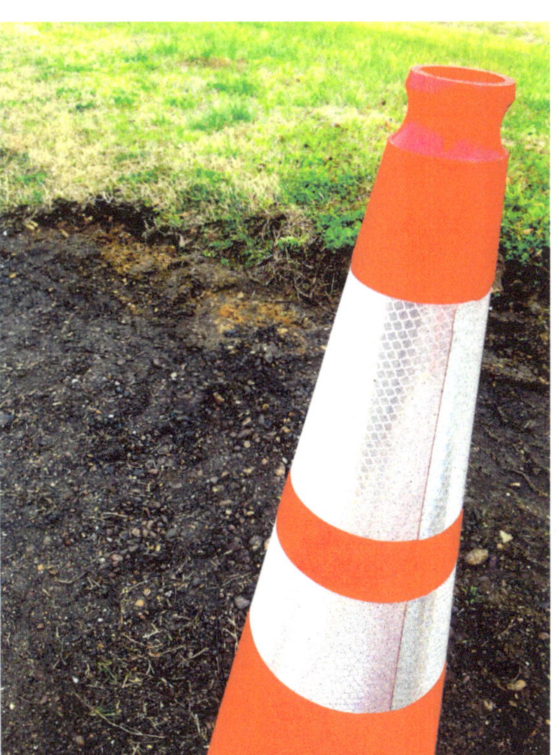

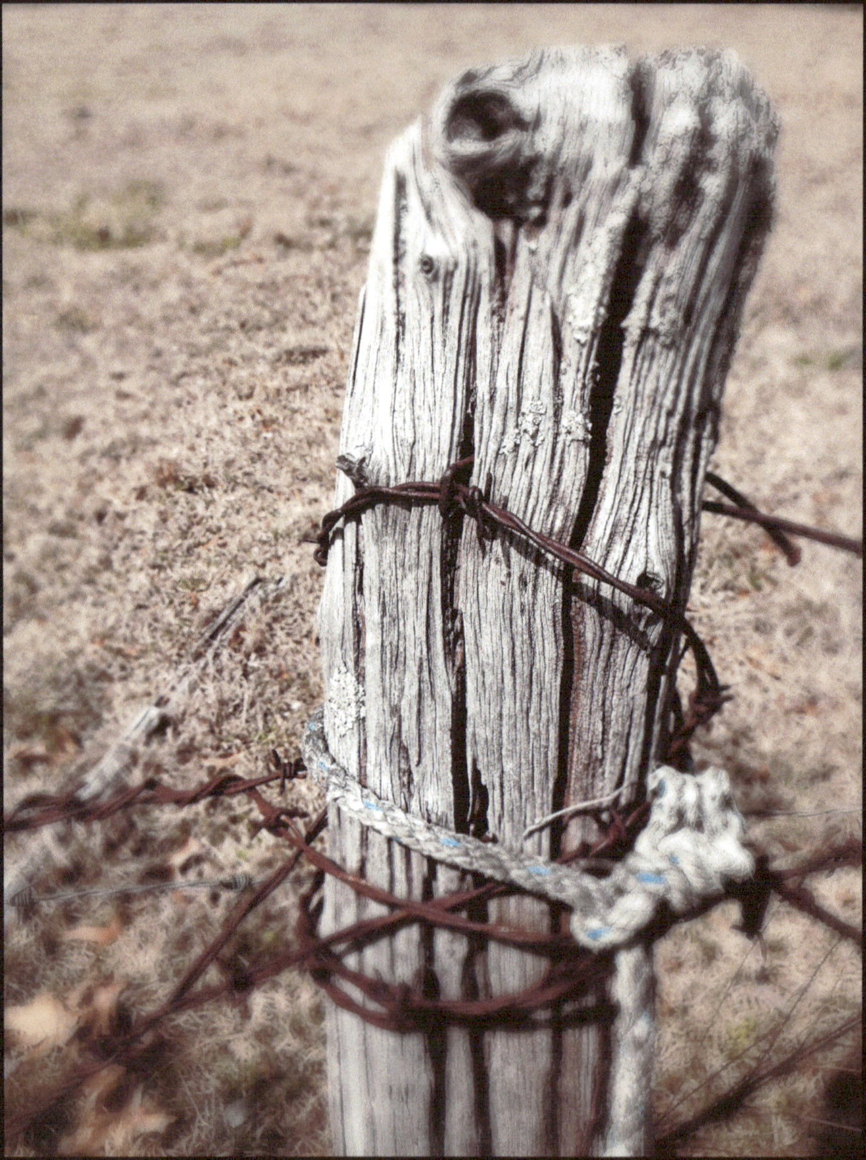

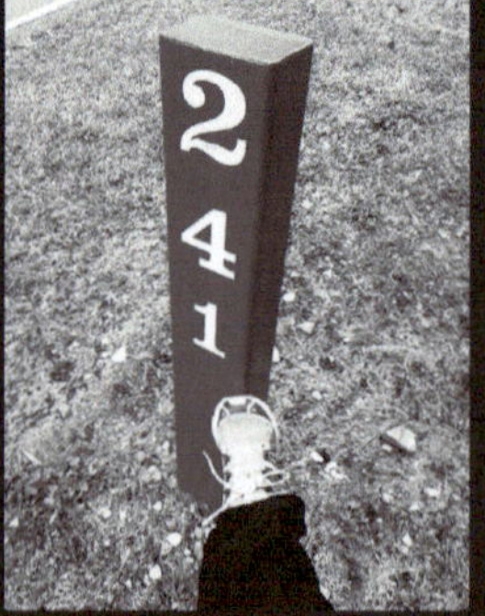
241

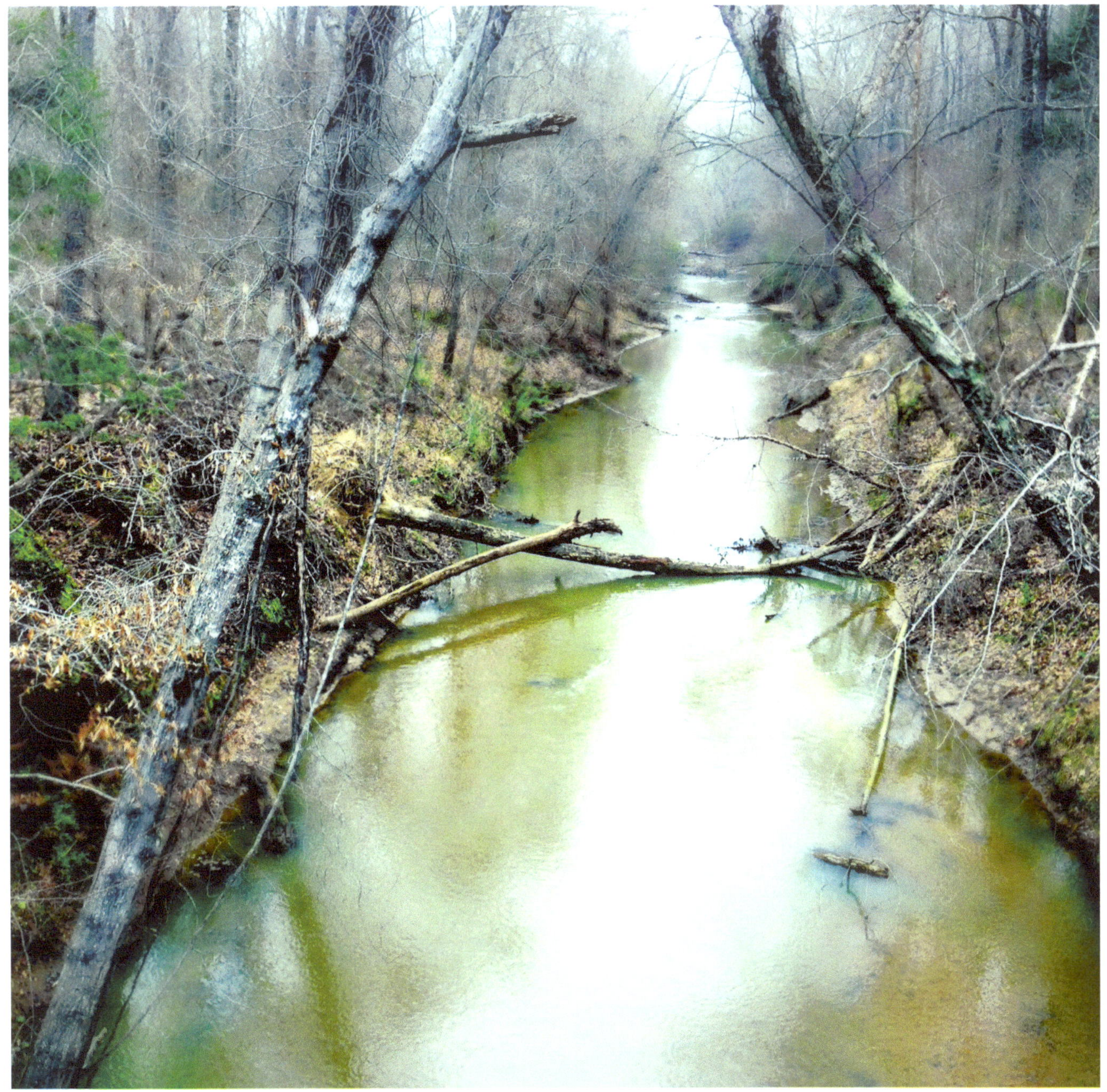

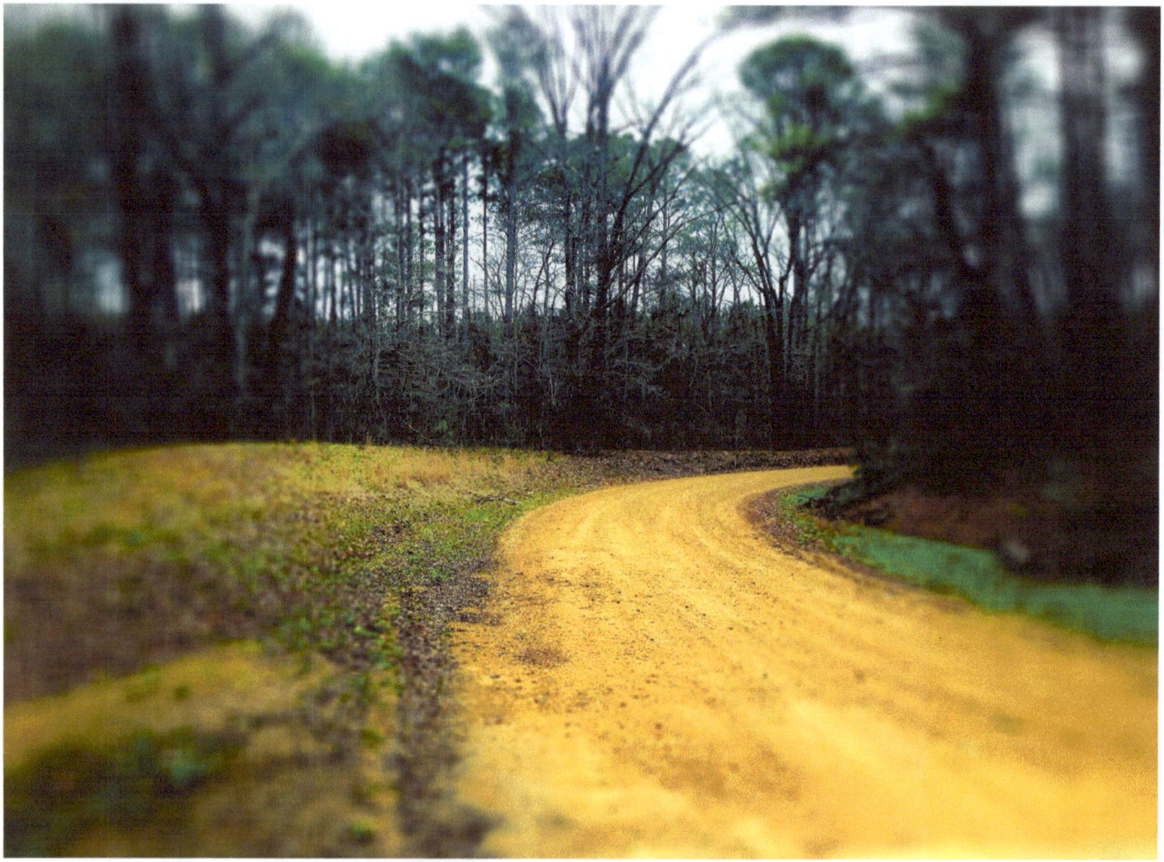

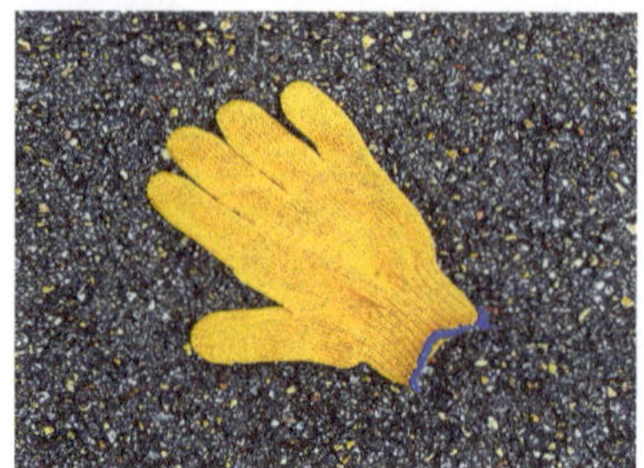

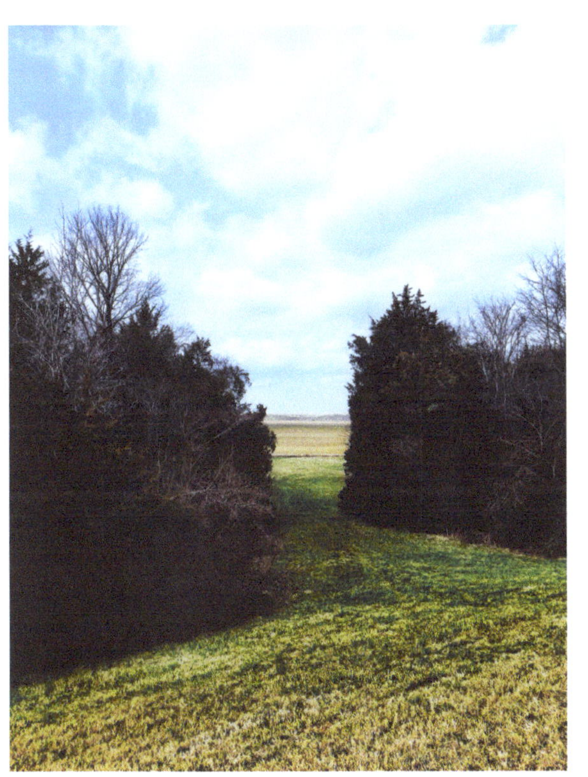

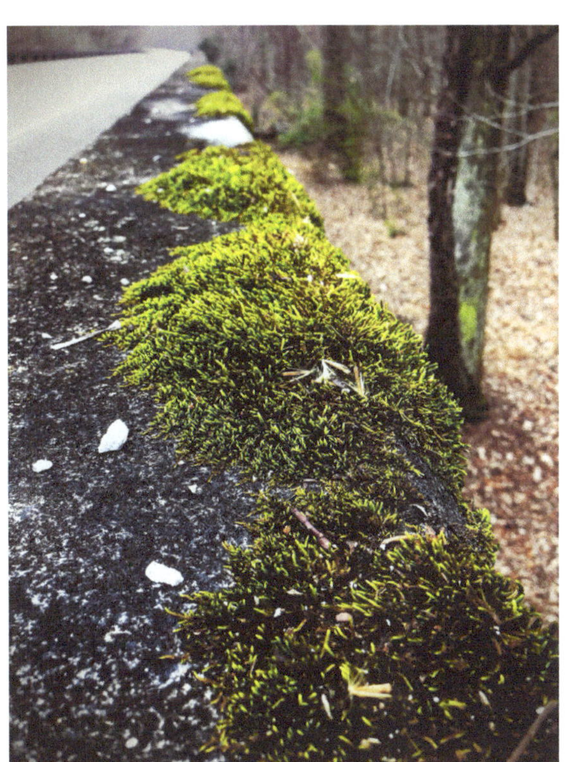

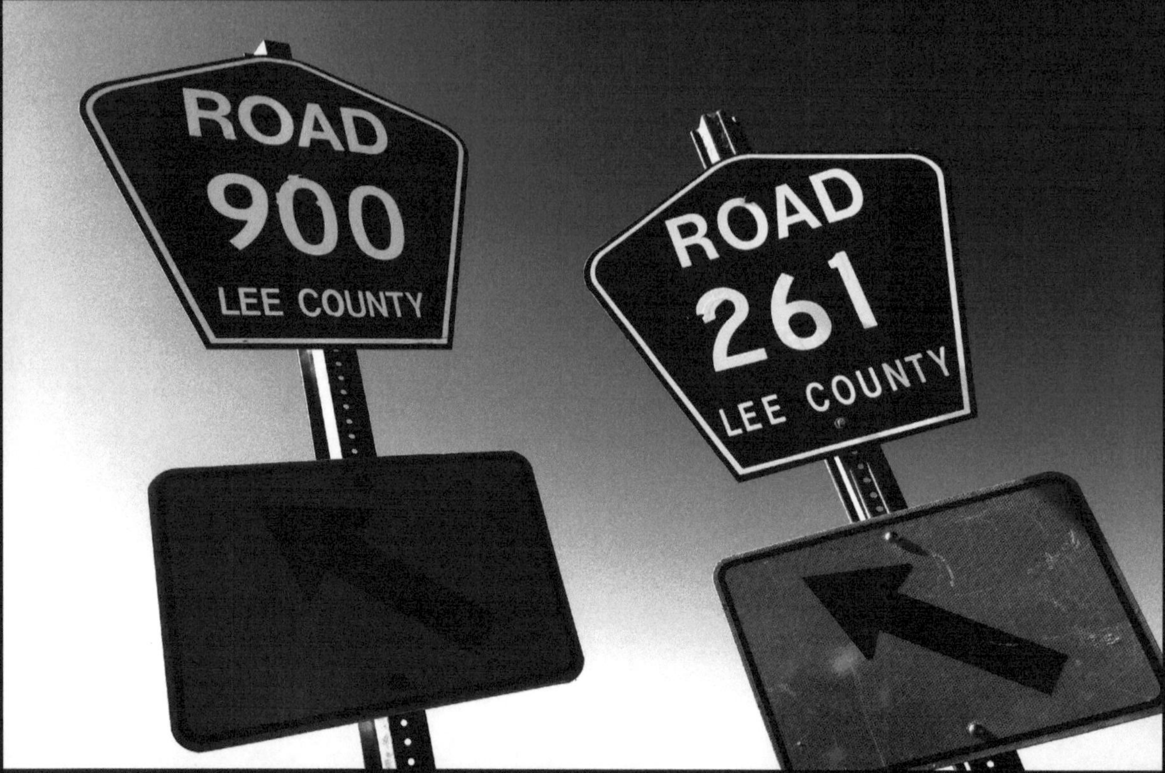

ROAD
900
LEE COUNTY
ROAD
261
LEE COUNTY

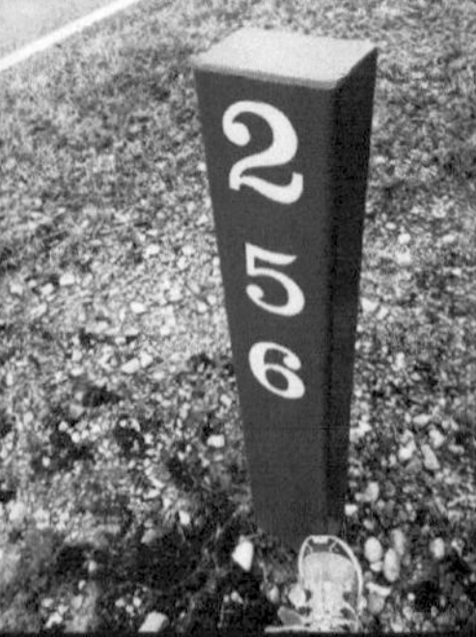
2
5
6

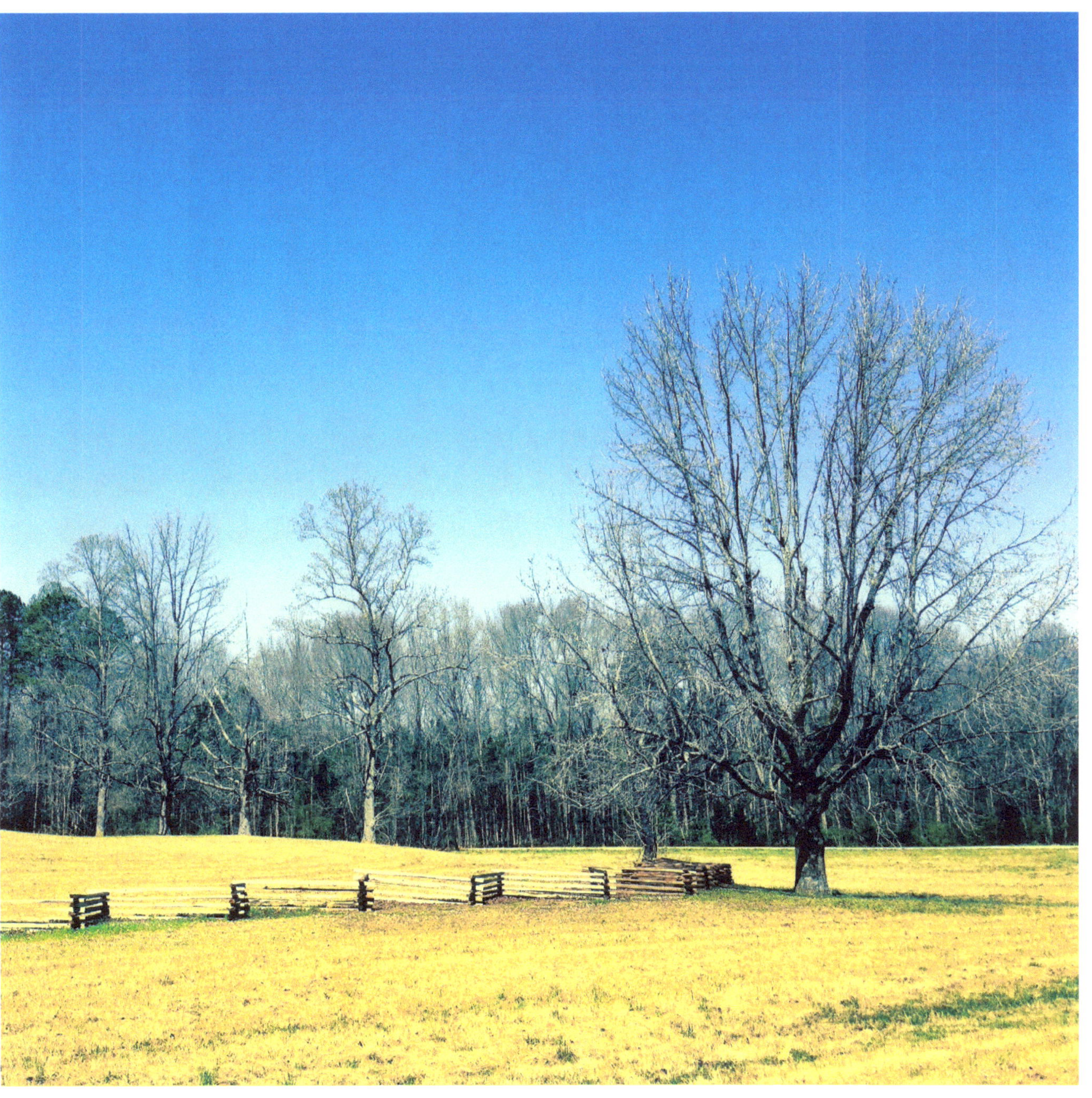

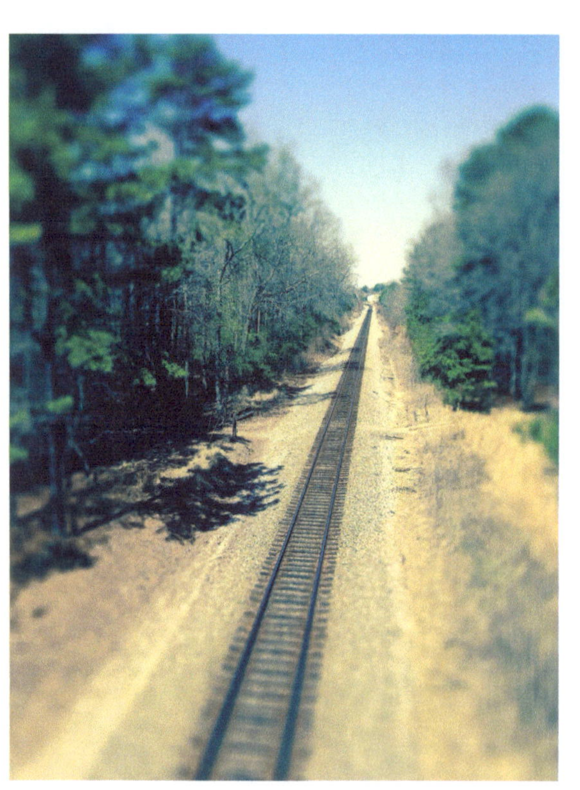

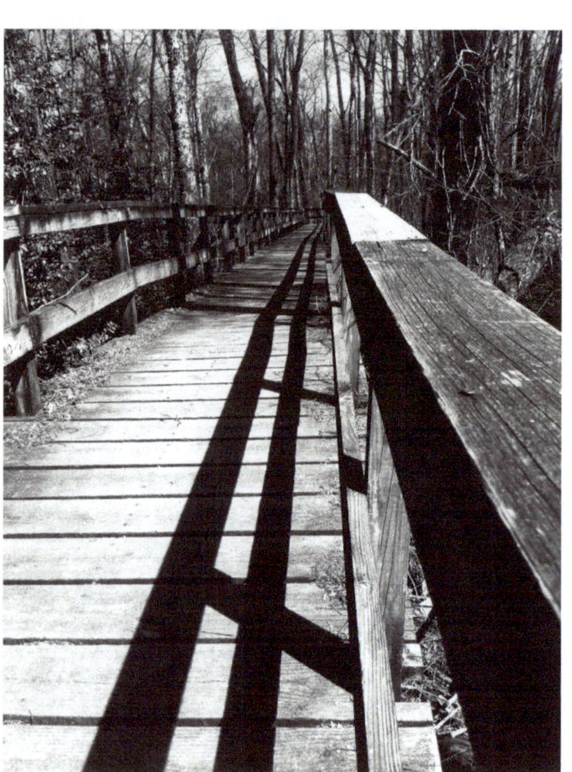

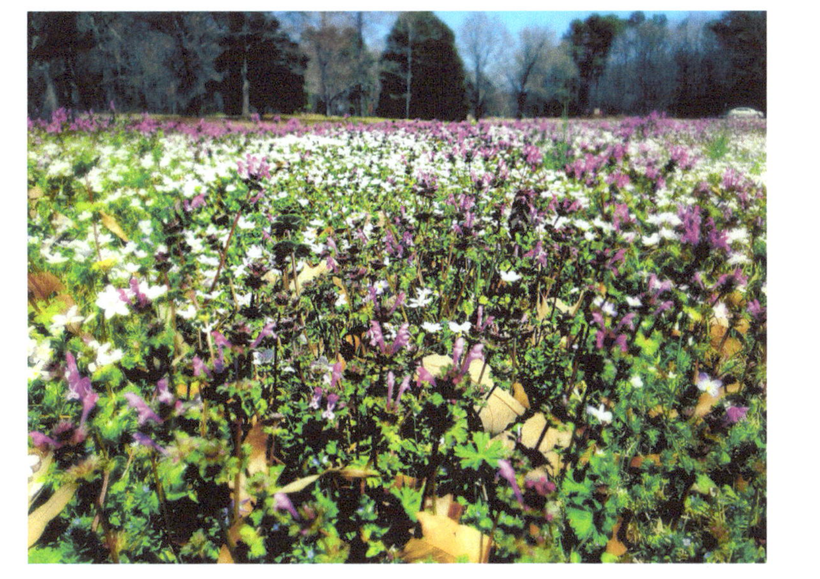

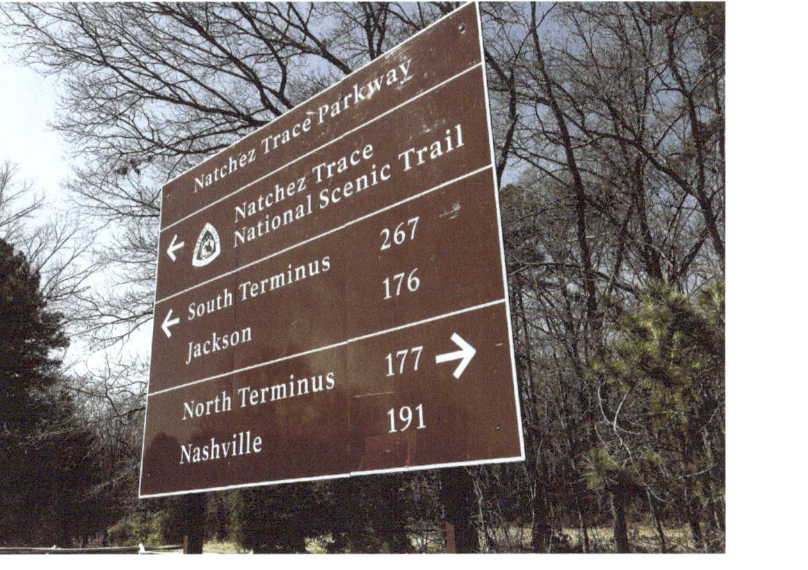
Natchez Trace Parkway
Natchez Trace
National Scenic Trail
South Terminus 267
Jackson 176
North Terminus 177
Nashville 191

TUPELO HARDWARE

In 1946, Elvis' mother, Gladys brought him here to buy a bicycle. Once they arrived, a 22-caliber rifle caught Elvis' eye, and he asked his mother to buy it instead. She wasn't happy about purchasing a gun so they compromised on a guitar. Forest L. Bobo, a long-time employee of Tupelo Hardware, sold the guitar to the young Elvis for $7.90.

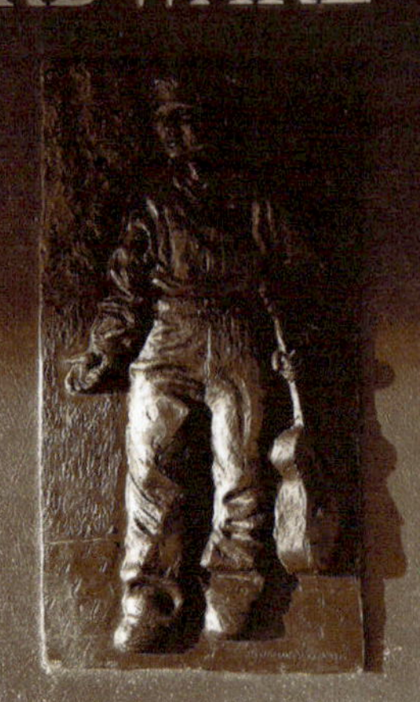

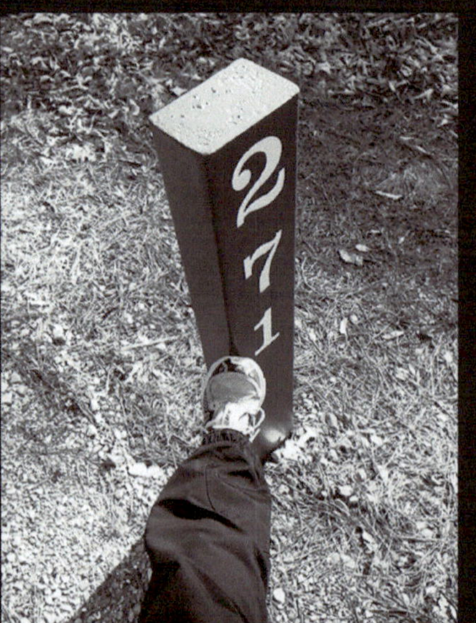

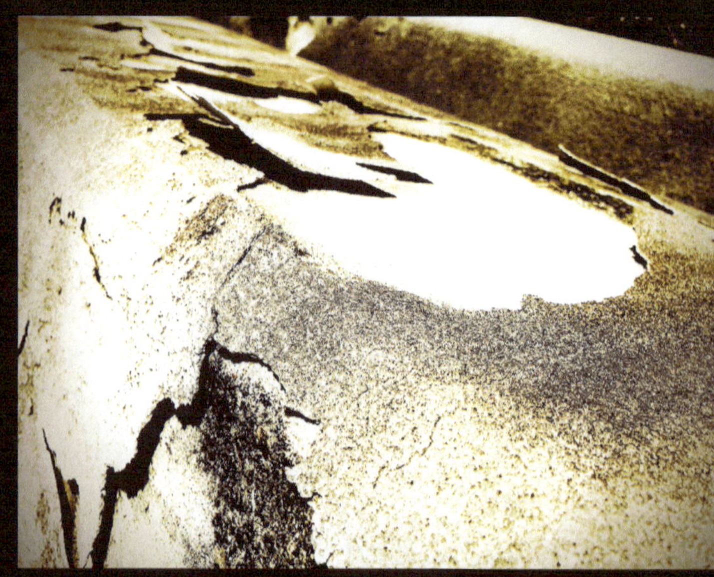

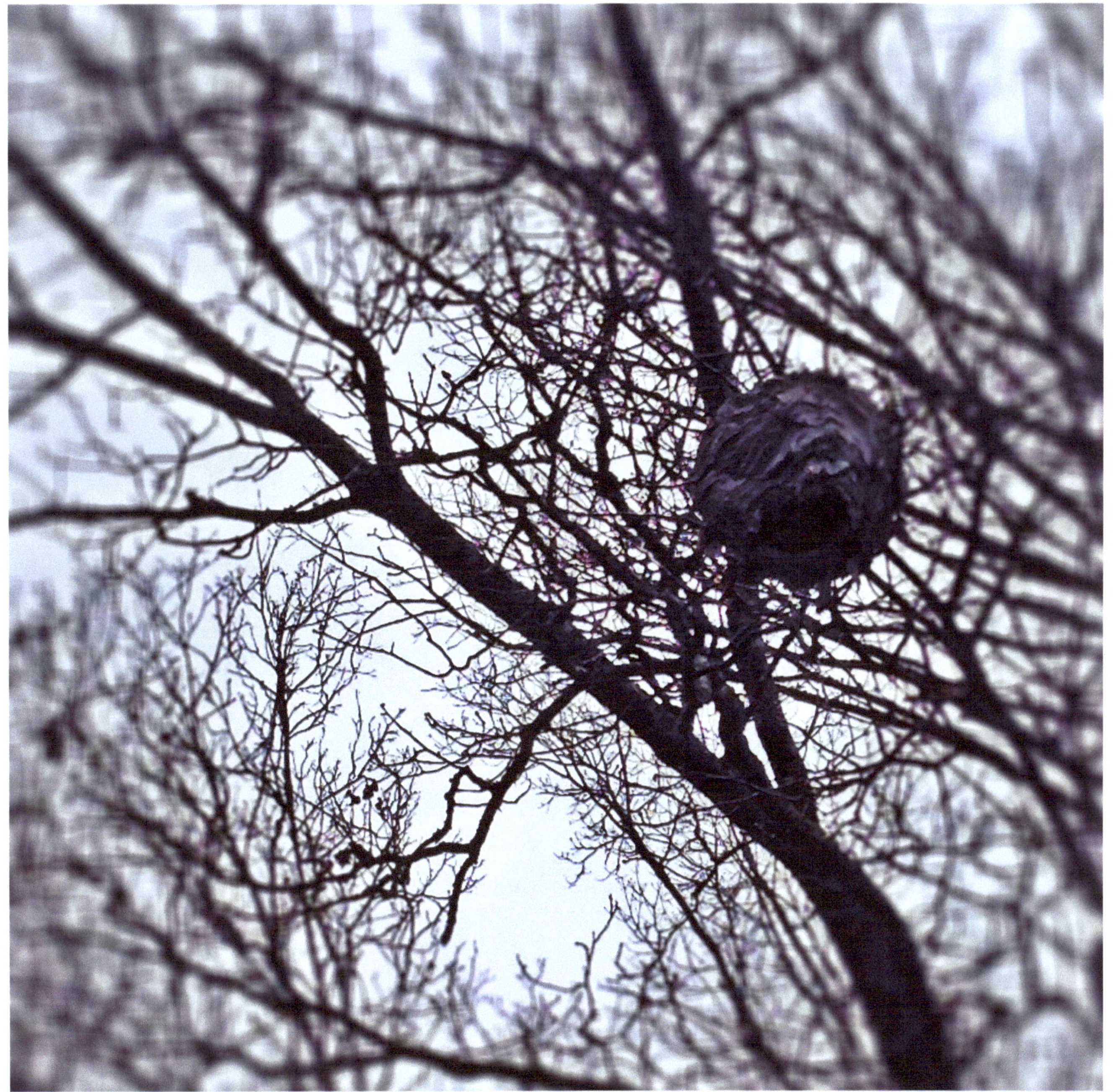

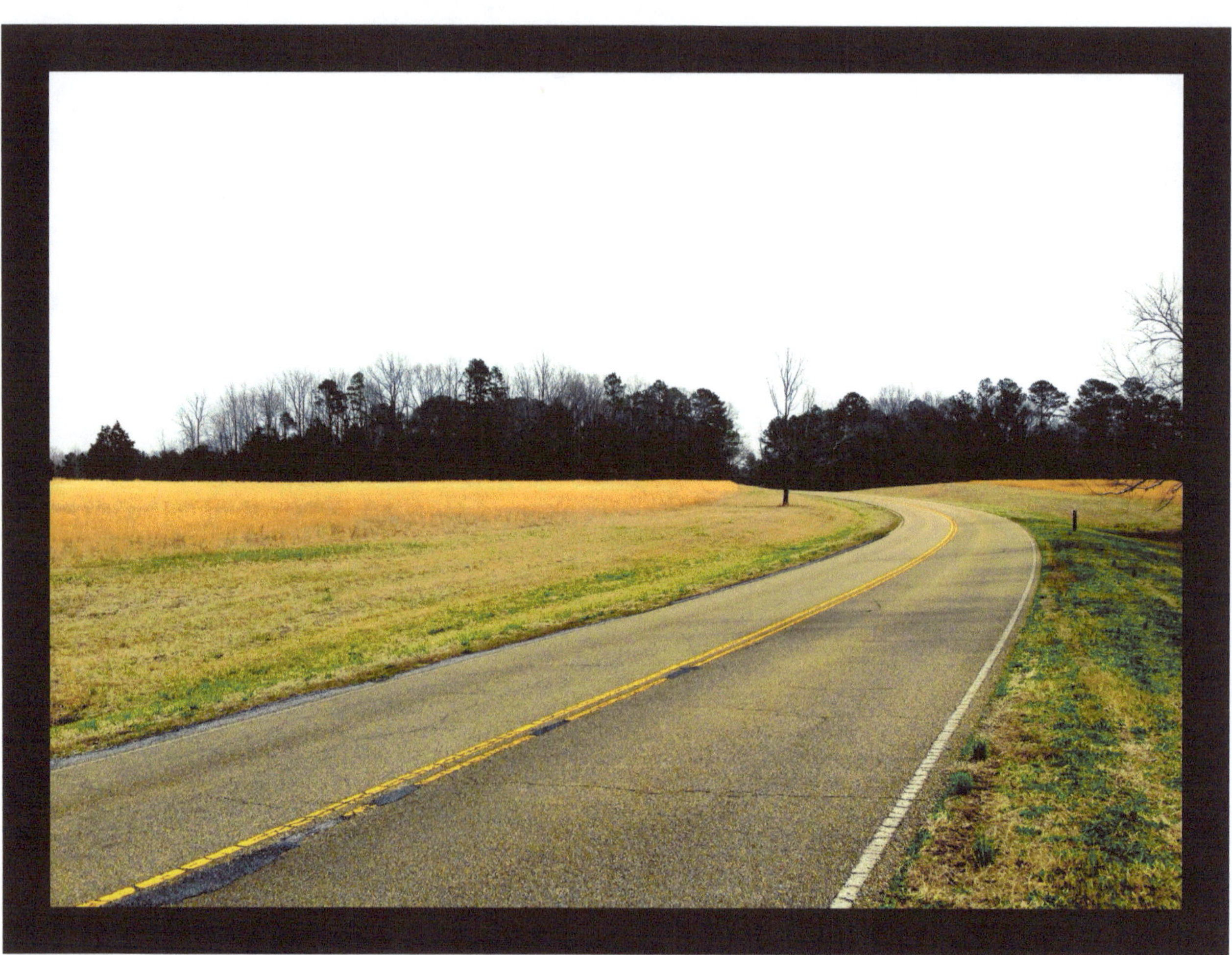

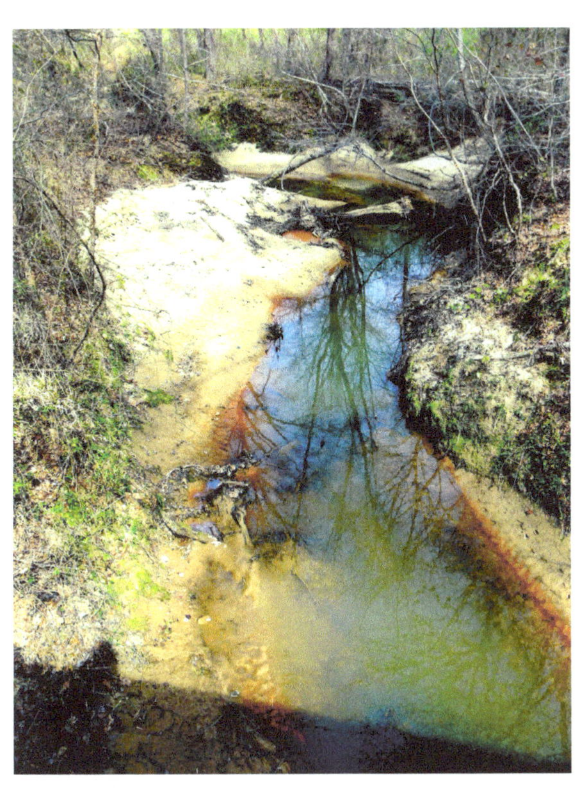

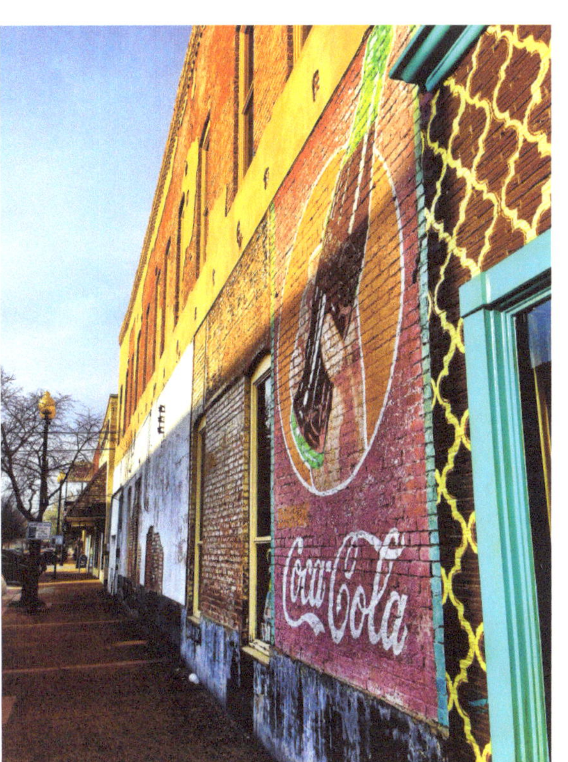
Coca-Cola

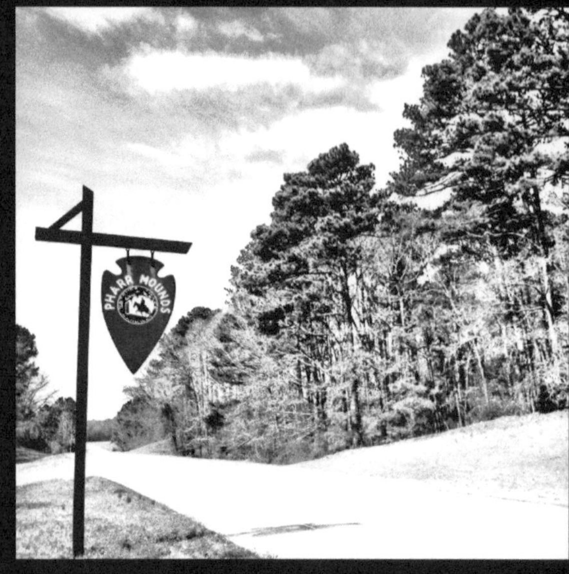
PHARR MOUNDS

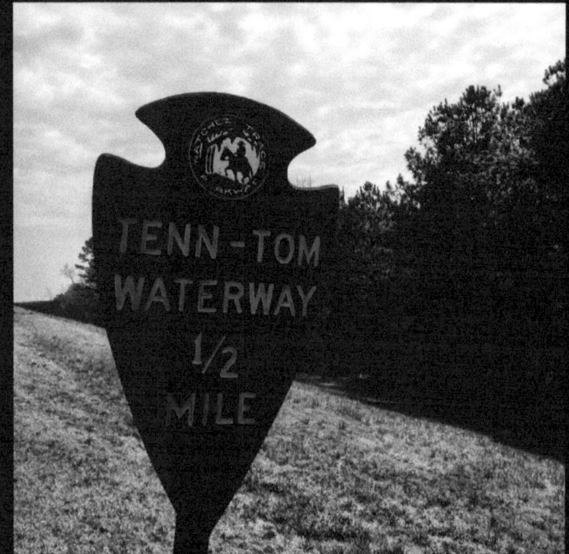
TENN-TOM
WATERWAY
1/2
MILE

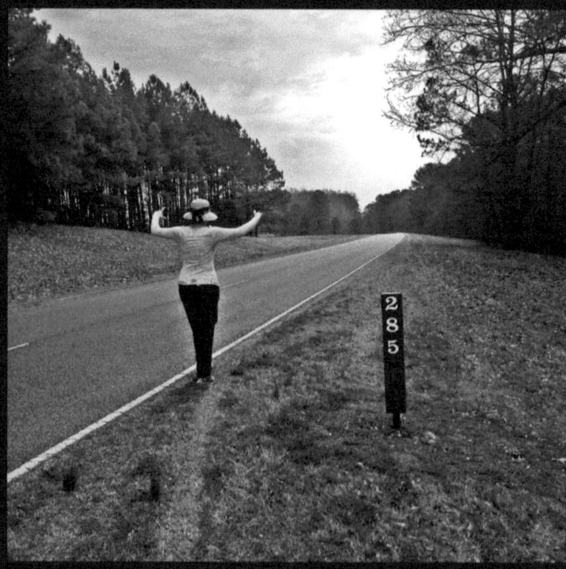
285

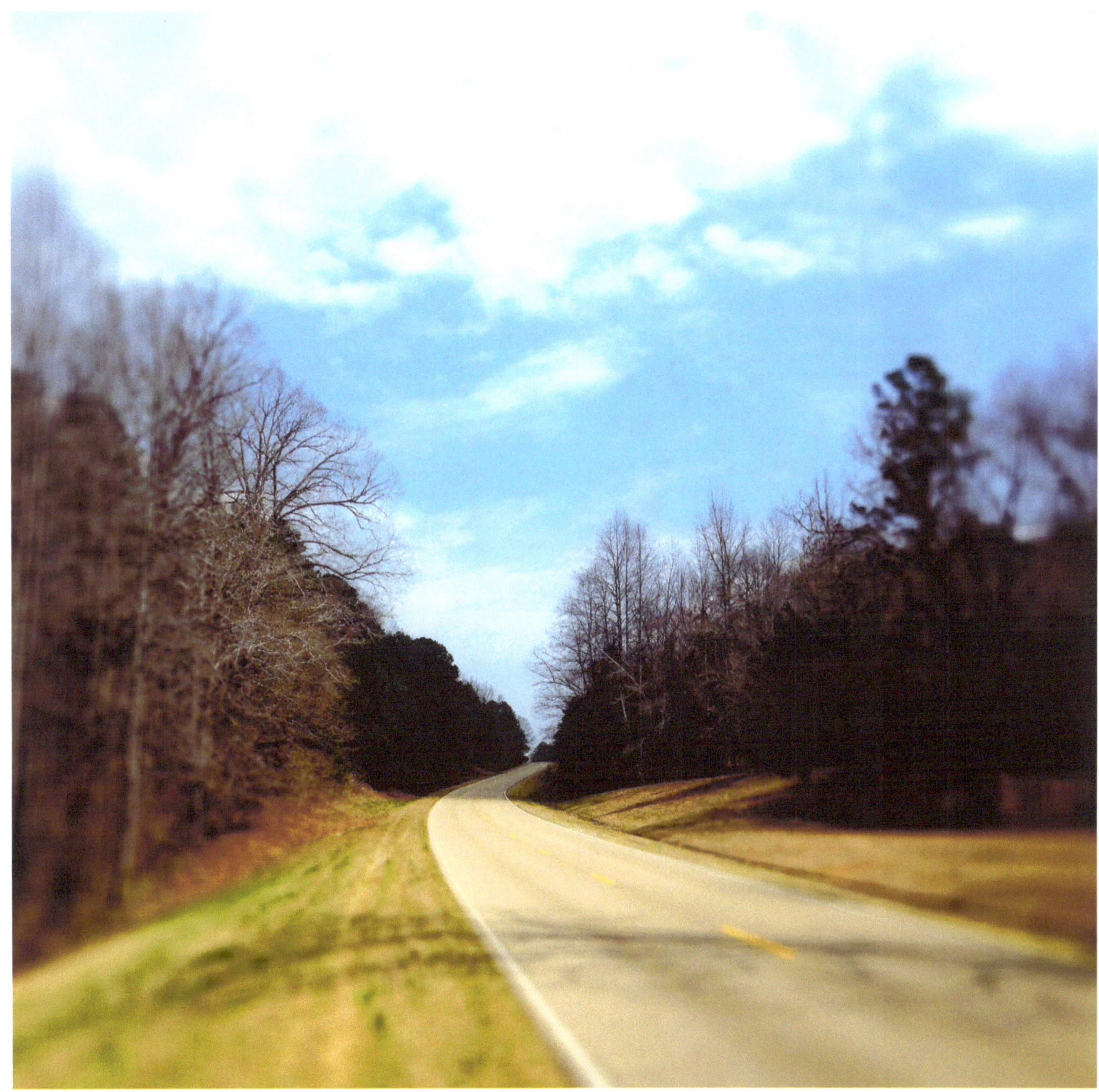

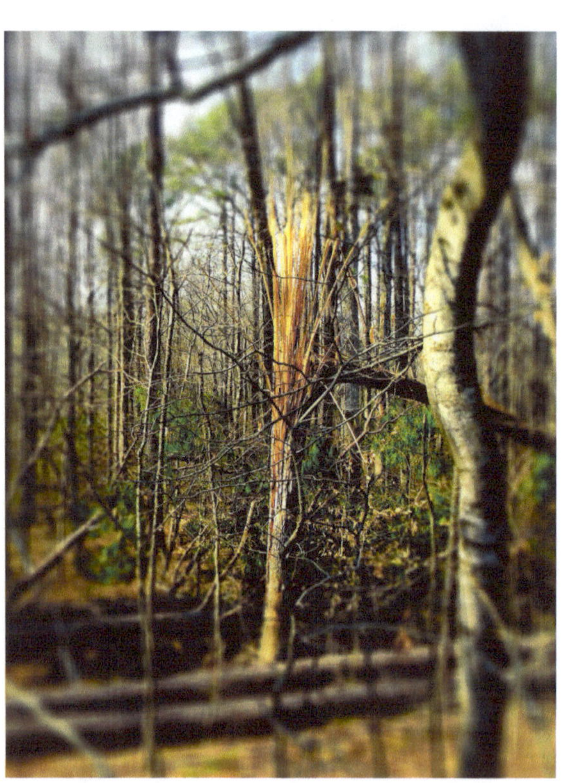
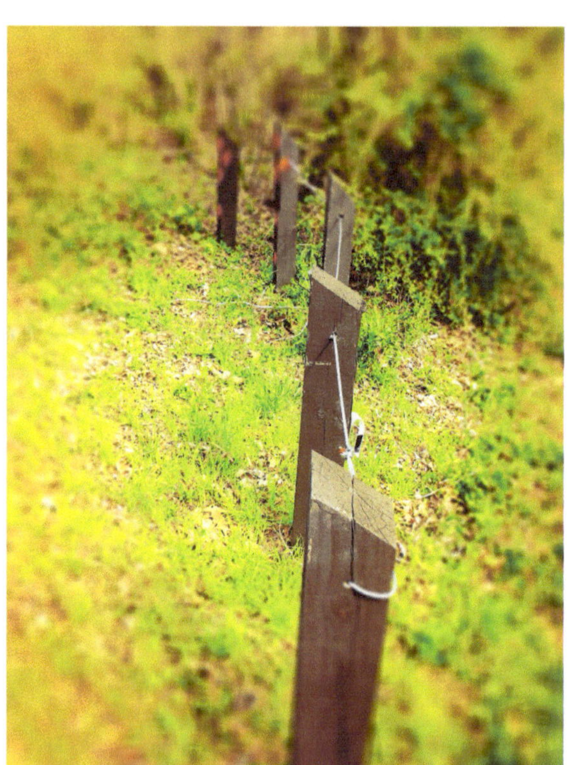

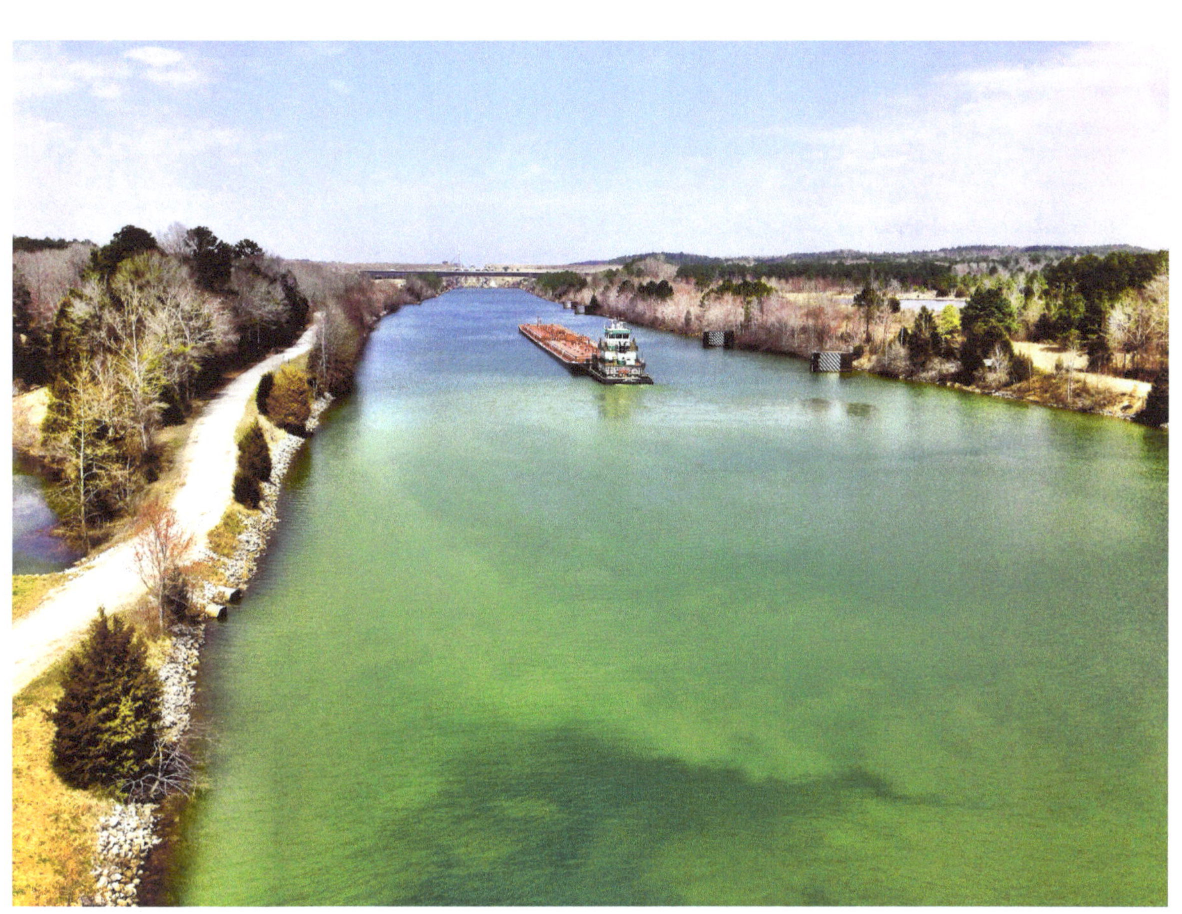

My birthday. I stumbled through the second mile of my walk, close to where Meriwether Lewis probably hit the Natchez Trace on the way to his death at Grinder's Stand on October 11, 1809. Cool air tingled on my face, more mid-October than late-March. I stooped to photograph what I thought was a piece of trash.

Only it wasn't.

There on the tarmac was a Lewis and Clark nickel. Tails up. Clark's words *Ocean in view! O! The joy!* screamed down through time. Clark's joy flooded my heart as I held it aloft and squealed aloud, "It's a birthday present. From Meriwether Lewis to me." I swear I heard Lewis whisper his affirmation.

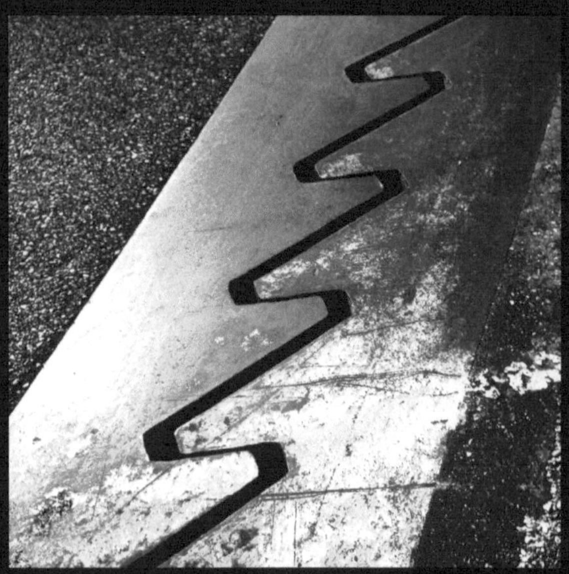

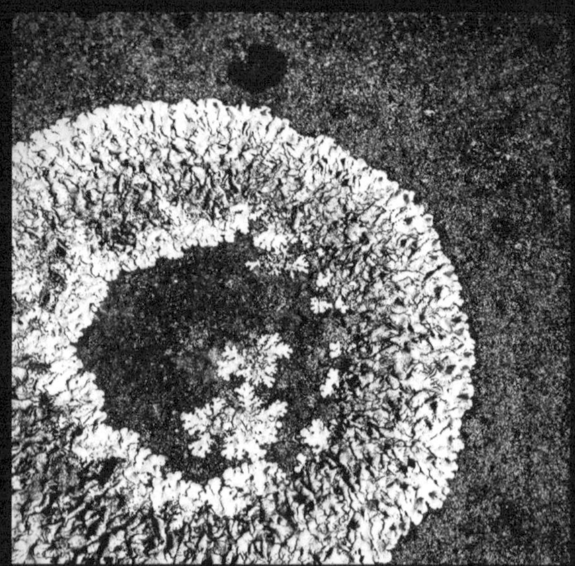

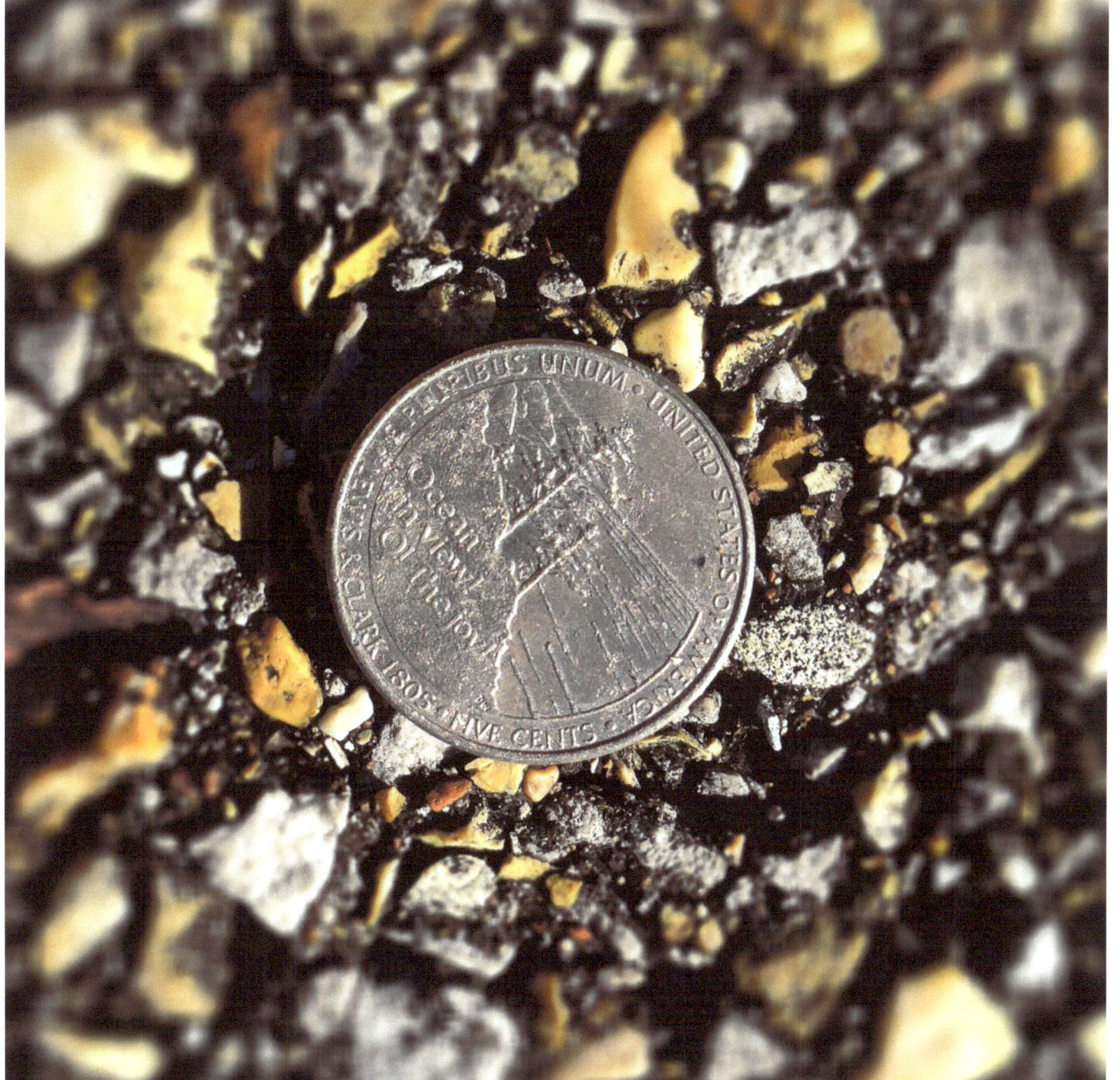
PLURIBUS UNUM
UNITED STATES OF AMERICA
CLARK 1805
FIVE CENTS
Ocean in view! O! the joy

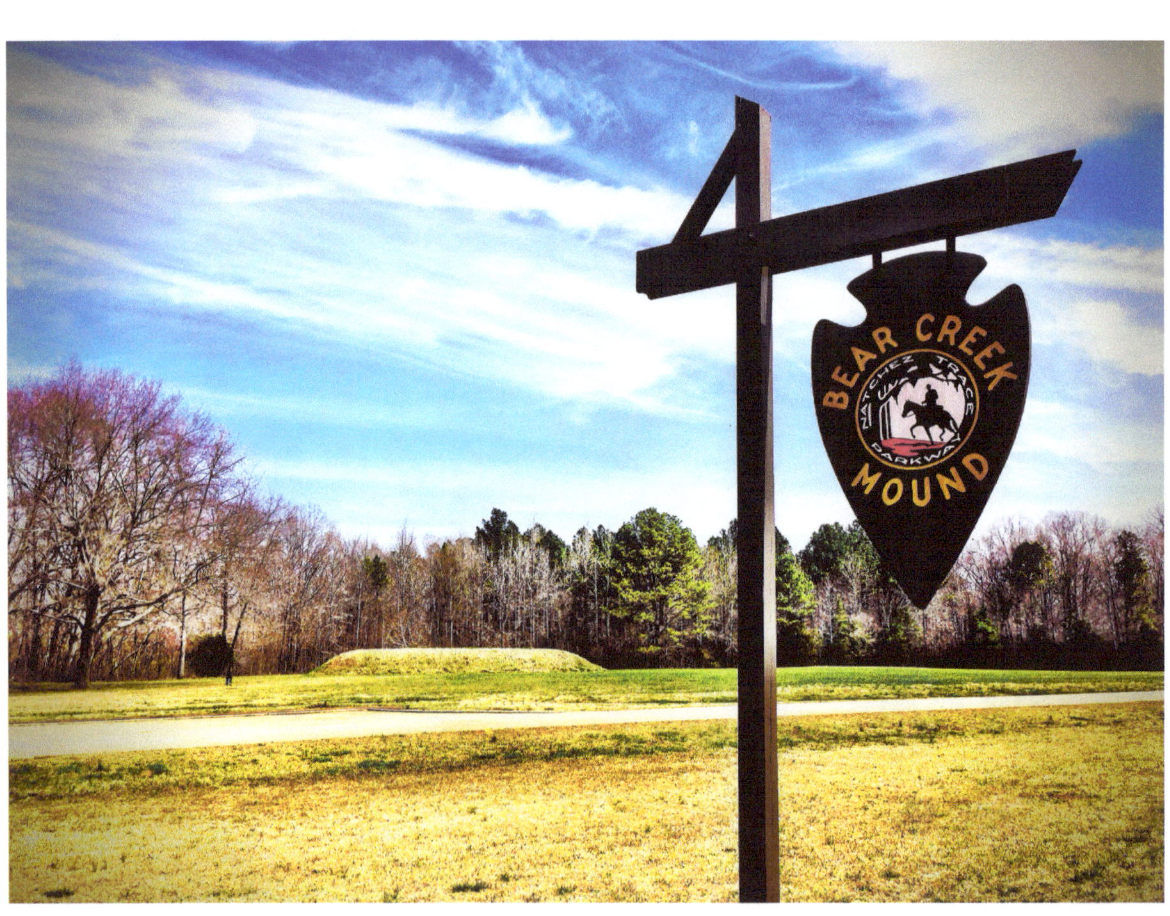
BEAR CREEK
NATCHEZ TRACE
PARKWAY
MOUND

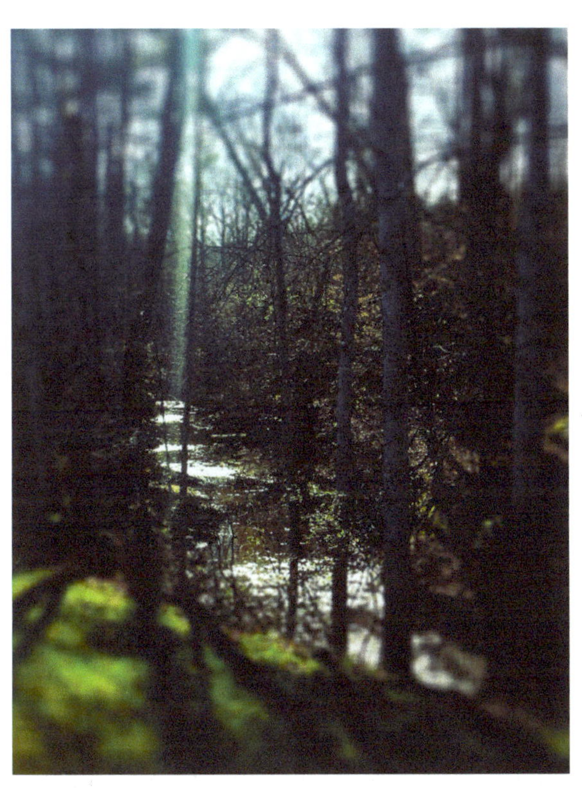

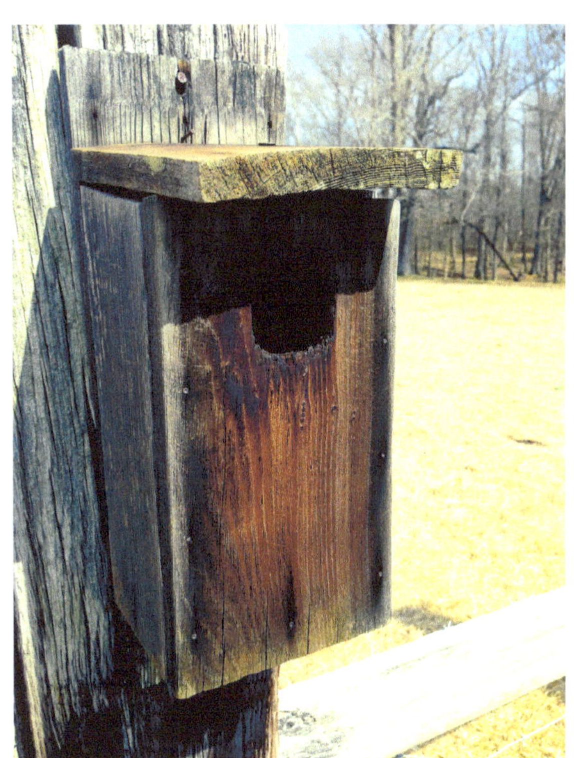

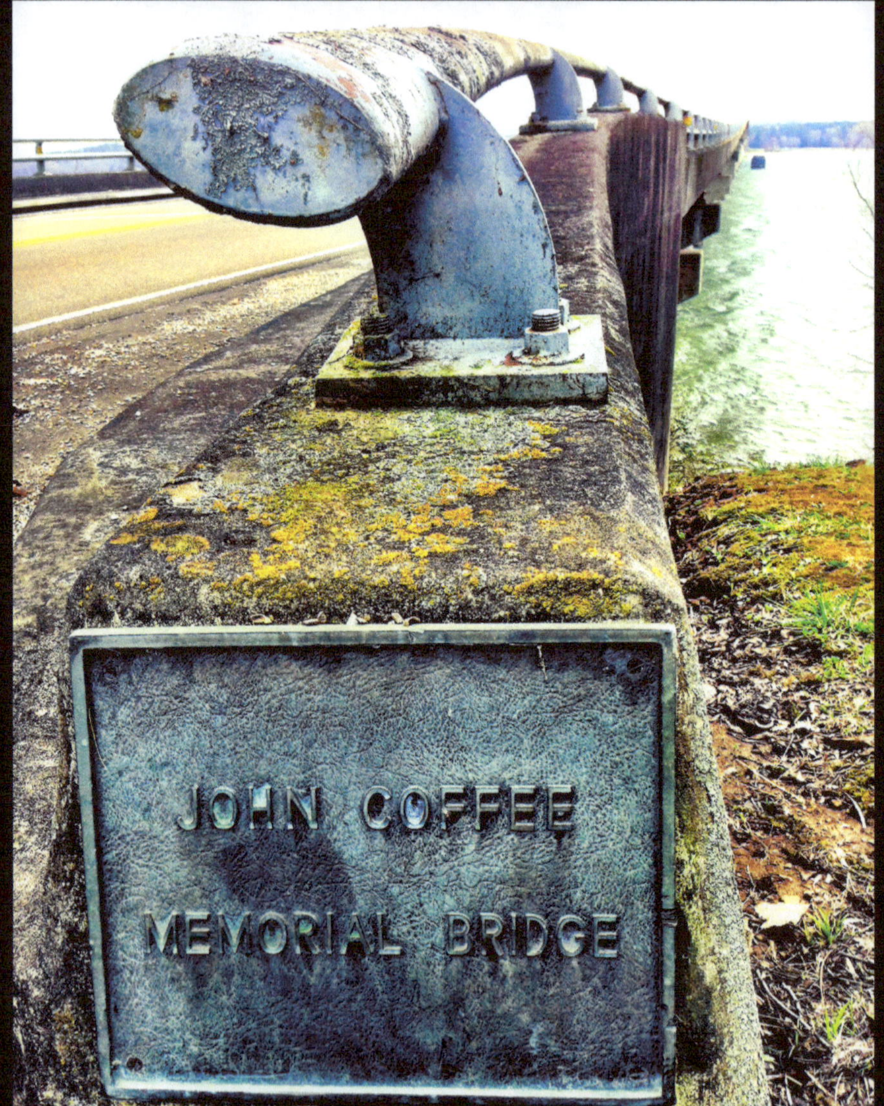
JOHN COFFEE
MEMORIAL BRIDGE

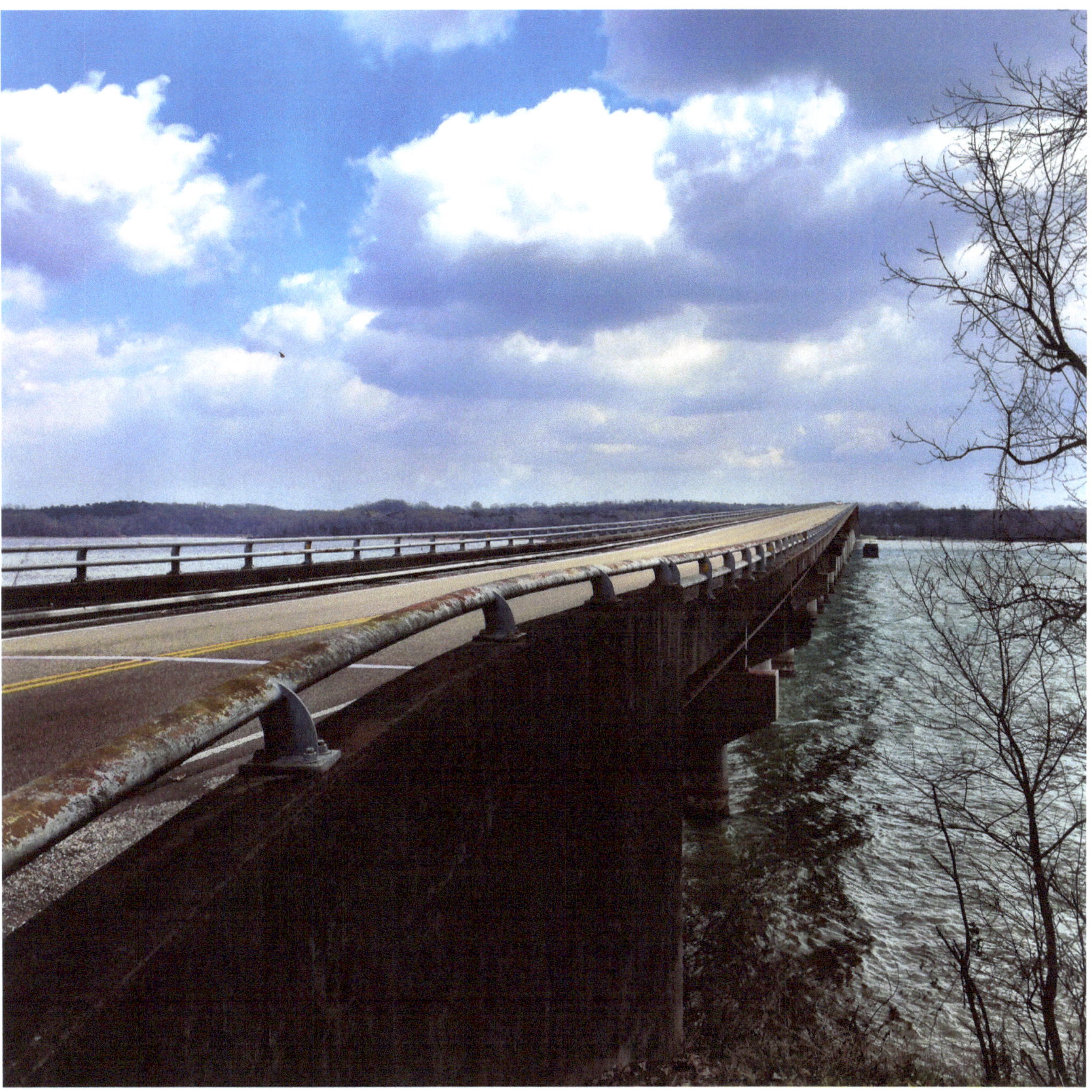

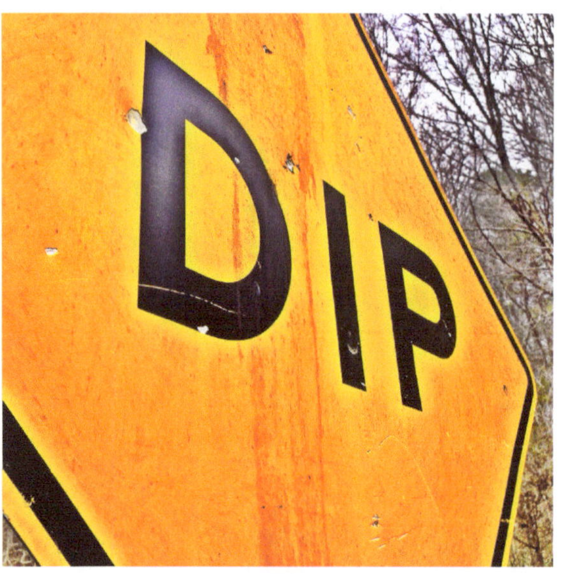
DIP

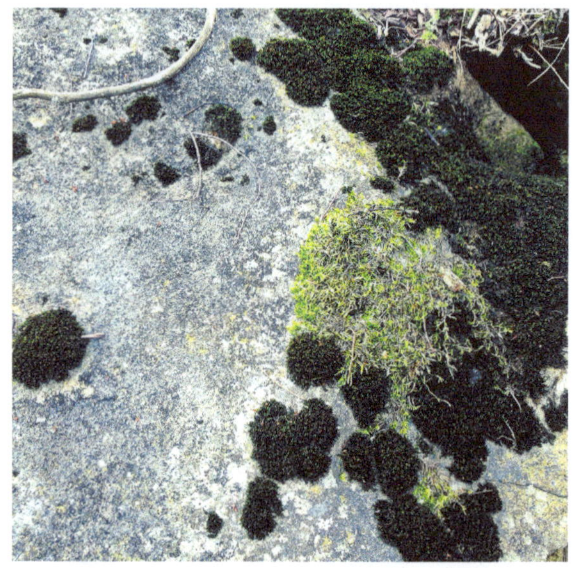

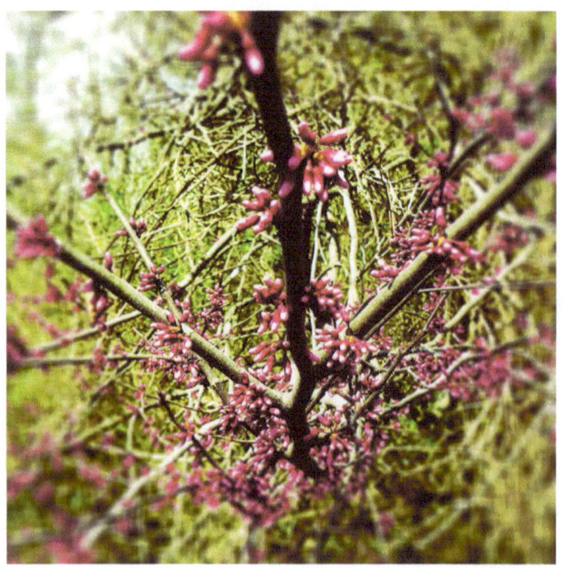

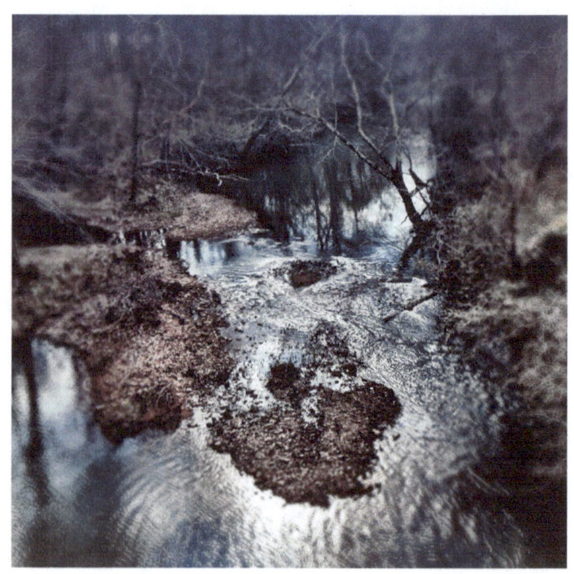

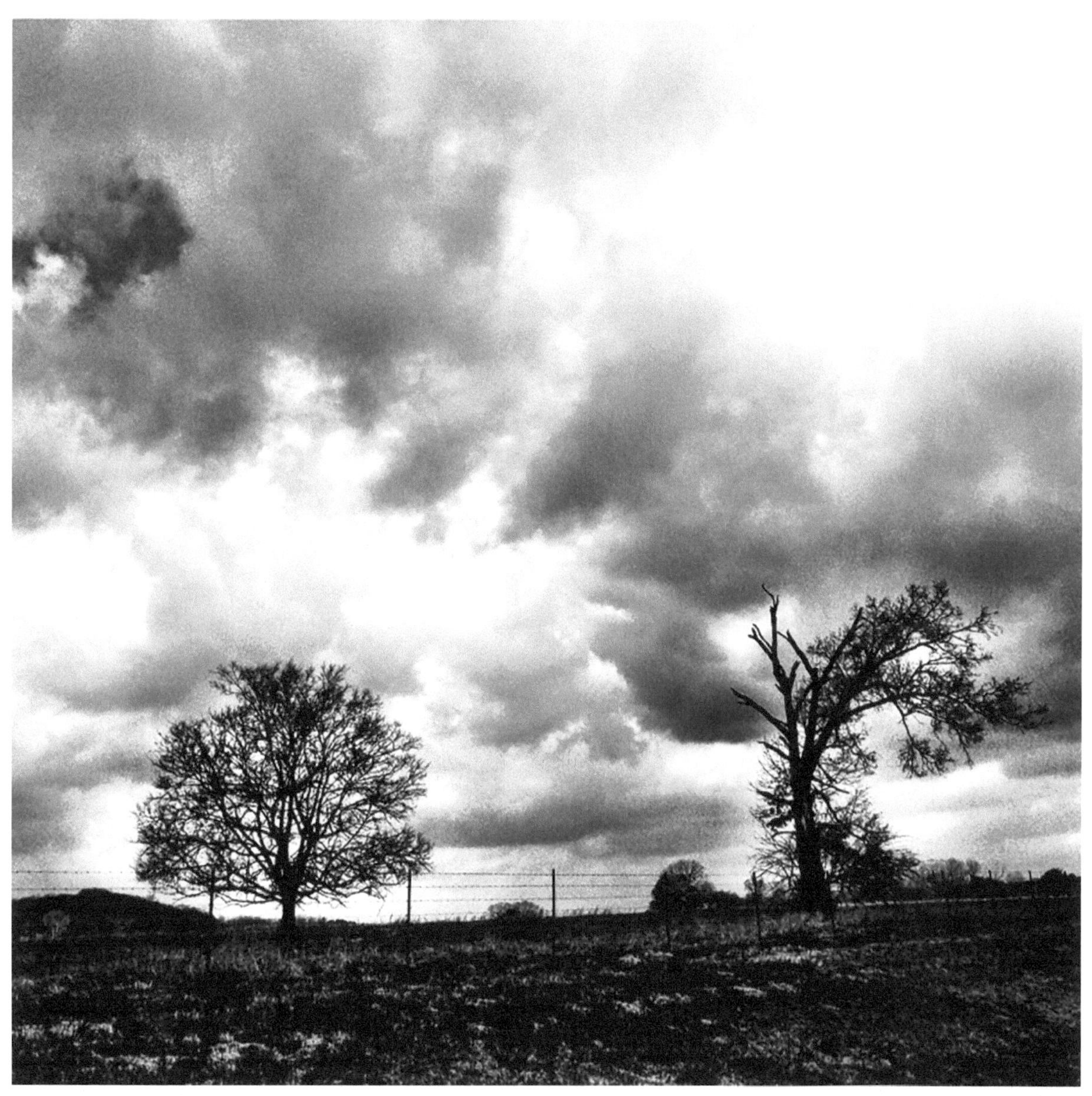

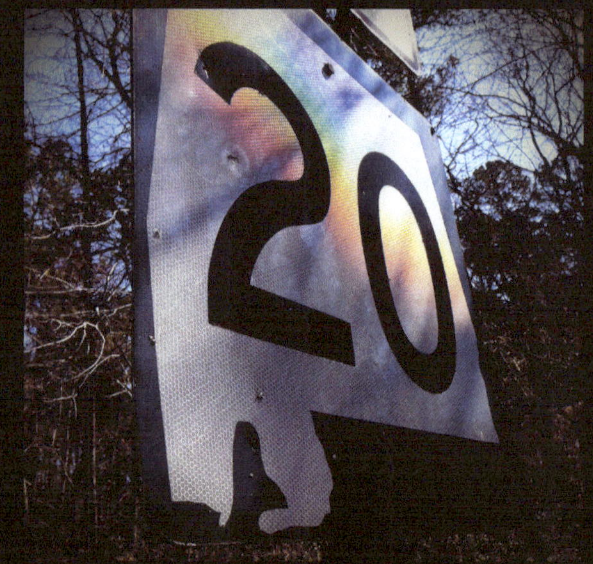
20
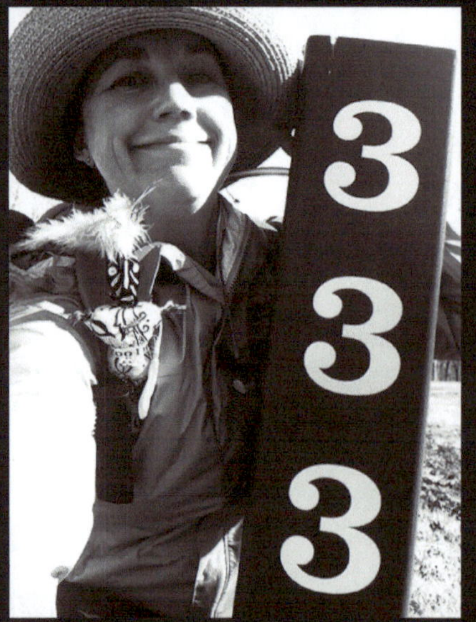
3
3
3
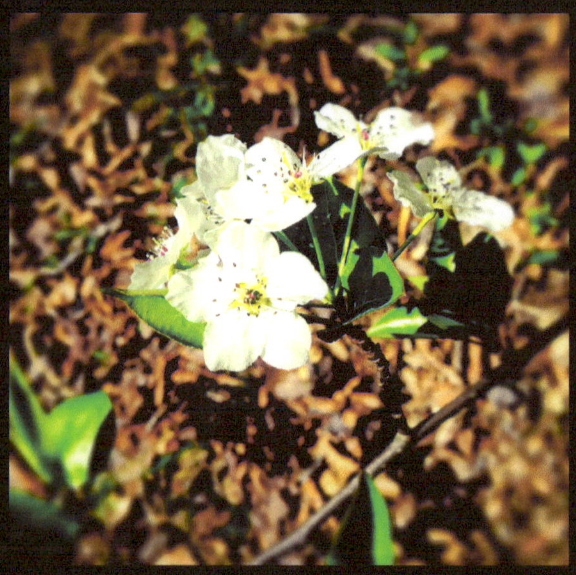

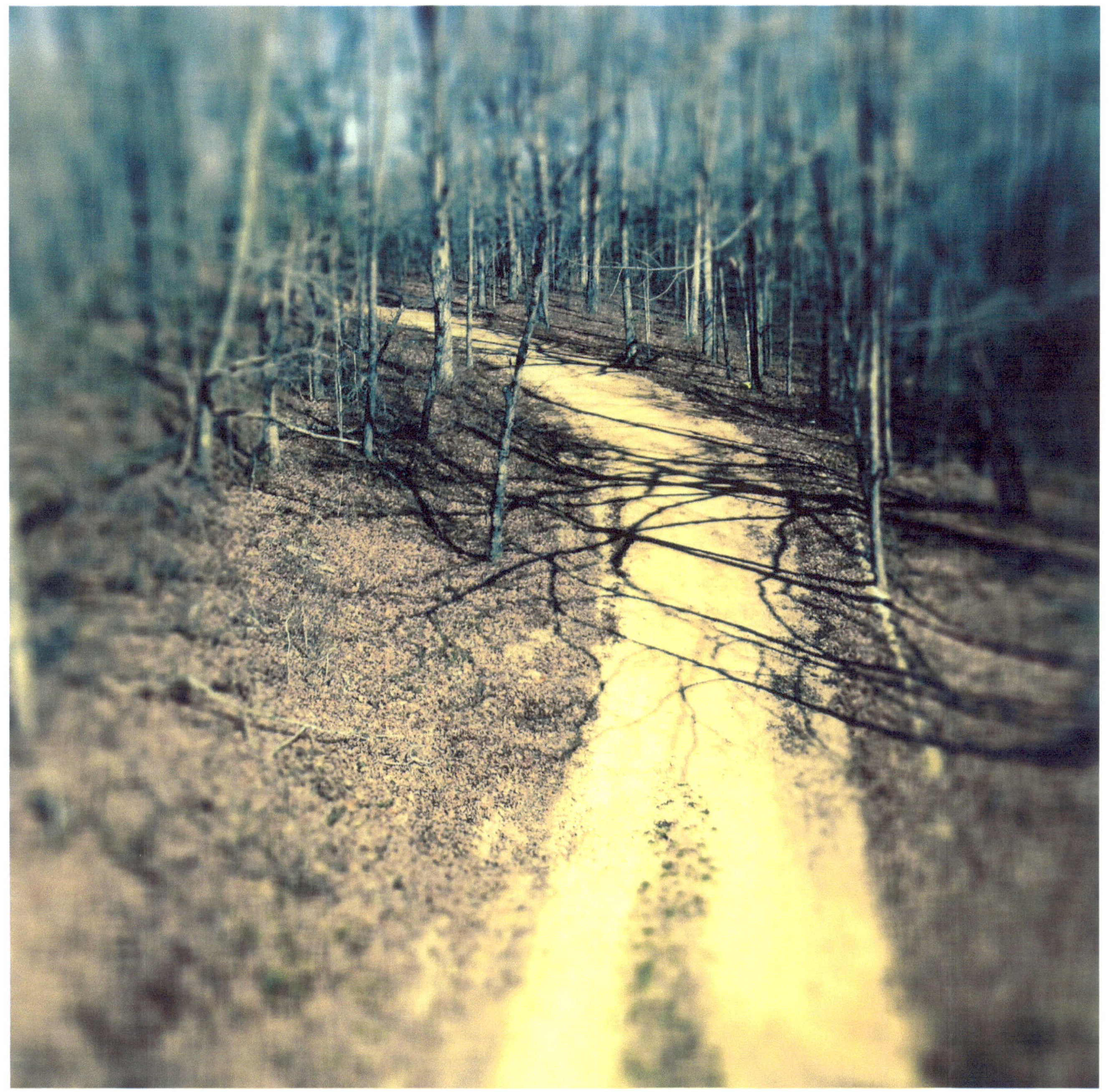

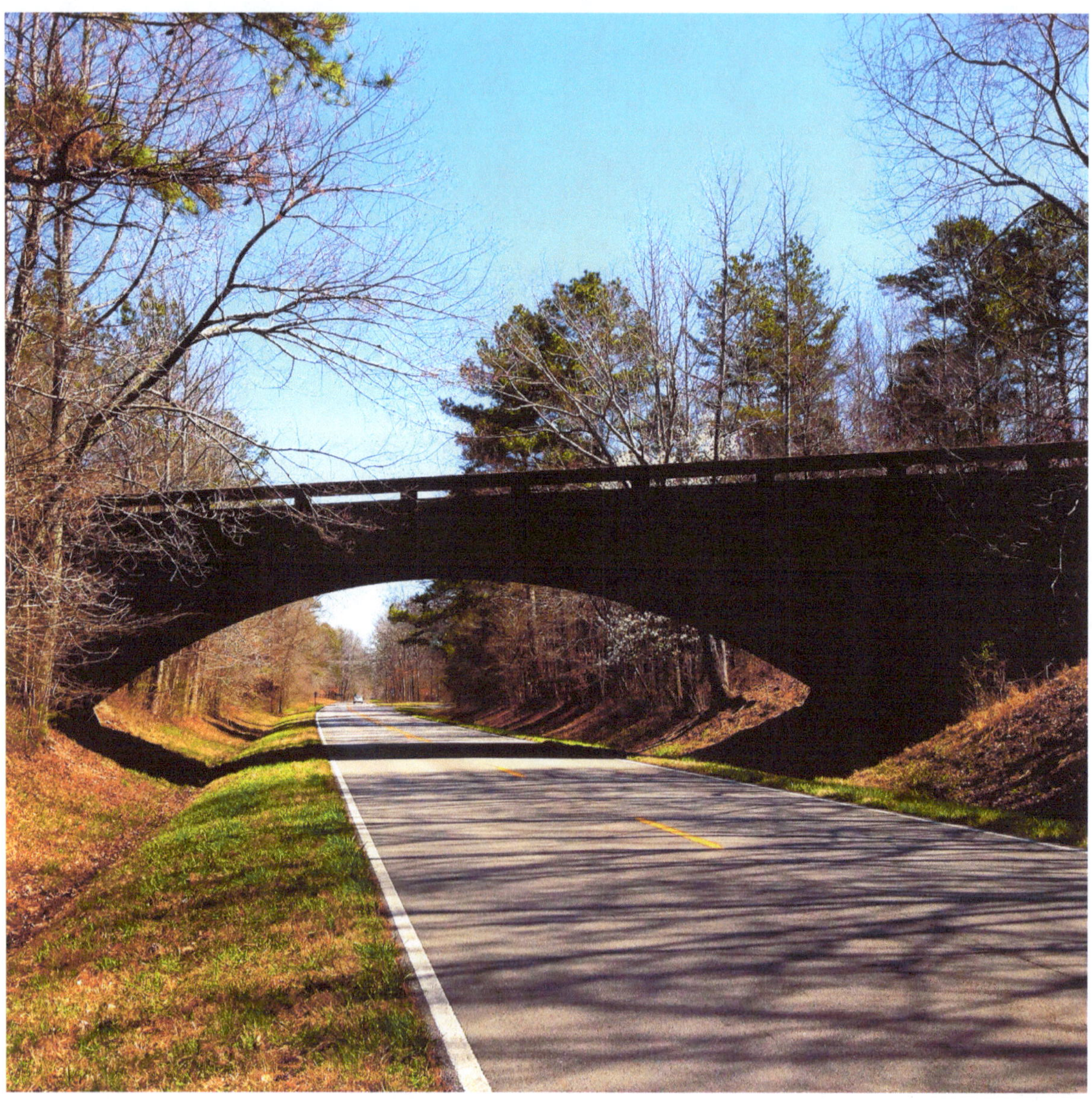

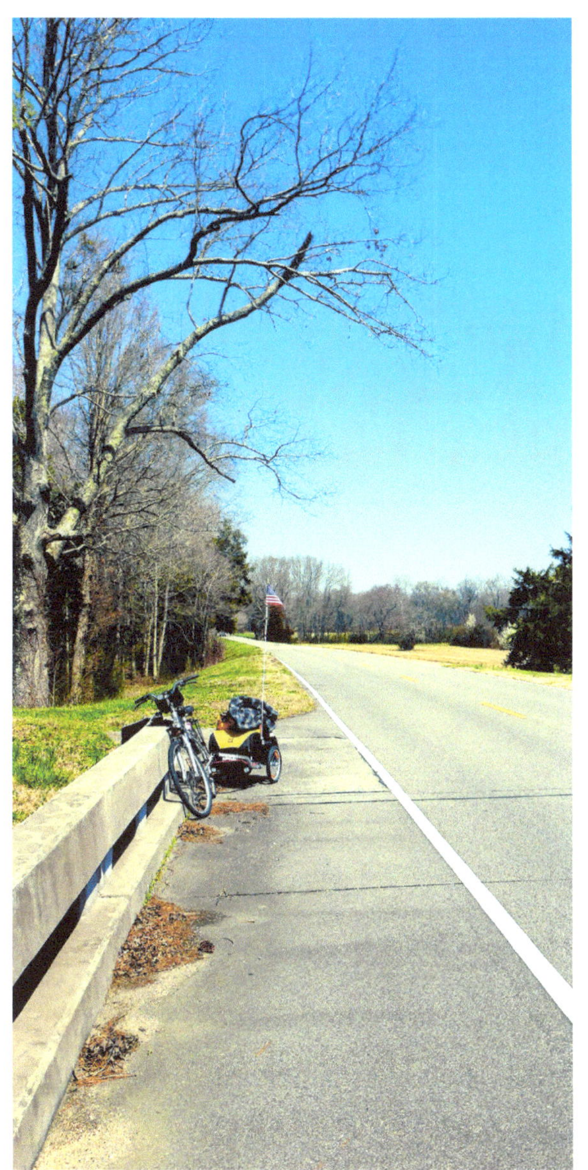

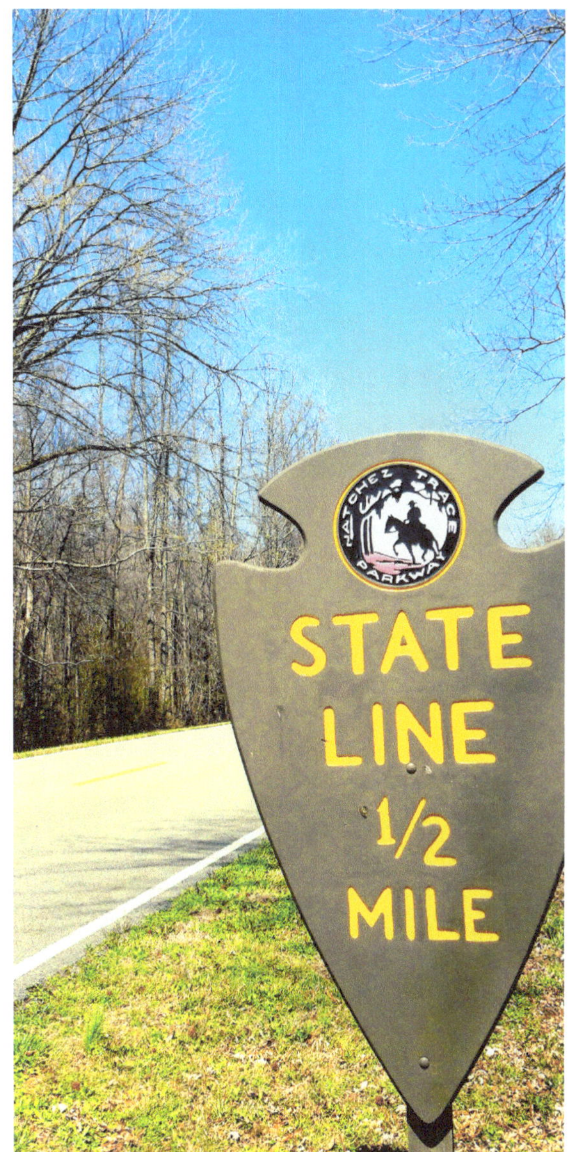
NATCHEZ TRACE
PARKWAY
STATE
LINE
1/2
MILE

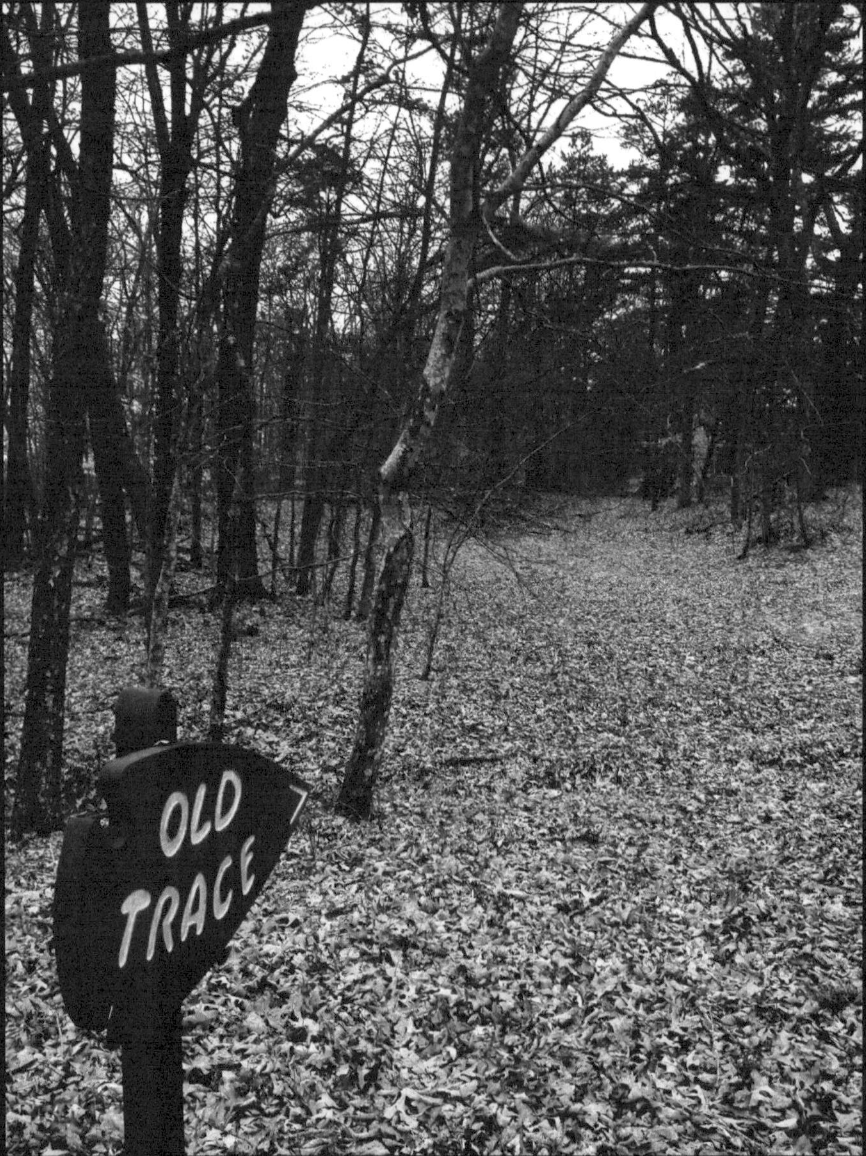

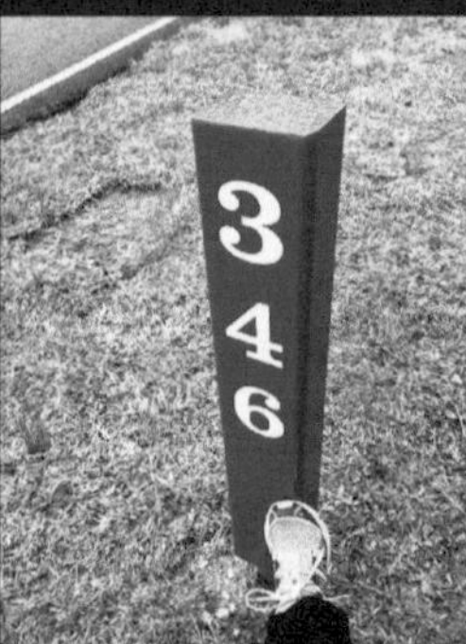
346

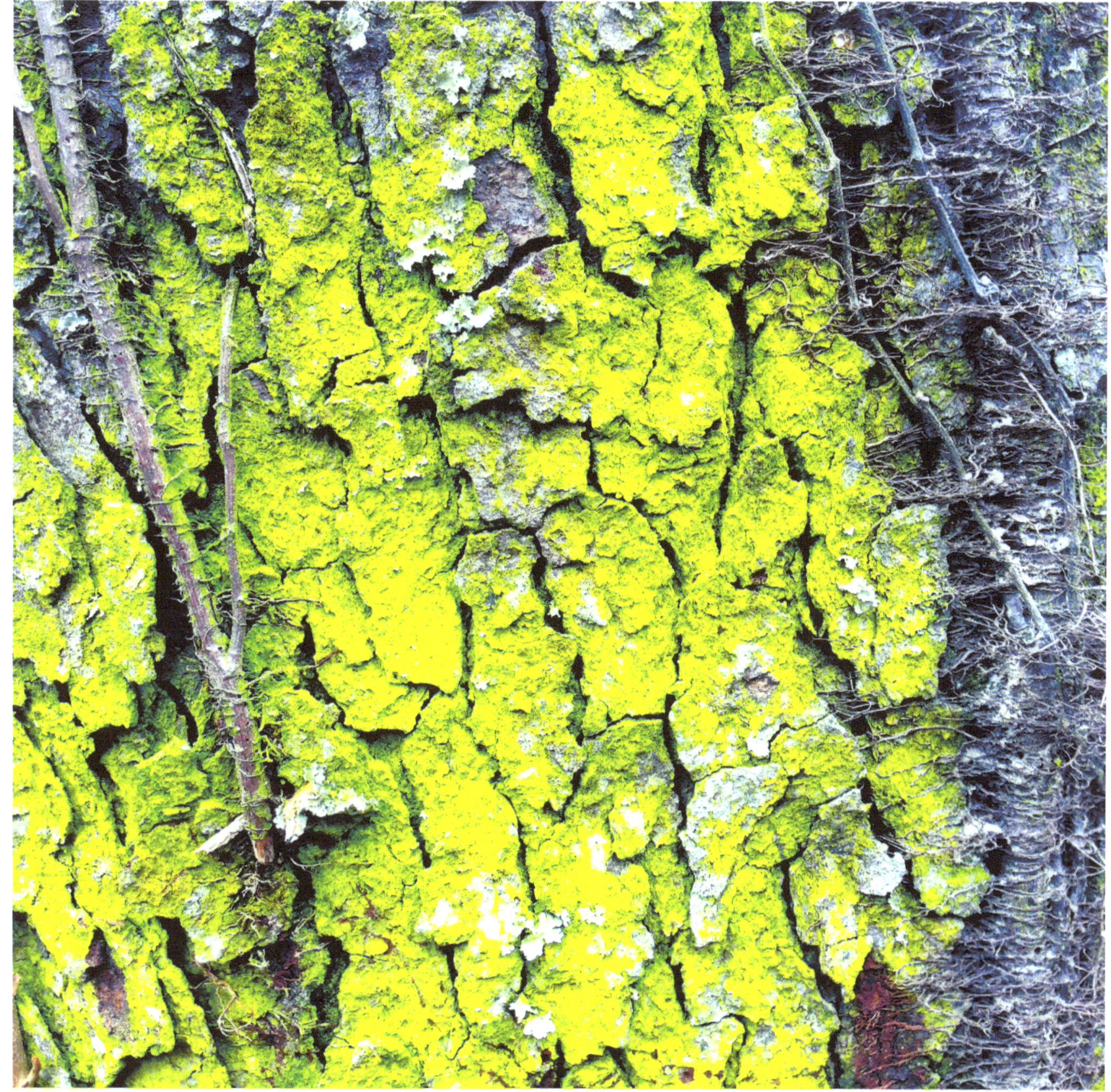

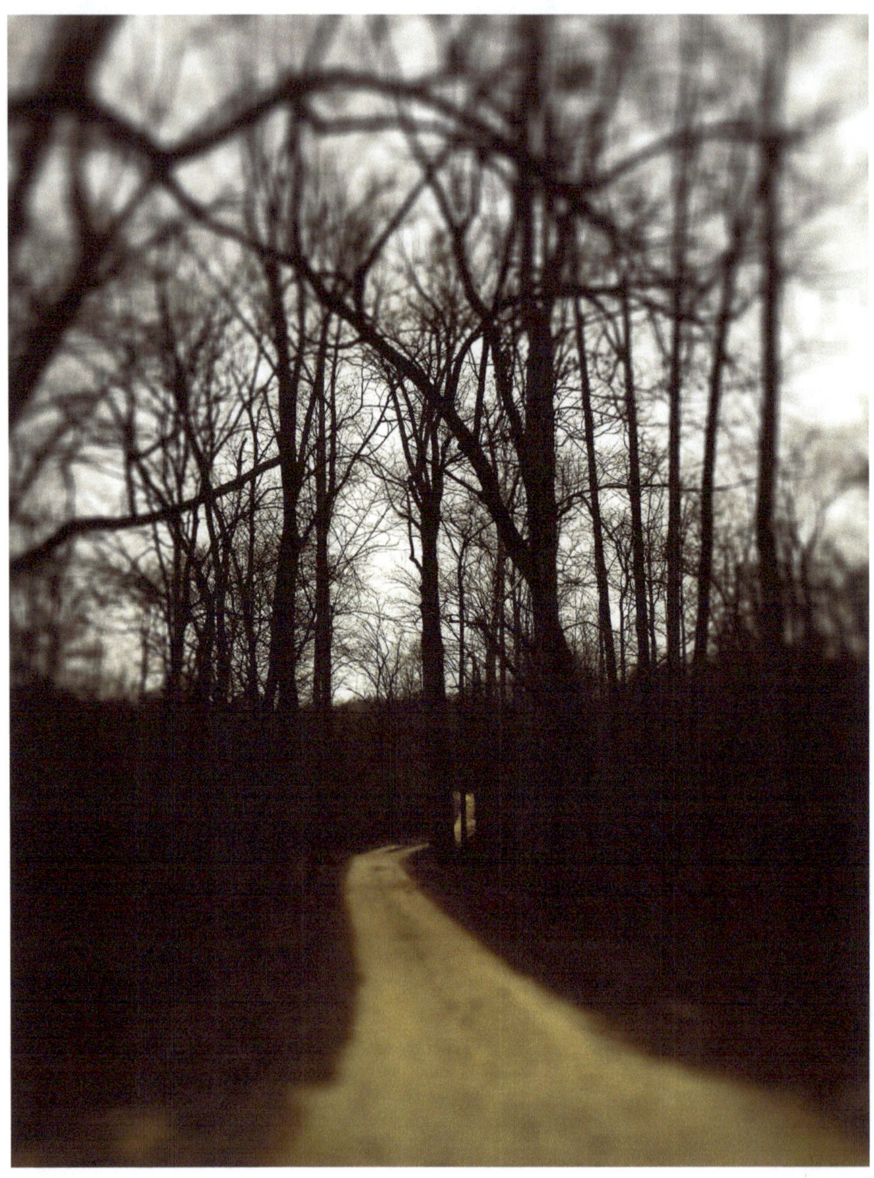

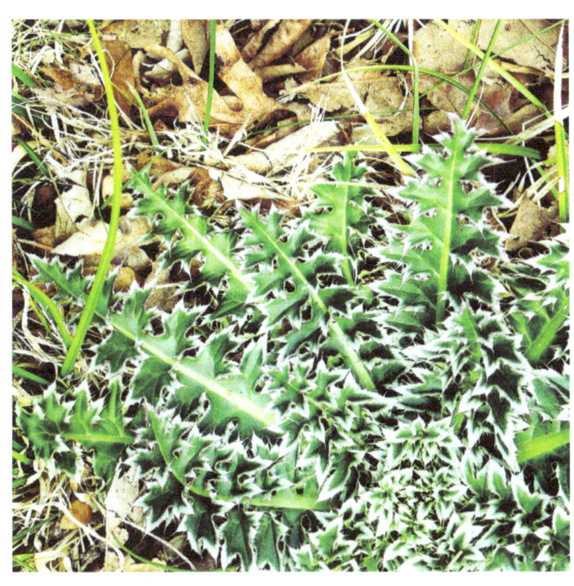

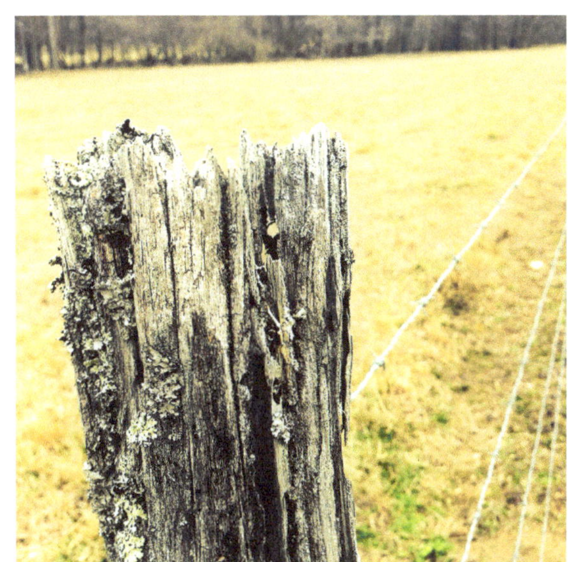

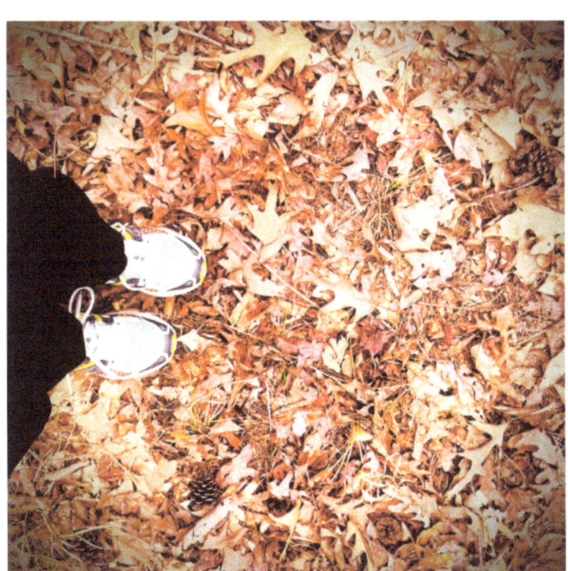

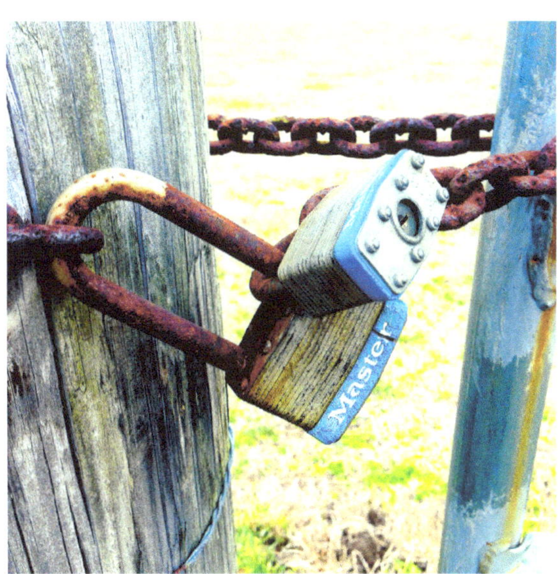
Master

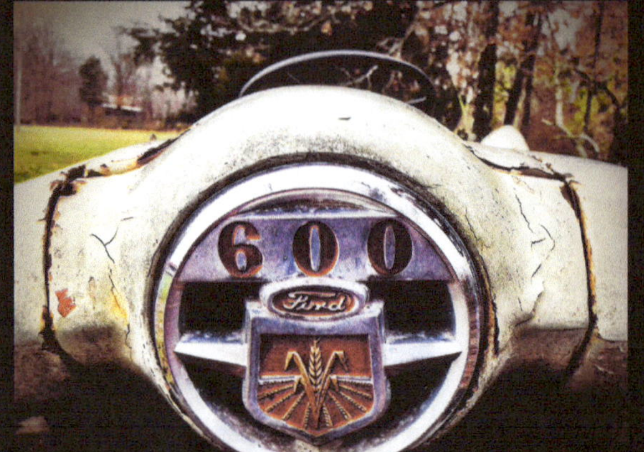
600
Ford

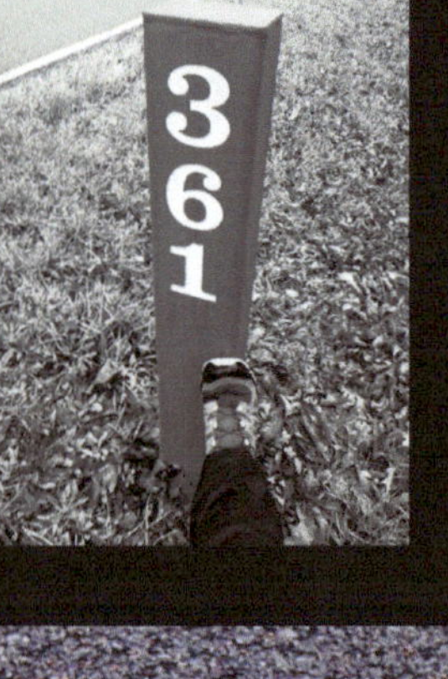
361

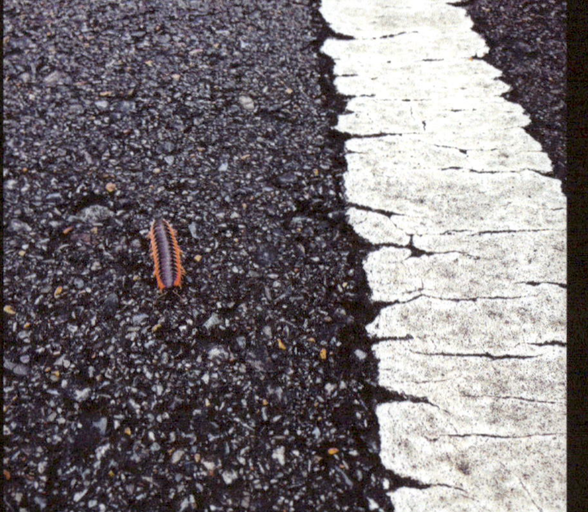

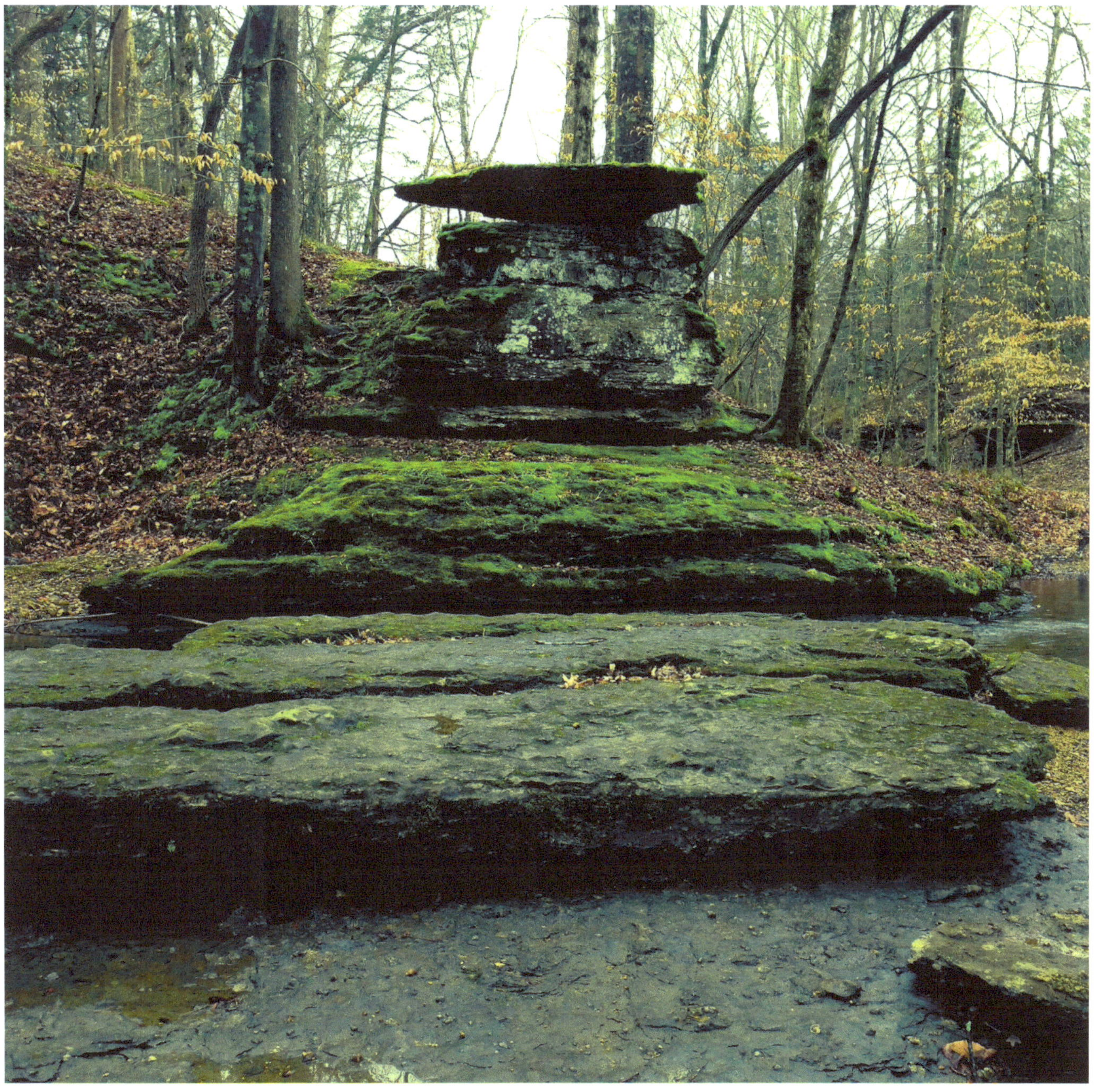

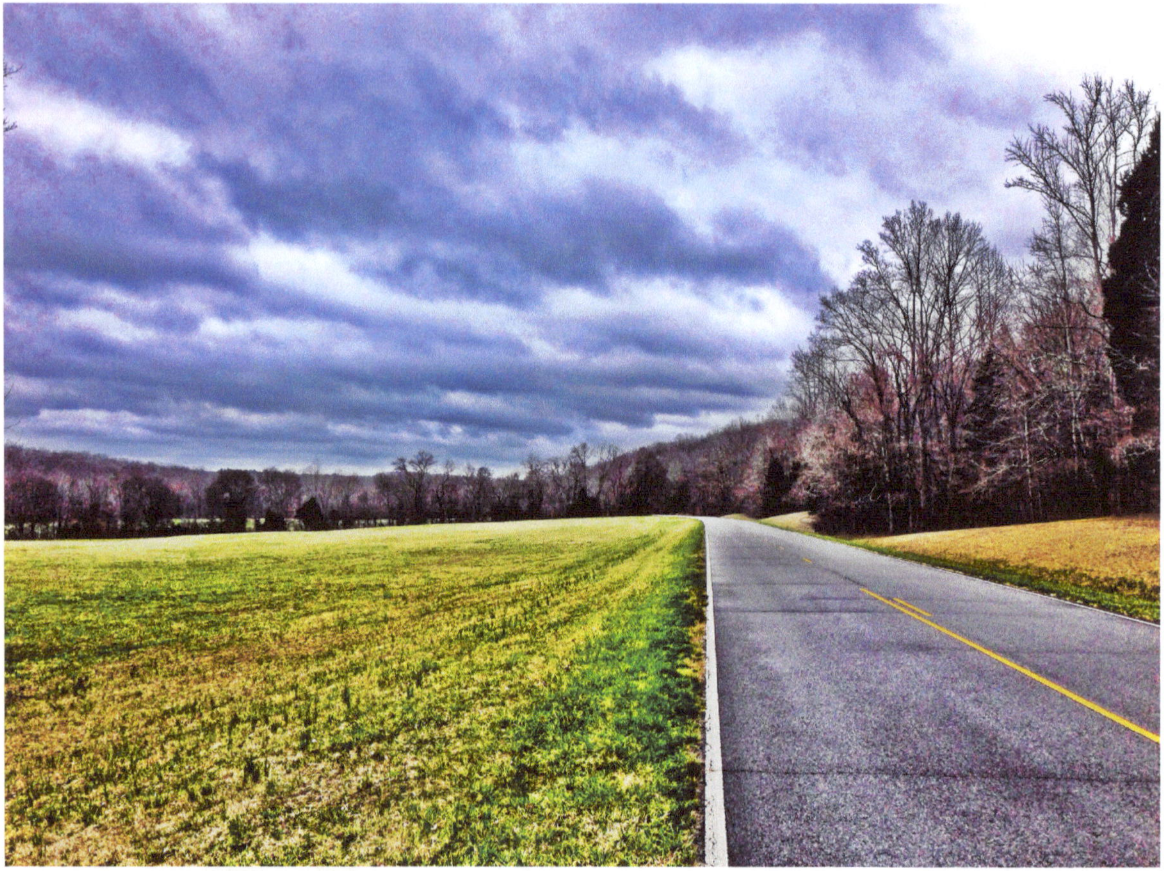

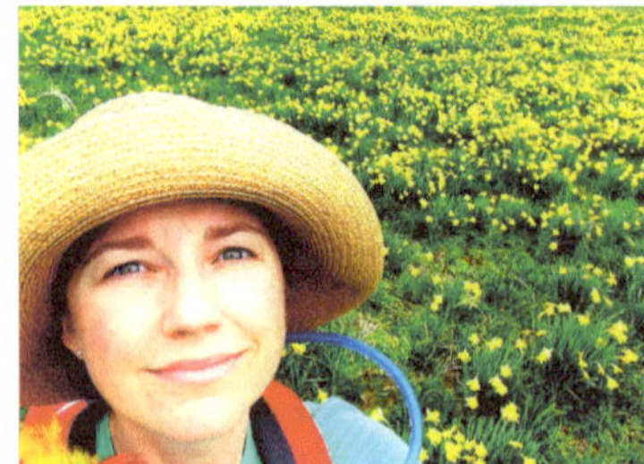

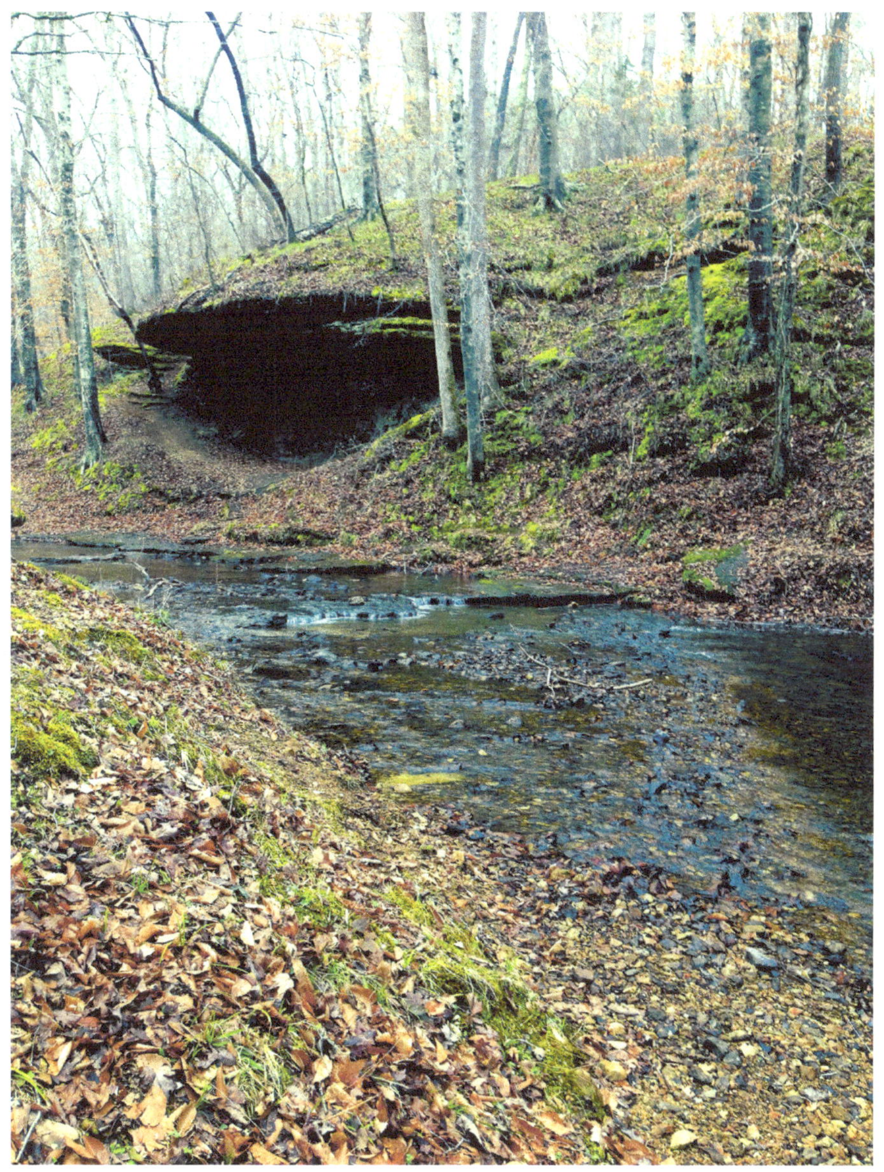

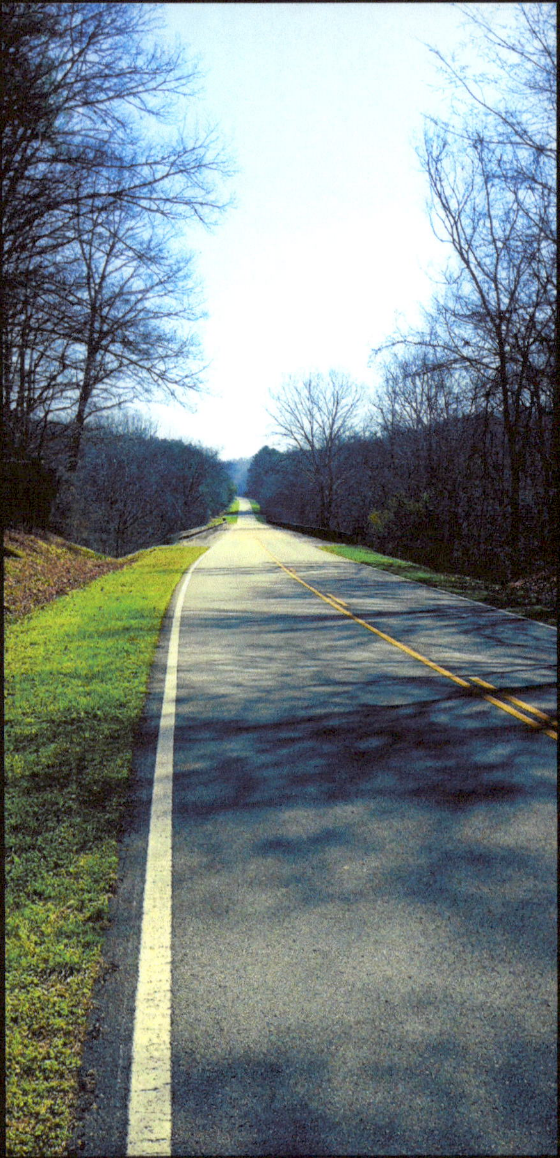

Dear Meriwether Lewis:

You gave me a gift. Maybe several.

Inspiration. You lent me your voice. Your story. You let me imagine what you might do if you had more time, a new purpose.

Fortitude. You gave me the strength to not give up, even when I stood on the side of the road and screamed, "I quit! I quit! I quit!" into a Mississippi swamp.

Connection. You led some of Clark's descendants to find me, as I stumbled through an open field. "Lewis was murdered!" We found connection in that thought, common ground in that idea.

You left me a nickel along the white line of the Natchez Trace. Tails-up, a gift on my birthday. I picked it up, and it will stay with me forever. Maybe you knew I had been carrying a similar nickel on my long pilgrimage to your gravesite. I left it there.

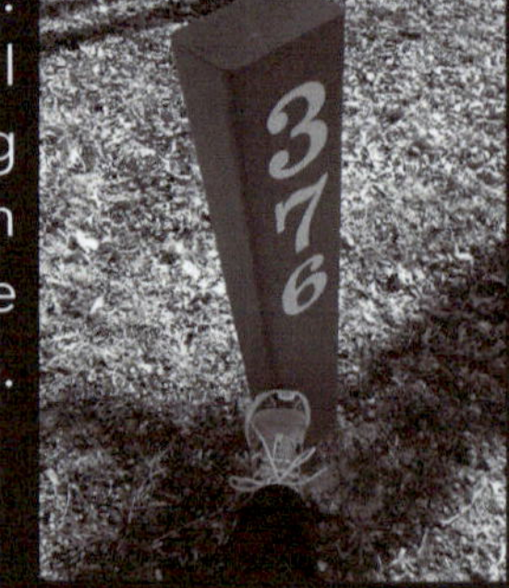

For you.

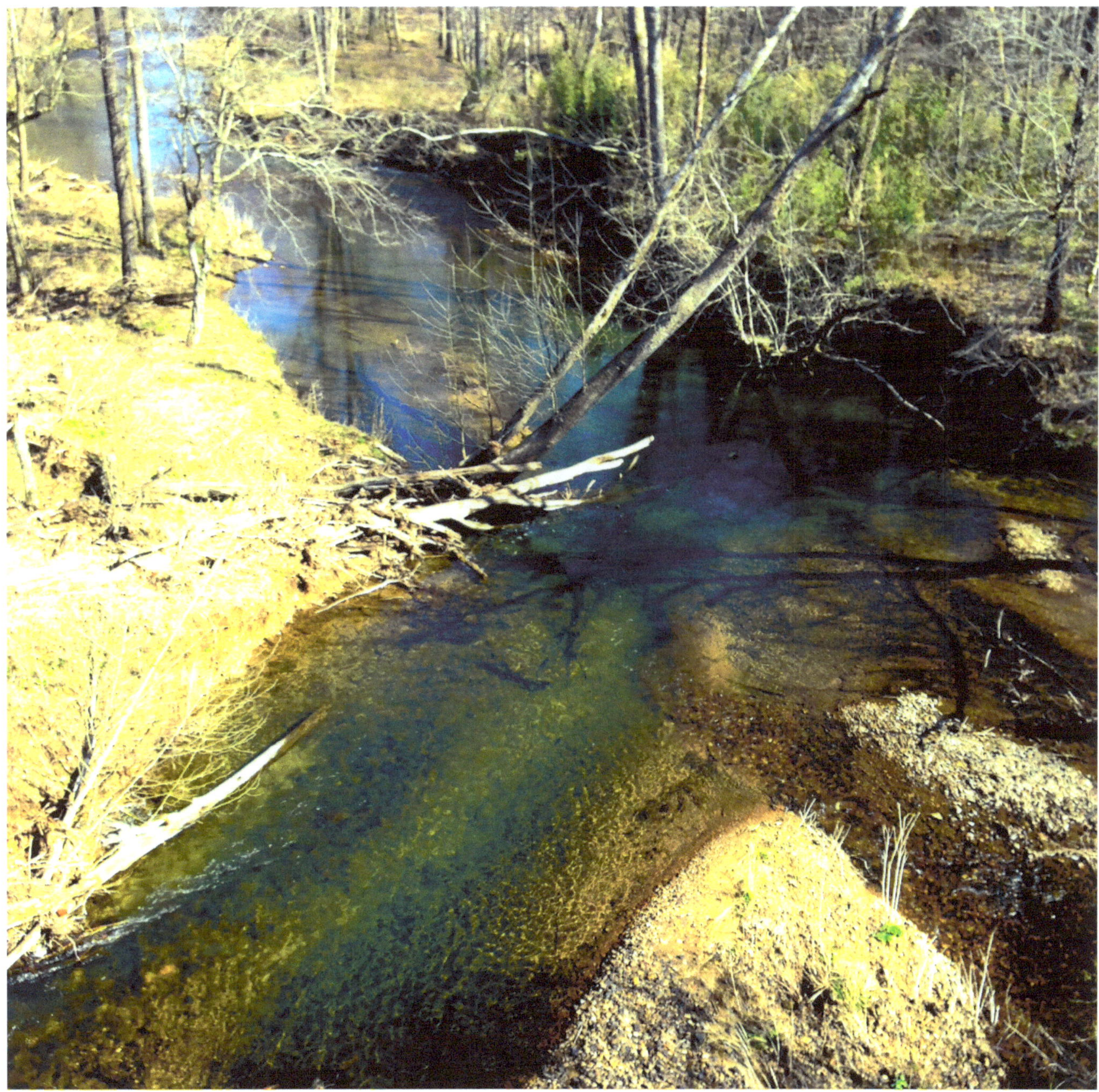

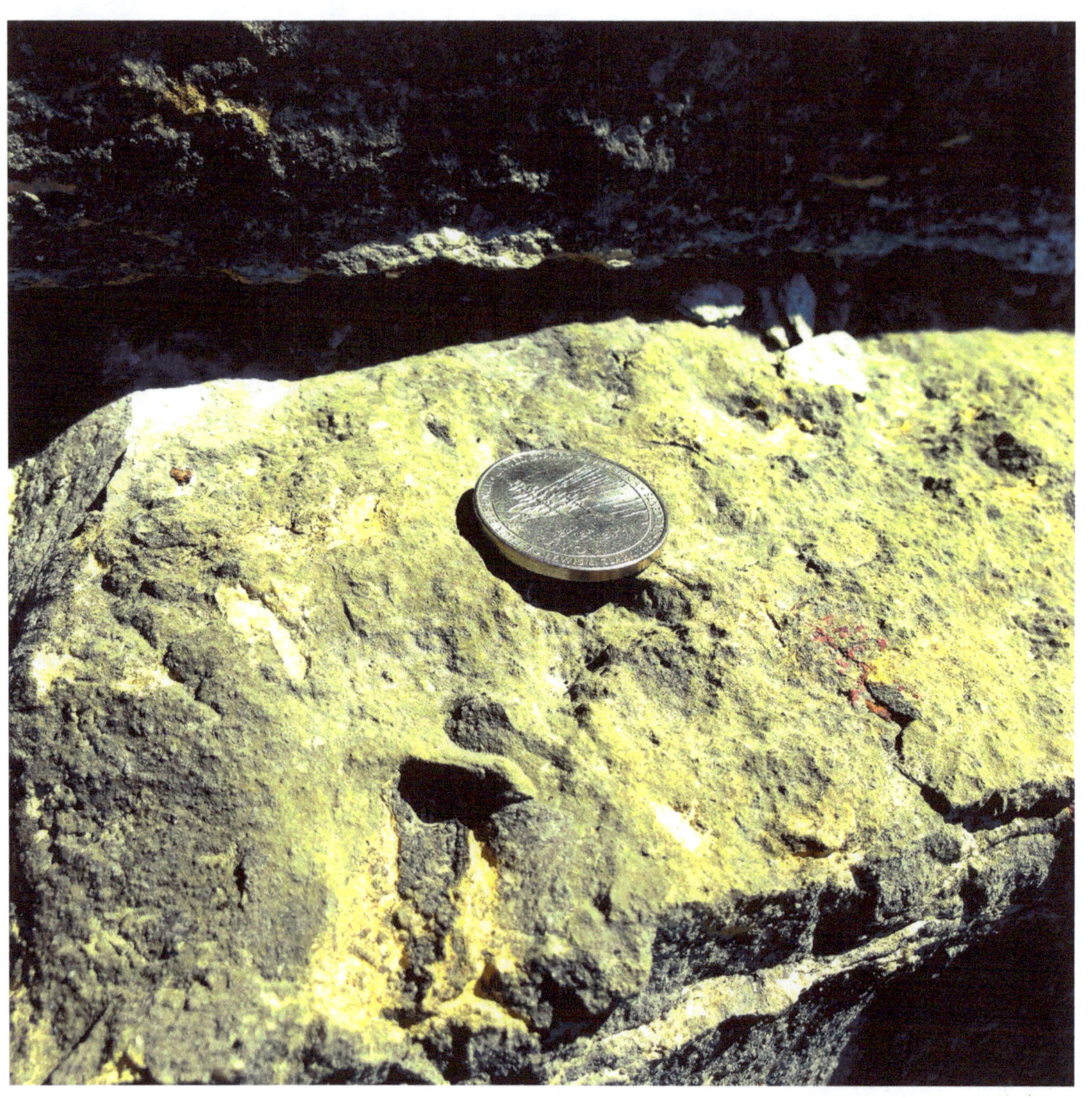

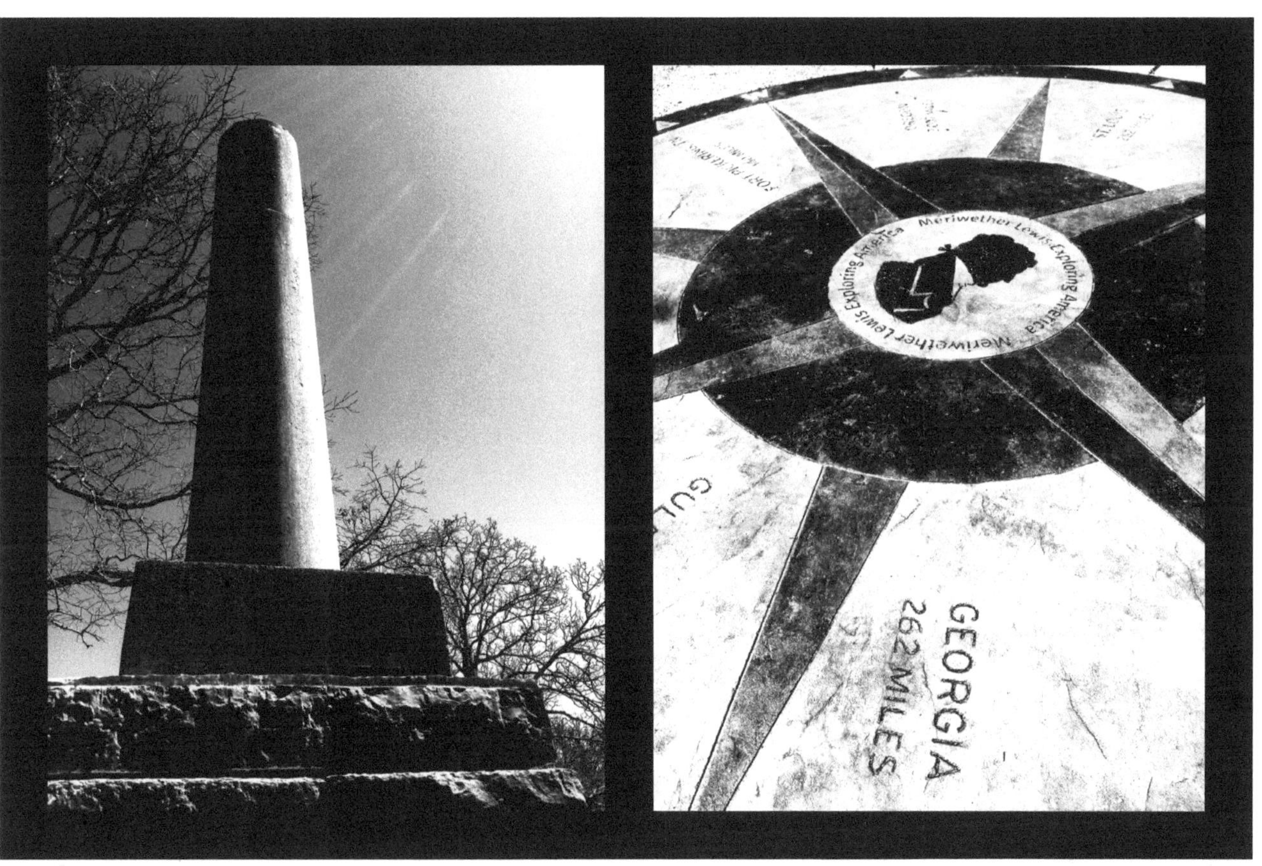

Meriwether Lewis Exploring America
GEORGIA
262 MILES

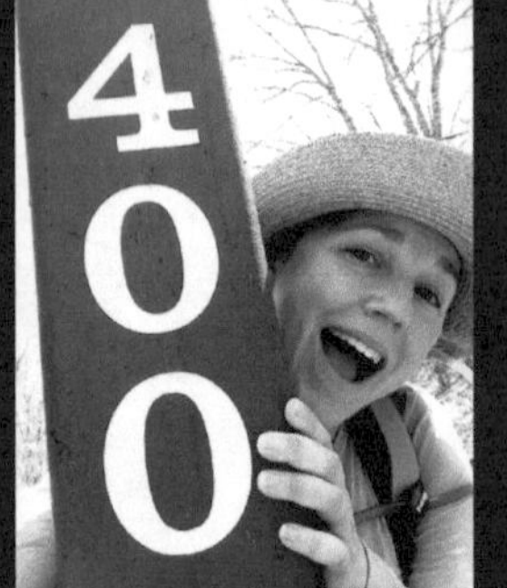
400

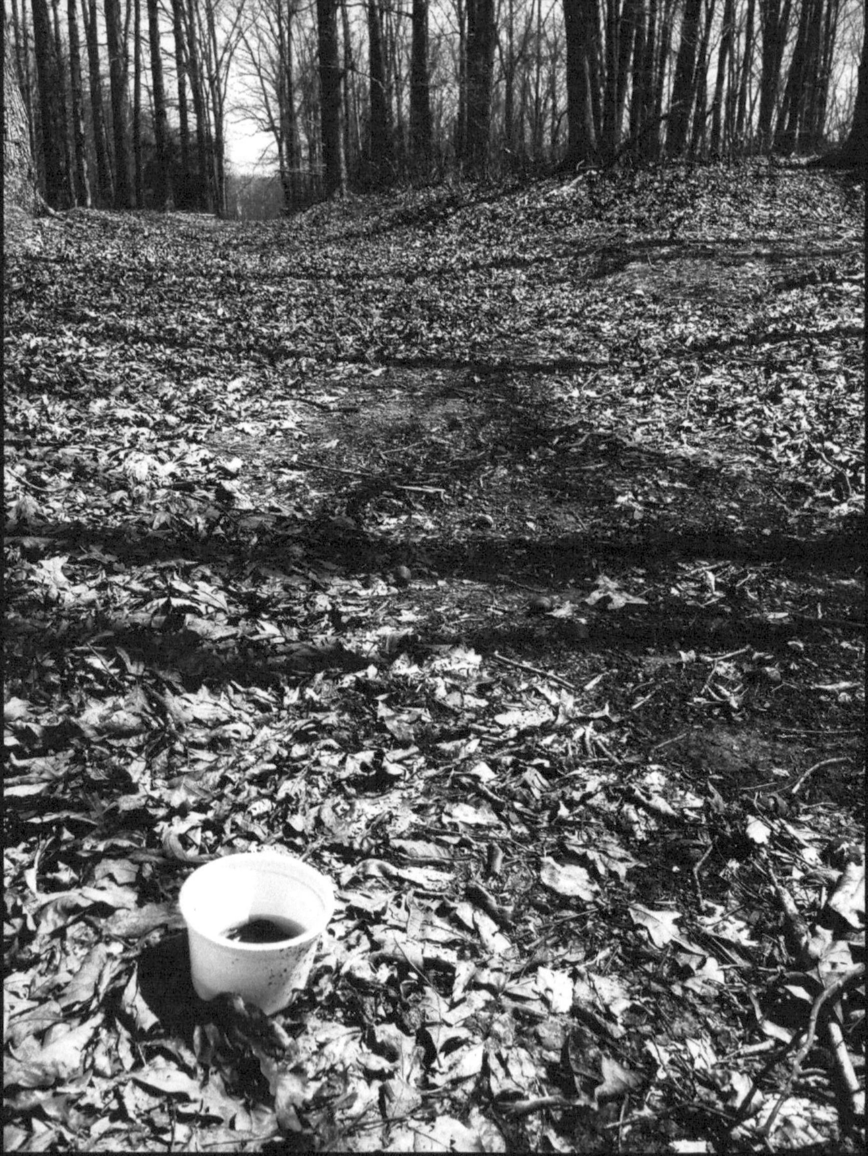

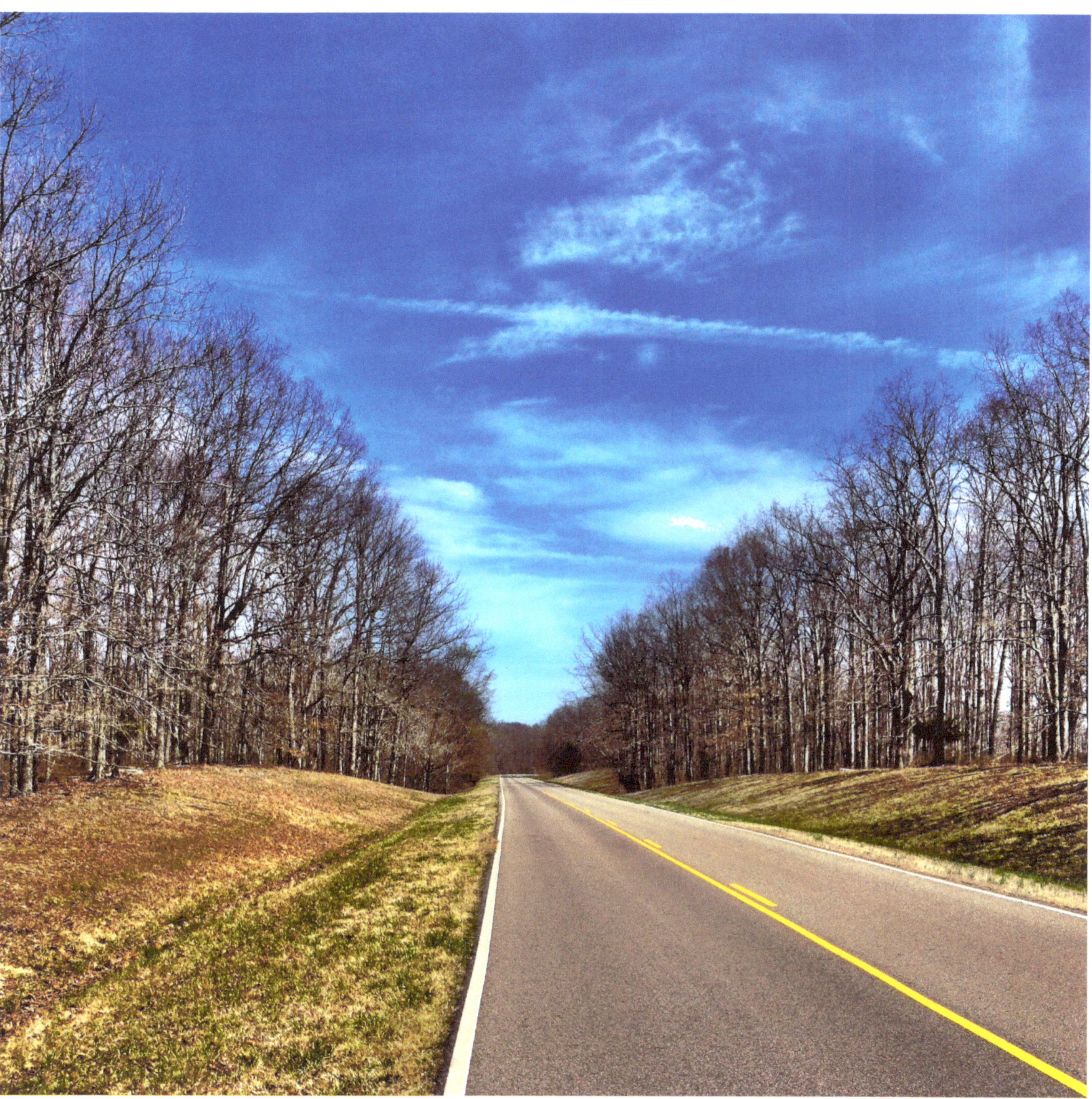

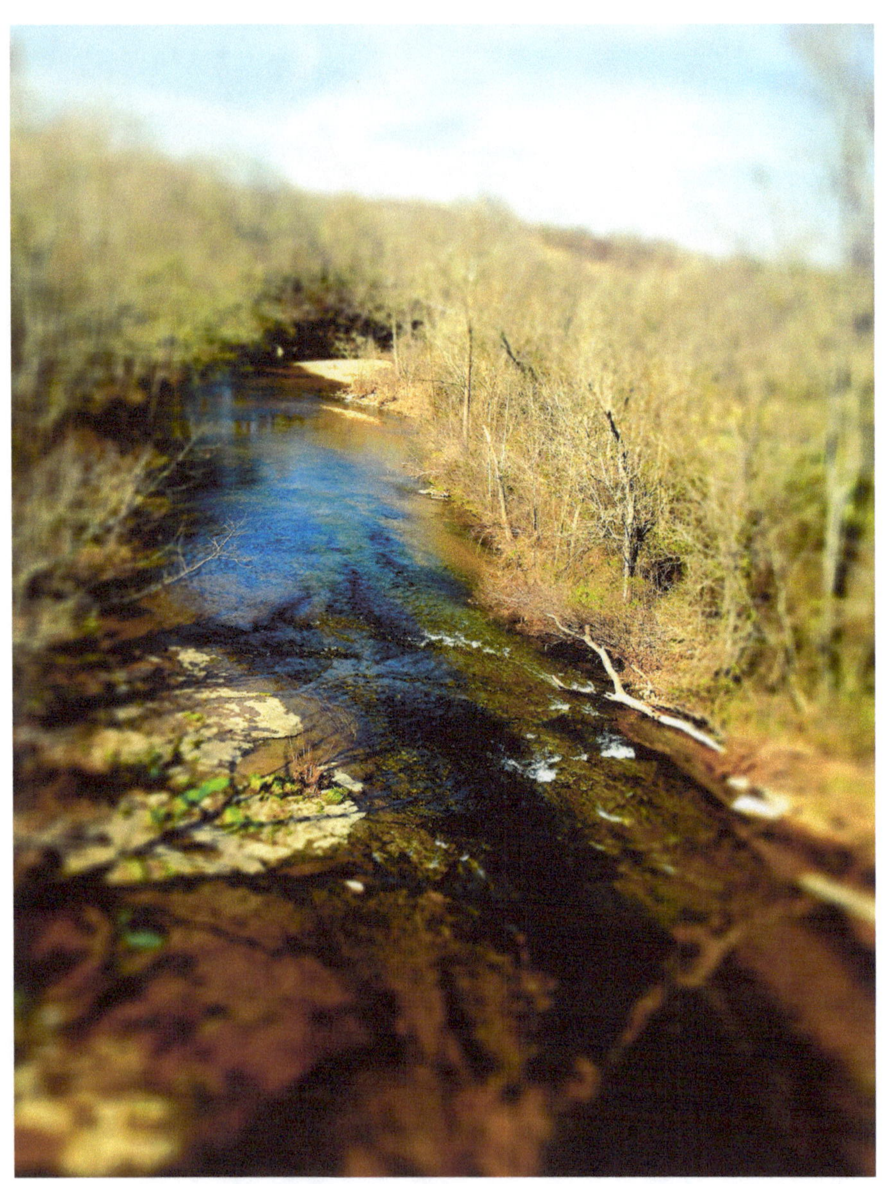

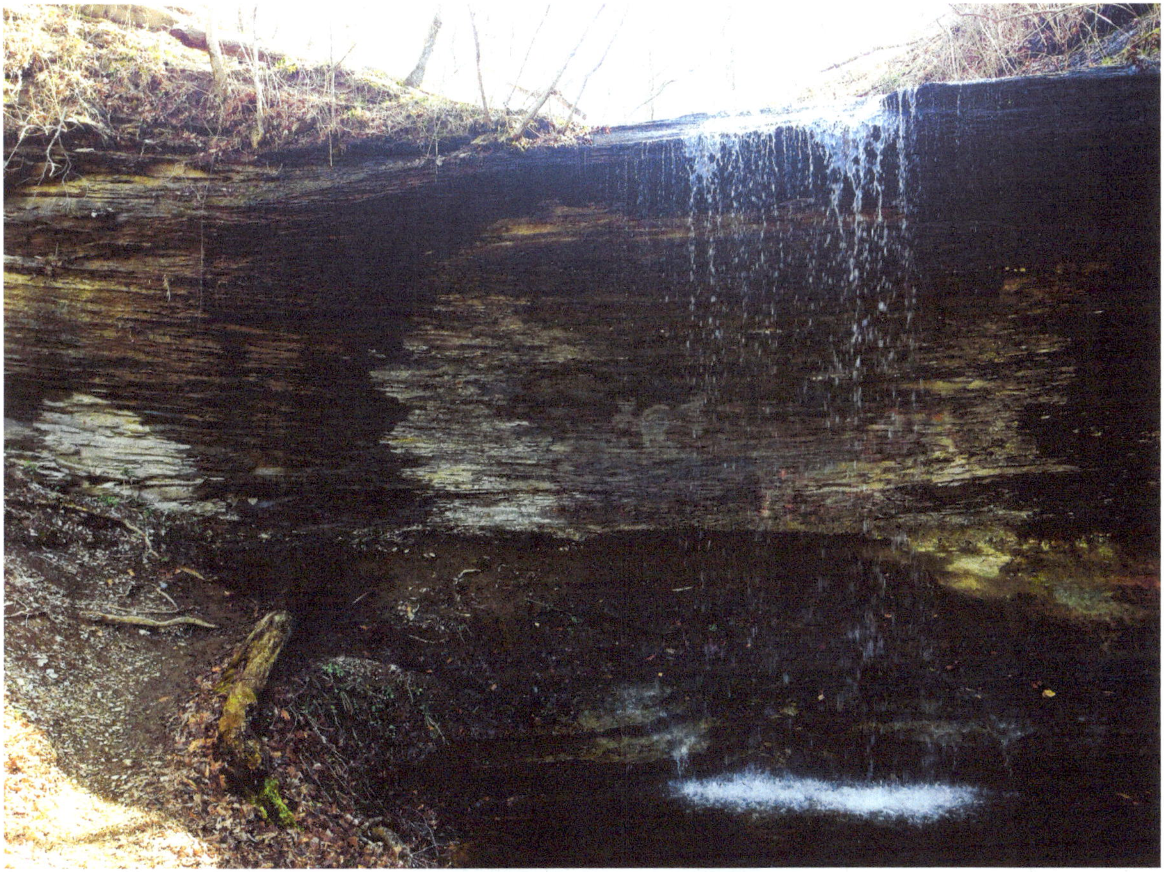

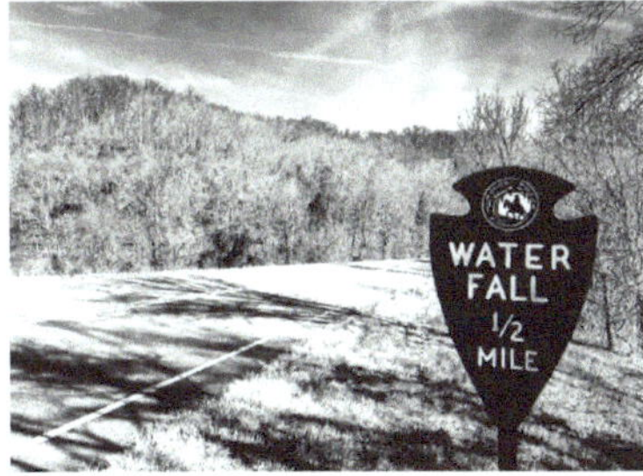
WATER
FALL
1/2
MILE

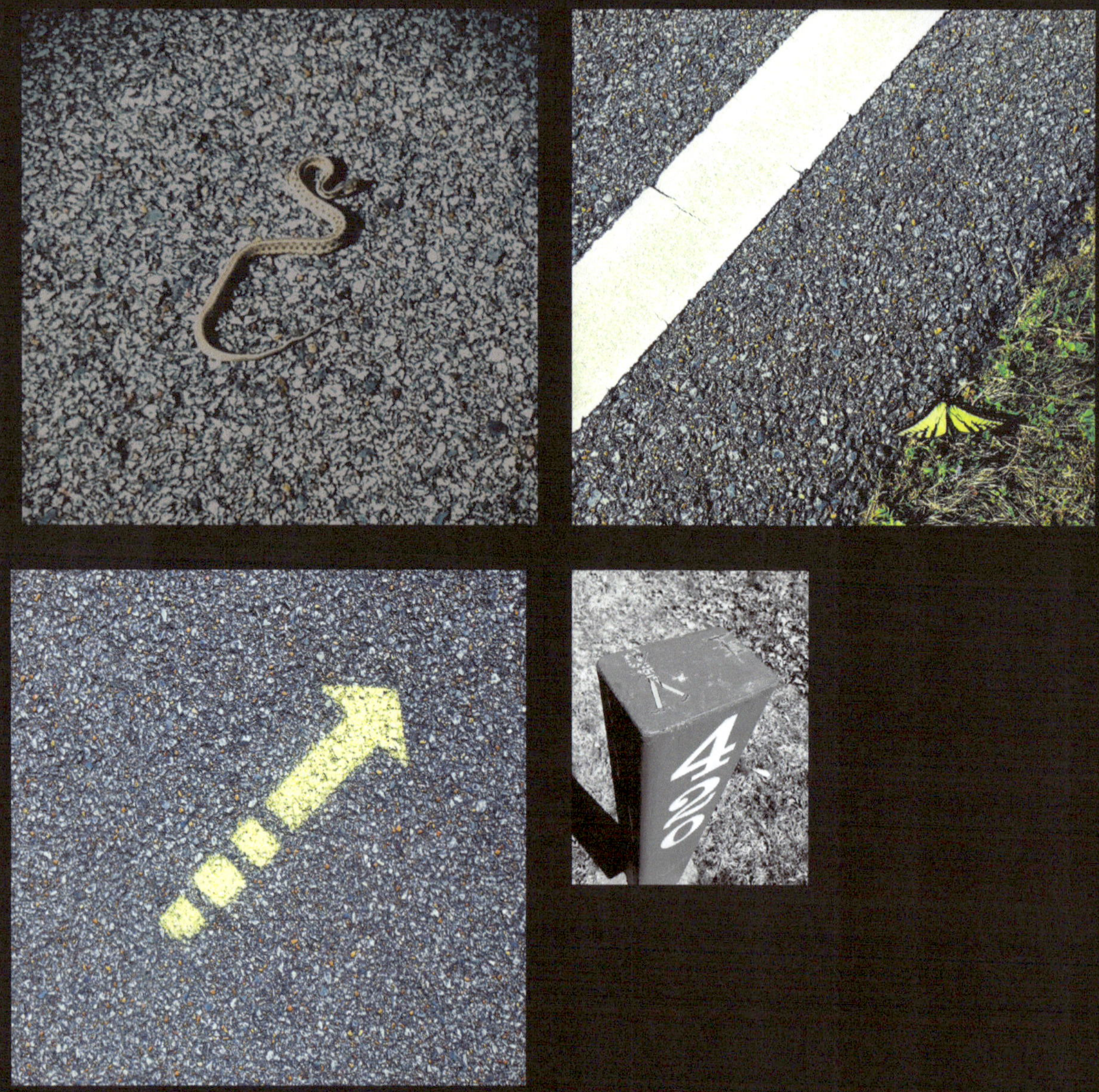
420

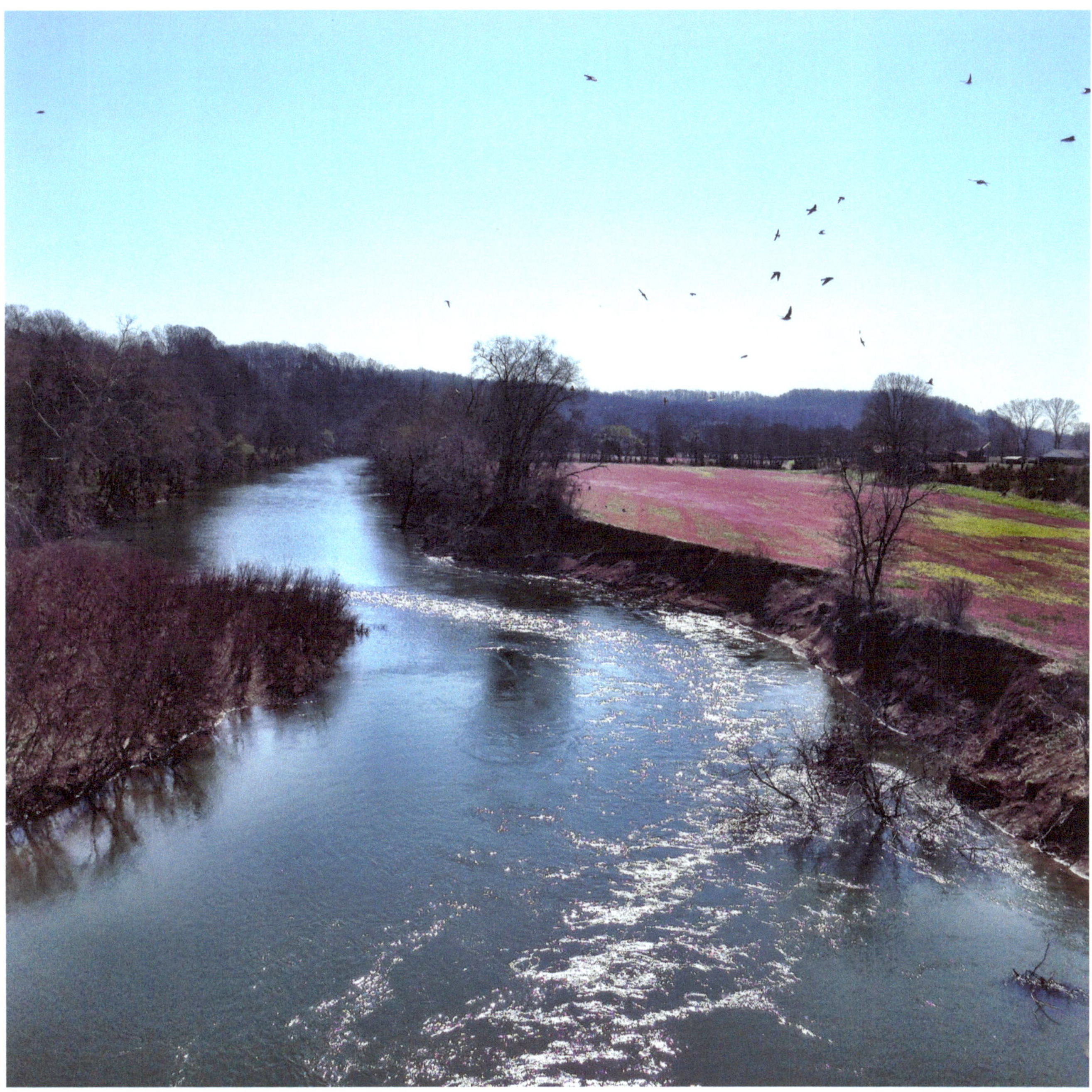

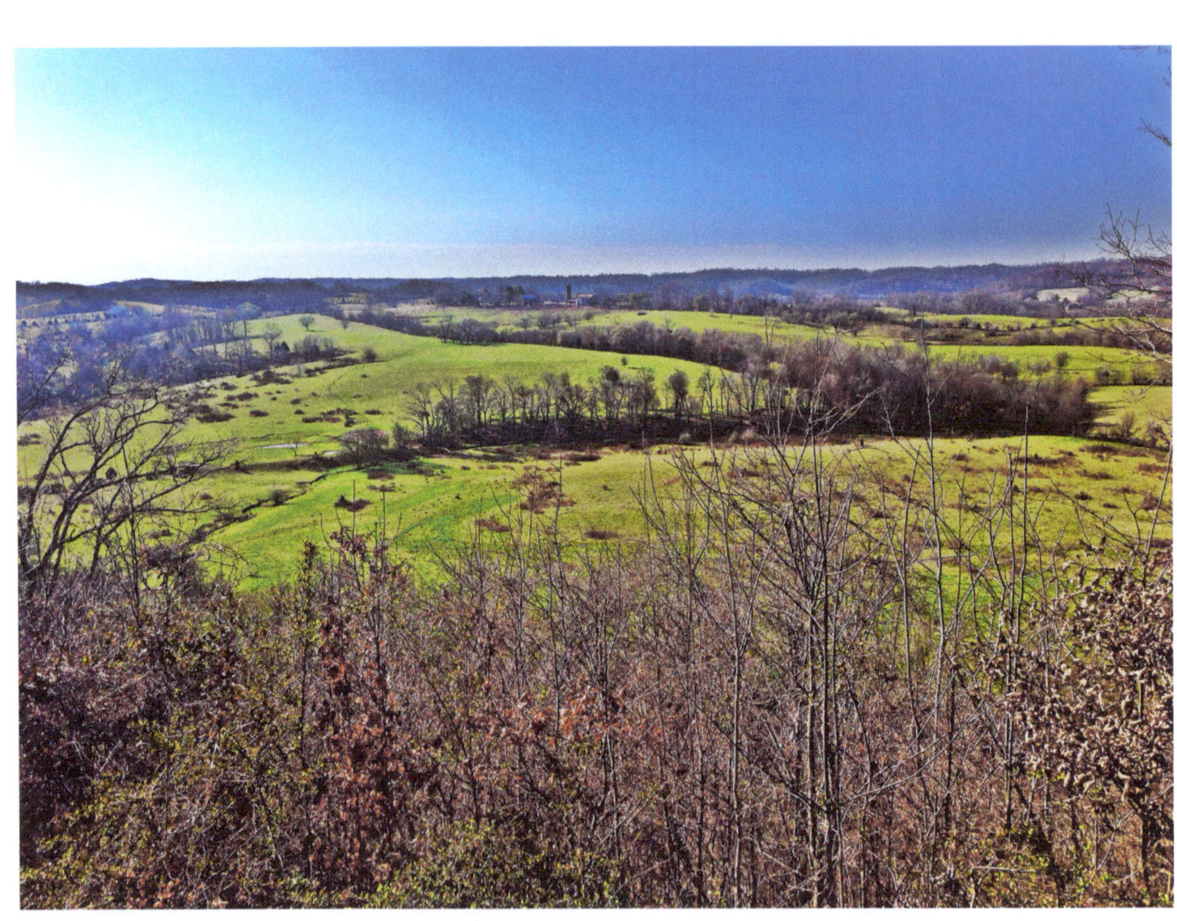

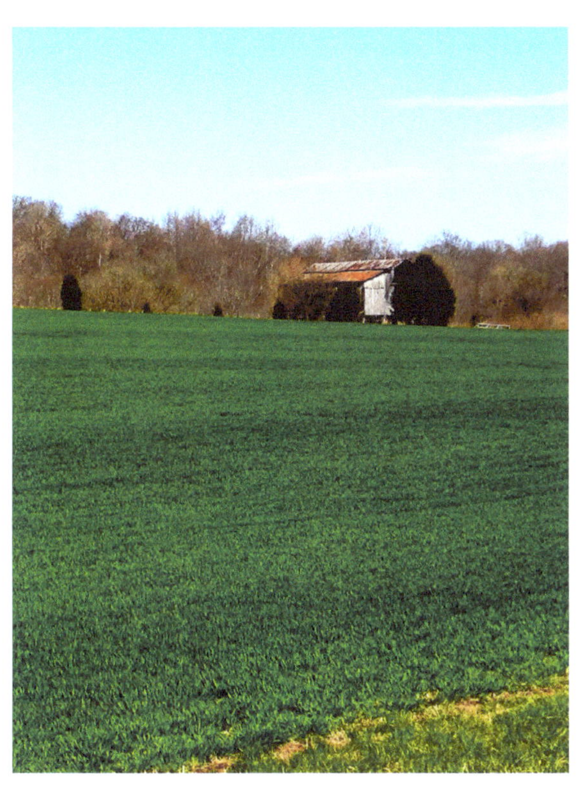

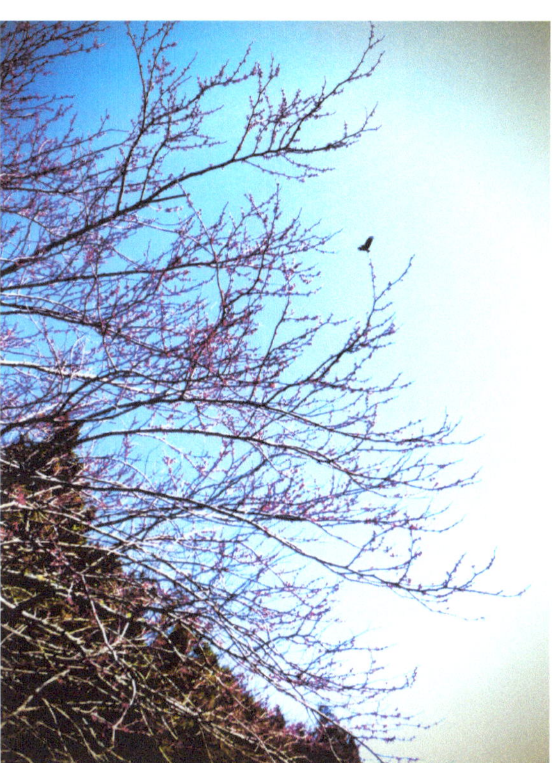

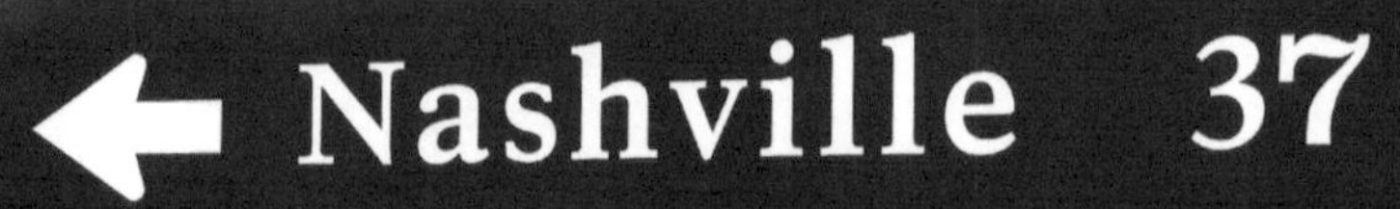
Nashville 37
Tupelo, MS 169

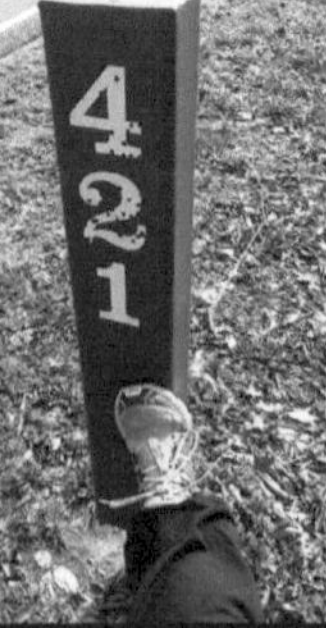
421

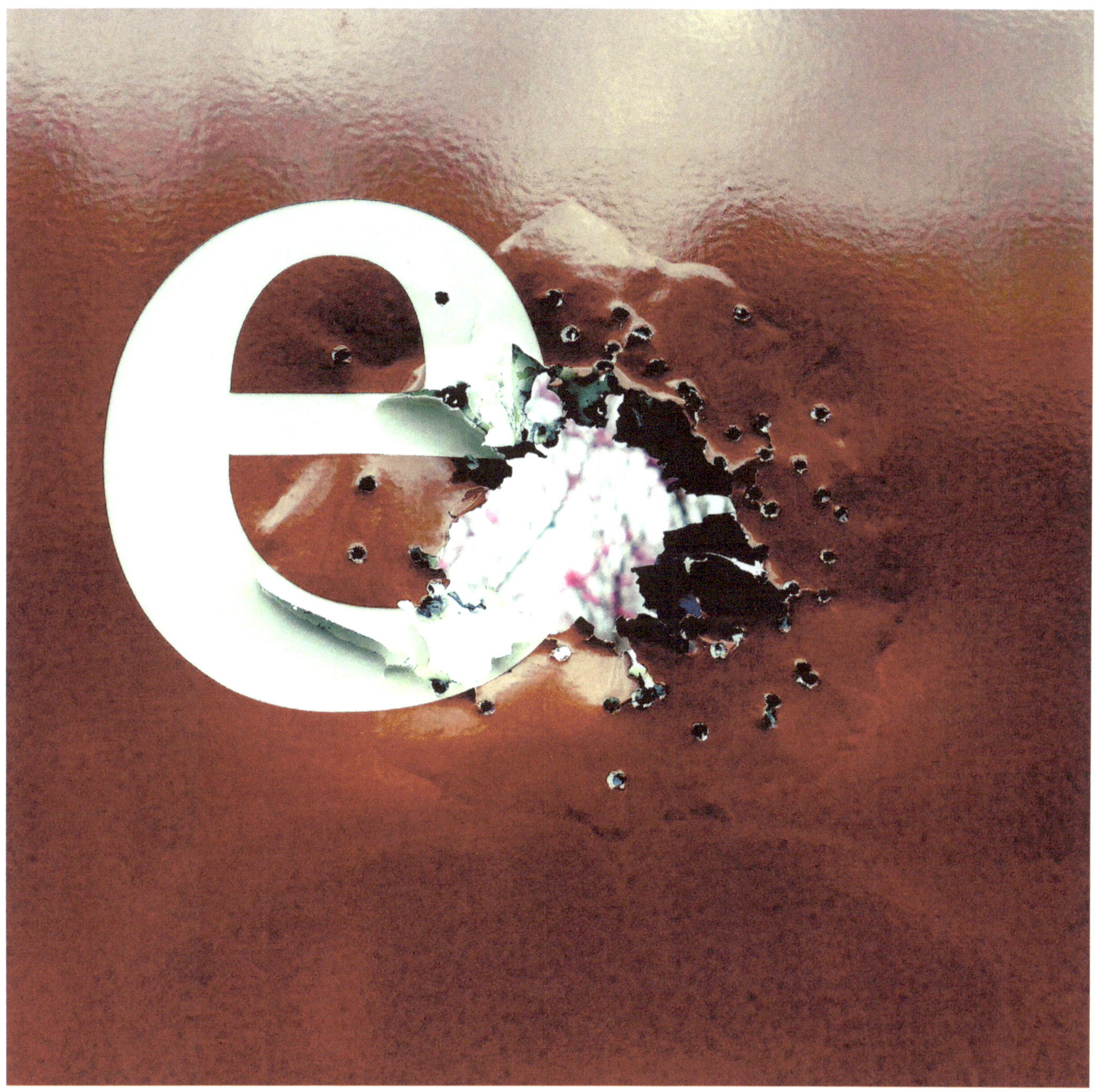

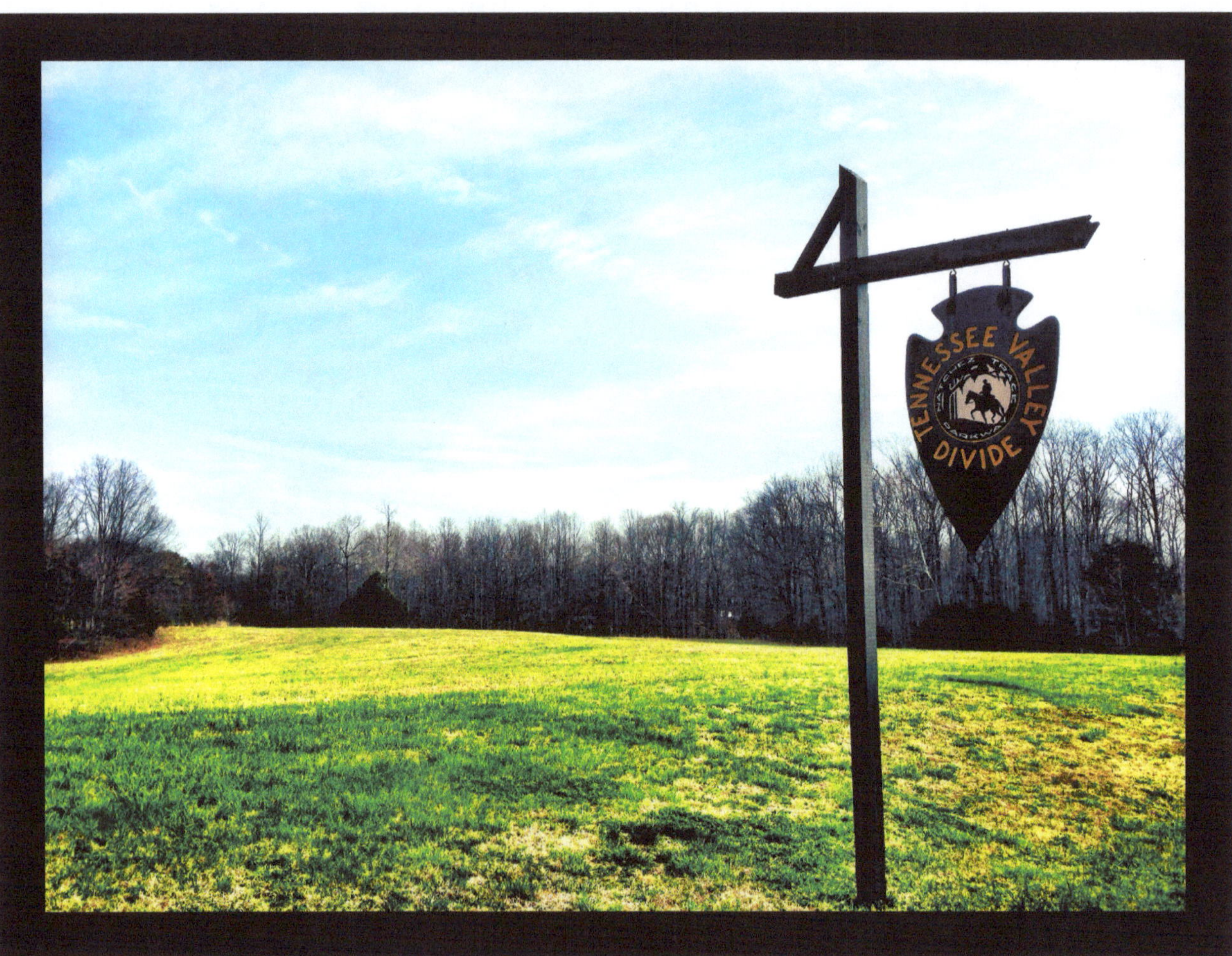
TENNESSEE VALLEY
DIVIDE

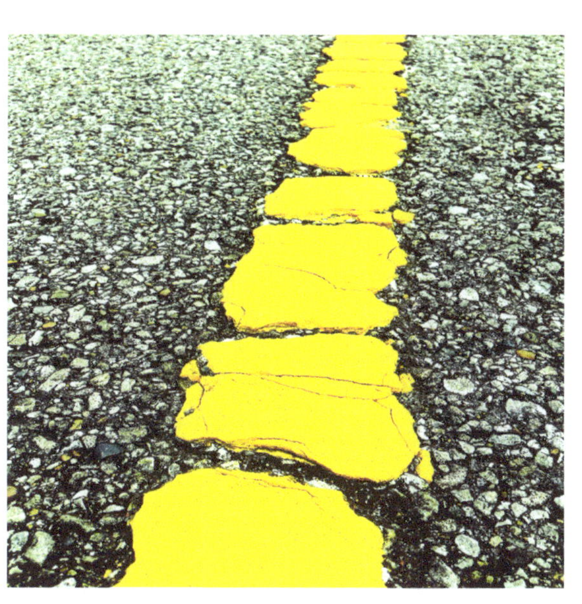

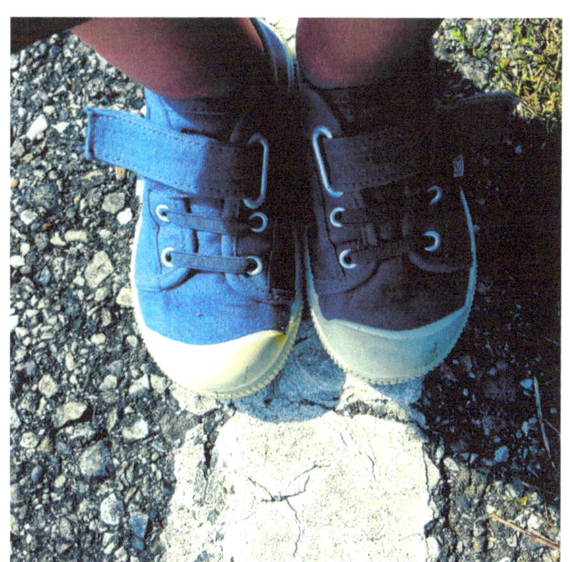

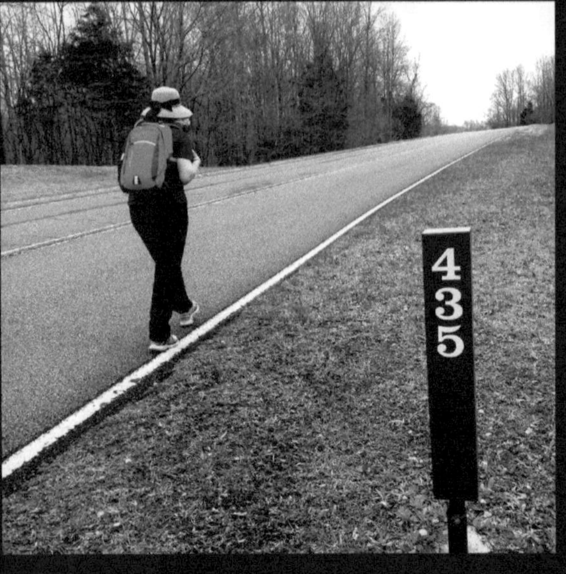
435

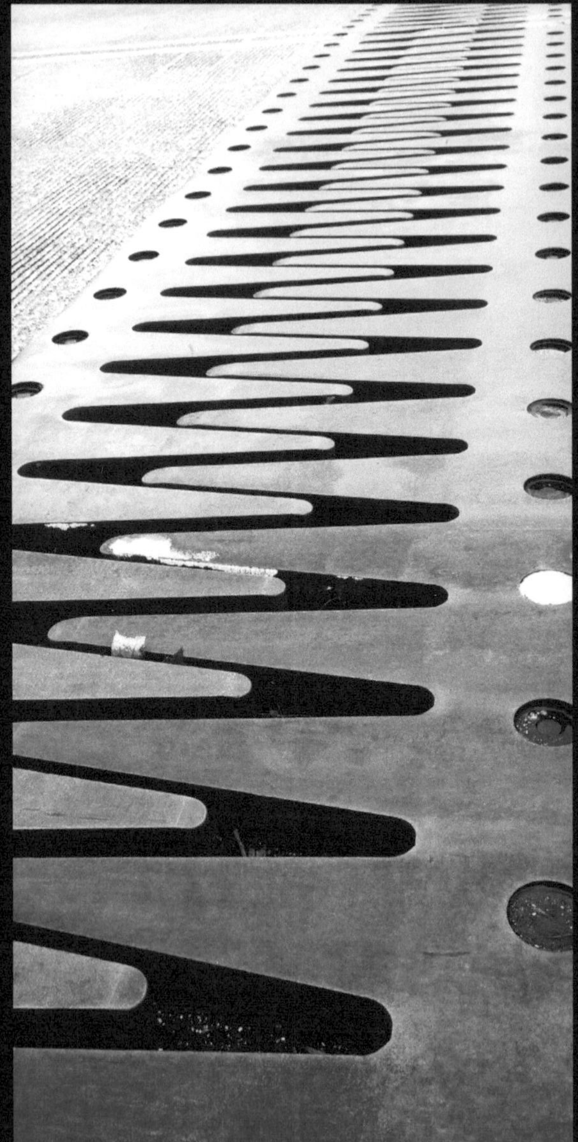

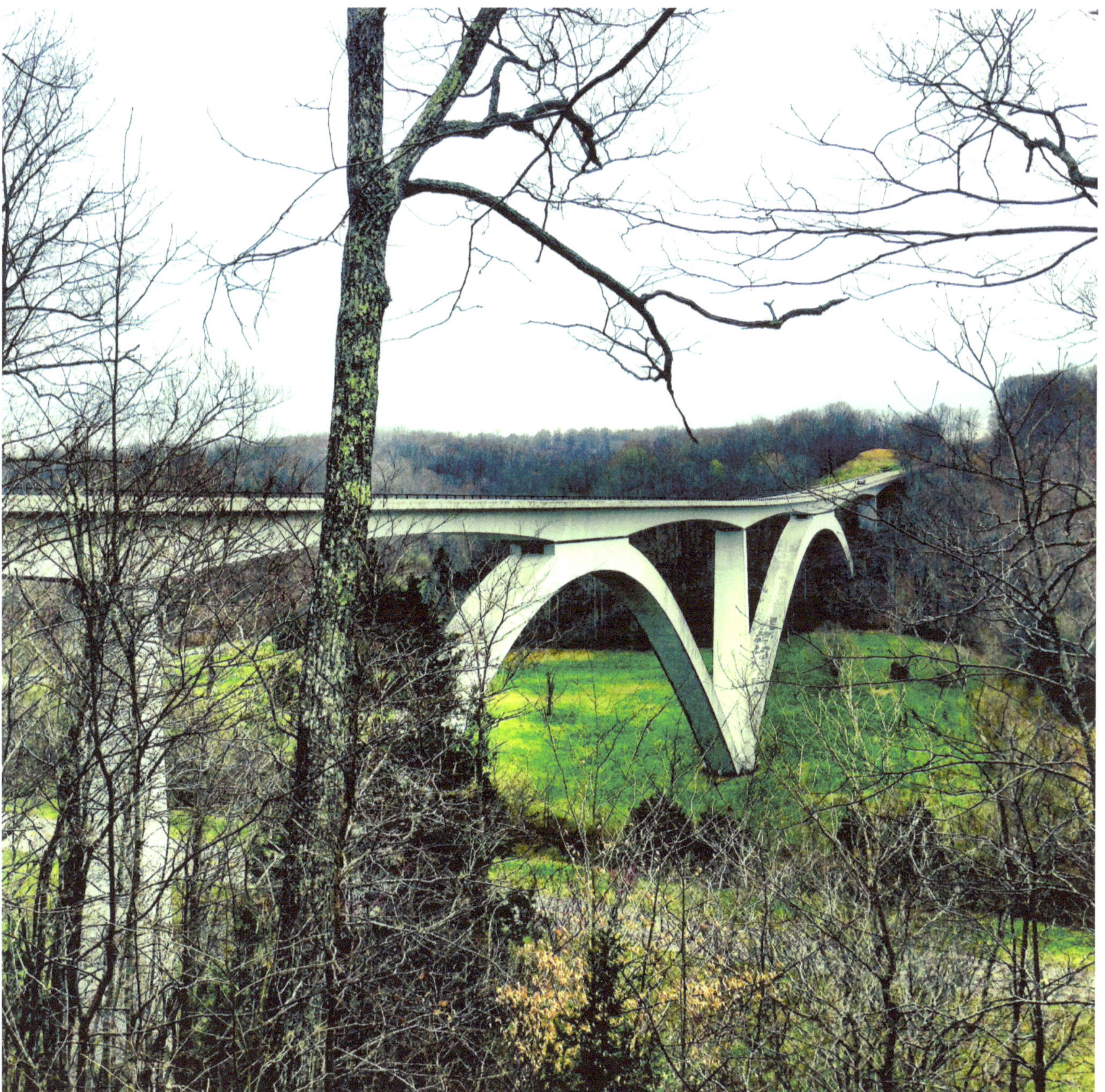

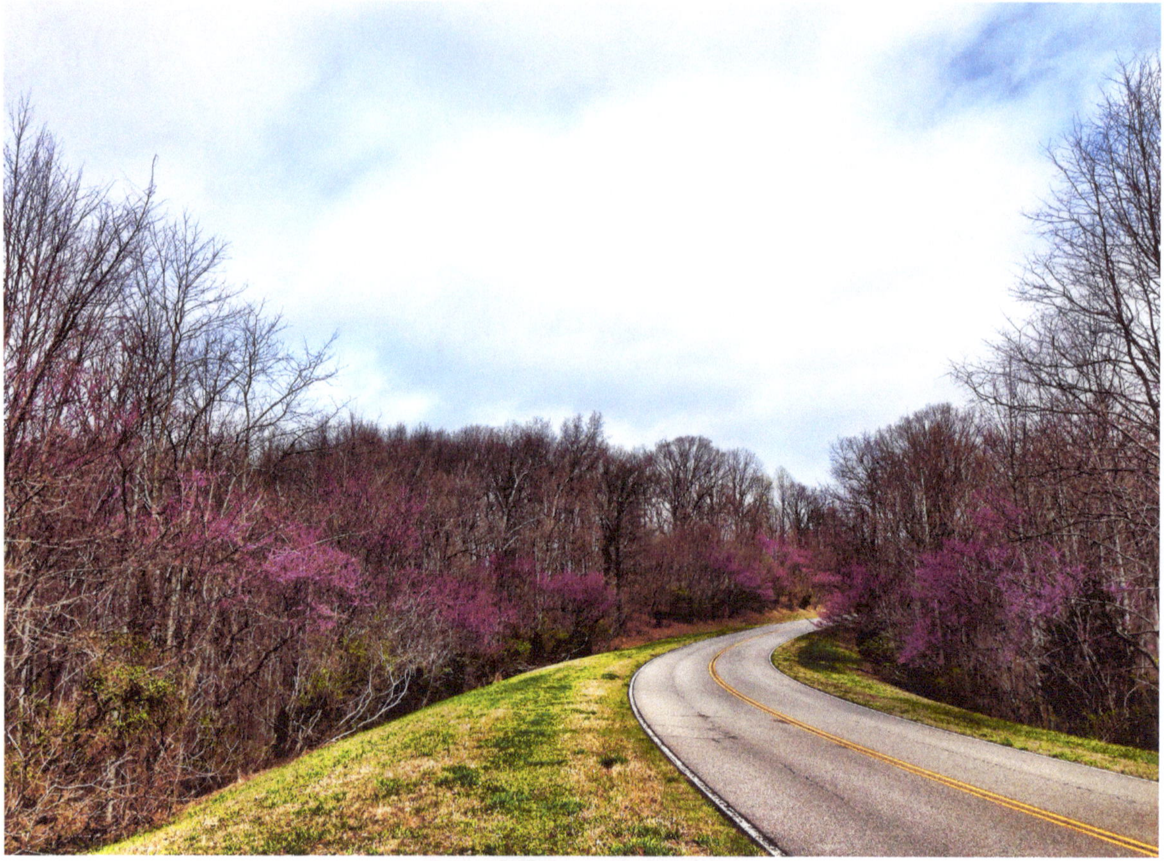

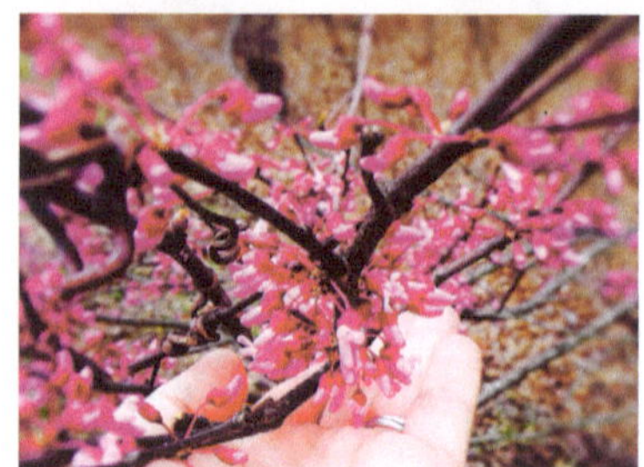

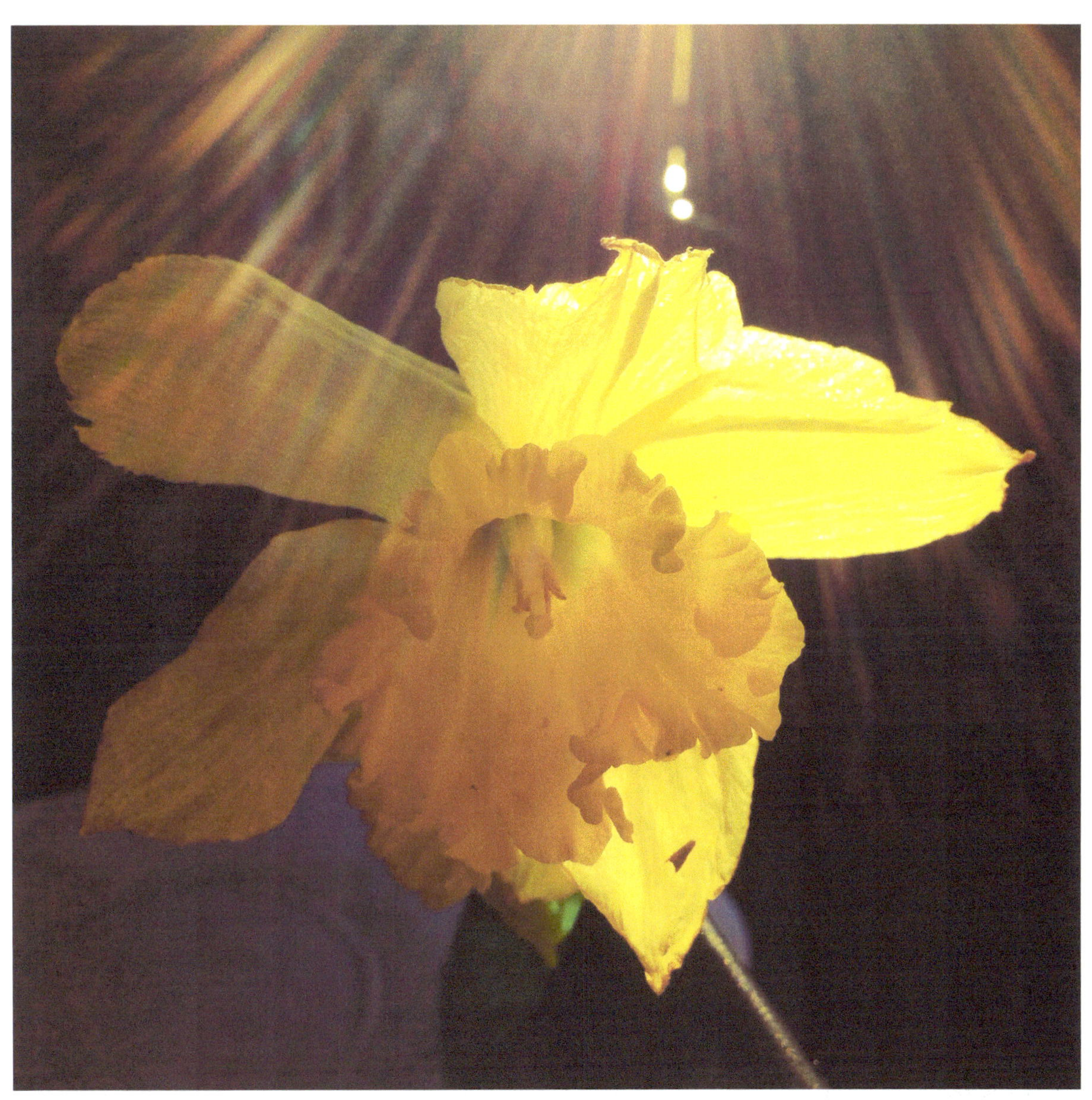

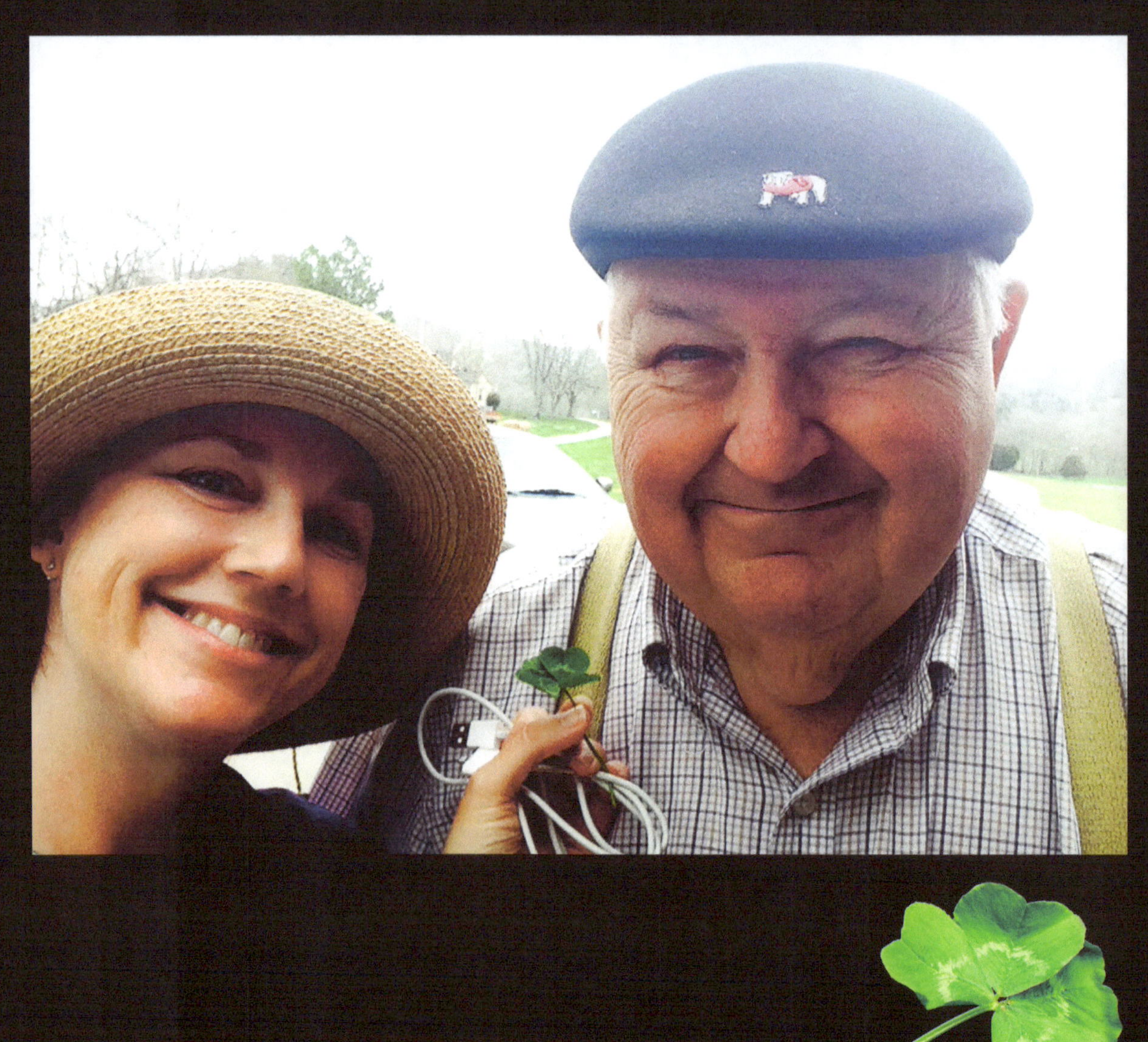

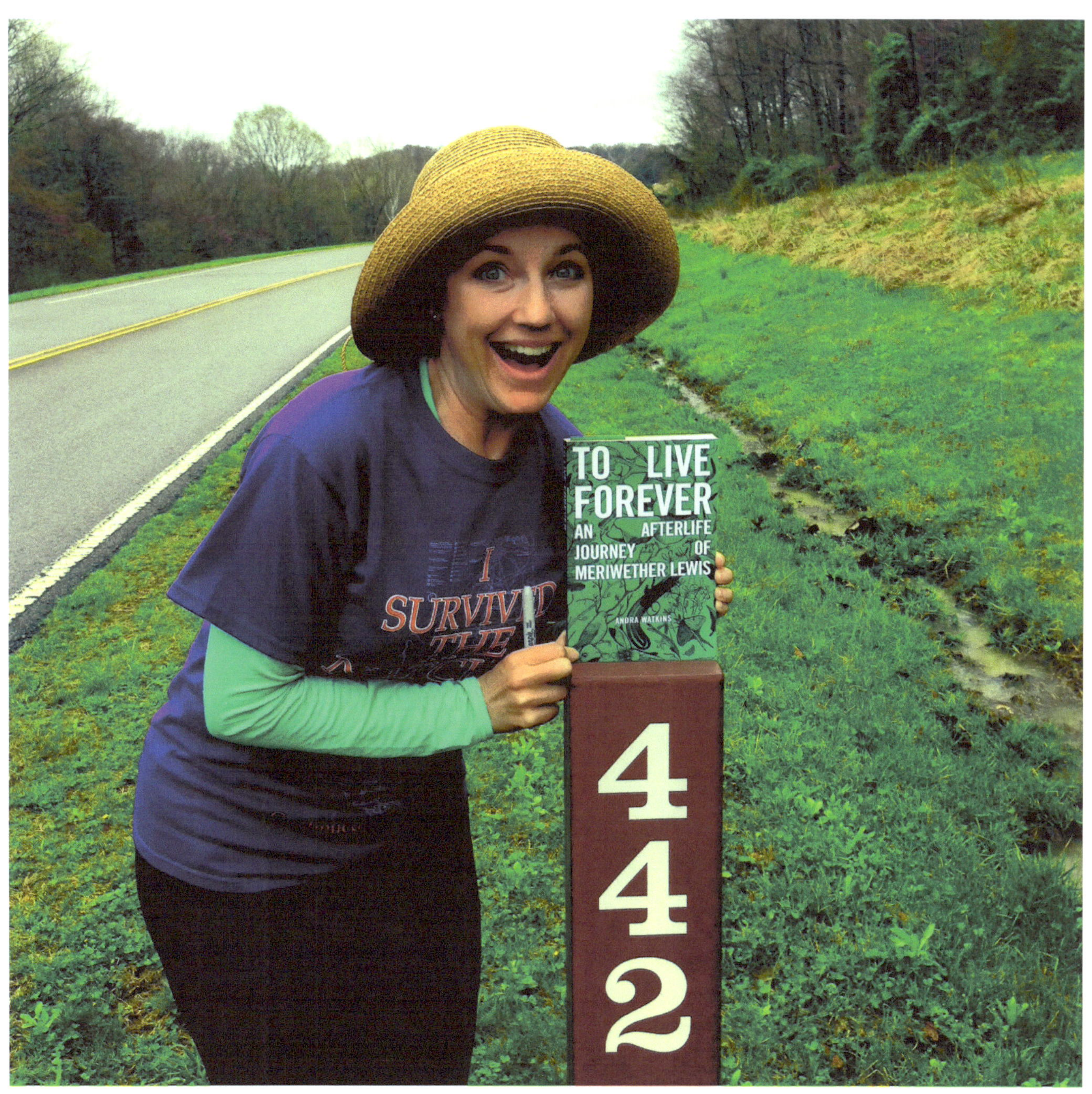
TO LIVE FOREVER
AN AFTERLIFE JOURNEY OF MERIWETHER LEWIS
ANDRA WATKINS
I SURVIVED THE
442

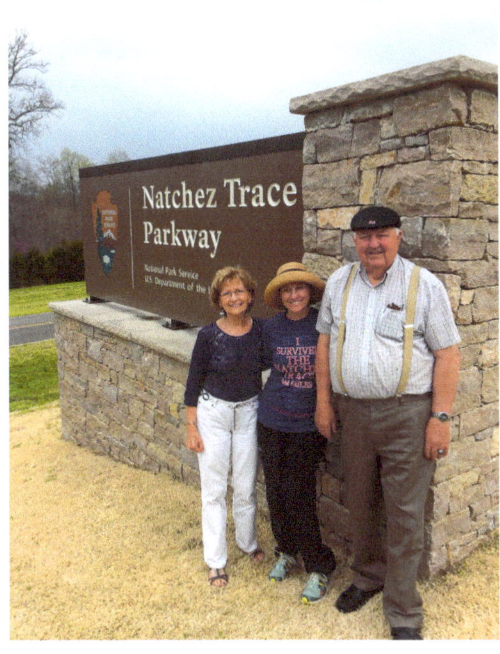

What did I expect to feel as I walked through a wooden gate and hoisted my foot onto milepost 442, the end of the Natchez Trace?

I couldn't feel anything. For the first time in five weeks, nothing hurt. My body was numb. But my mind buzzed with the trip's revelations about Mom. About Dad. About myself. My heart overflowed with joy. "I'd like to go to that big stone sign a couple of miles back and take some pictures."

I wasn't ready to say goodbye to the Natchez Trace.

We drove through misting rain. When I looked into the trees, I was transported to points on the Trace's 10,000 year timeline. I focused on hardwood and leaves and slivers of sky, and for a few seconds, if I closed my eyes, I traveled through Time.

For 442 miles, I tried to honor the countless men who walked the Natchez Trace, alone or in packs, to build the frontier states of the USA. I listened to the voices of Native Americans who were displaced. "See what we did?" They whispered from ancient mounds and buried places. Quebecois French mingled with conquistador Spanish on the wings of thousands of migrating birds. I heard sounds I didn't recognize, rhythms I never expected.

And, at the end, I only had one plea. I hoped the Trace seared us into its soul. When people traveled it in a thousand years, maybe a few of them would hear my parents and me. In fallen leaves and birdsong. In the echo of their own footsteps. In a field of daffodils winking in the breeze.

I stood next to the Natchez Trace Parkway sign, flanked by my parents. When I smiled into the camera, with one arm around each of them, I made one final addendum. I wanted to recall every molecule of our adventure. The sound of my father's laugh. How my mother said my name. Through tears, I hugged my parents and branded them into the corridors of my brain.

Because when someone remembers us, we live forever.

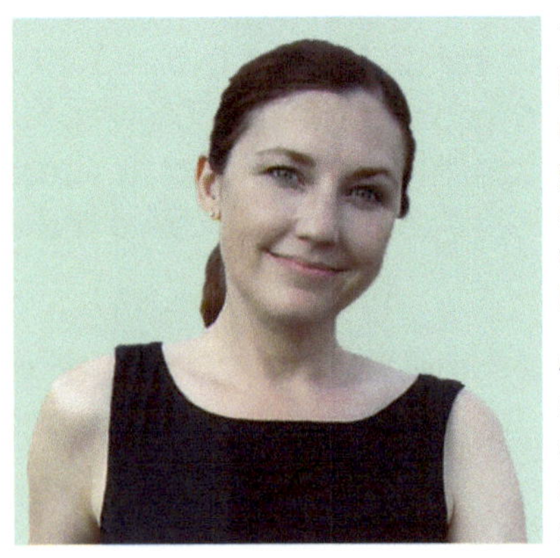

The Huffington Post says "Andra Watkins will soon explode on the literary scene with her captivating storytelling, and her sweet and occasionally oh-so-perfectly-salty Southern charm." Her memoir garnered five stars from *Portland Book Review.* A sought-after speaker, Andra's events compel attendees to Make a Memory that will change their lives. If you have an opportunity to meet Andra, DON'T MISS IT.

Andra lives in Charleston, South Carolina, and can be contacted at andrawatkins.com. A non-practicing CPA with a degree in accounting from Francis Marion University, she's still mad at her mother for refusing to let her major in musical theater because her mom was convinced she'd end up starring in porn films.

"One literary ride you don't want to miss!" -*The Huffington Post*

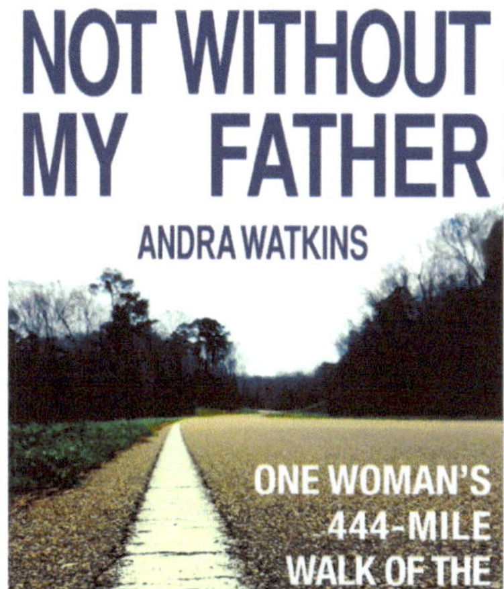

Can an epic adventure succeed without a hero? Andra Watkins needed a wingman to help her be one of the only living persons to walk the historic 444-mile Natchez Trace as the pioneers did. She planned to walk fifteen miles a day. For thirty-four days. After striking out with everyone in her life, she was left with her disinterested eighty-year-old father. And his gas. The sleep apnea machine and self-scratching. Sharing a bathroom with a man whose gut obliterated his aim.

As Watkins trudged America's forgotten highway, she lost herself in despair and pain. Nothing happened as planned, and her tenuous connection to her father started to unravel. Through arguments and laughter, tears and fried chicken, they fought to rebuild their relationship before it was too late. Watkins invites readers to join her dysfunctional family adventure in a humorous and heartbreaking memoir that asks if one can turn *I wish I had* into *I'm glad I did*.

Not Without My Father: One Woman's 444-Mile Walk of the Natchez Trace is available in paperback or e.book from: Ingram Book Company; Baker & Taylor; Barnes & Noble; Amazon; iTunes; Kobo; bookstores and libraries everywhere.

"A thoroughly enjoyable reading adventure unlike any other. Give it a try....I DARE YOU!" -*Cassandra King, New York Times Bestselling Author*

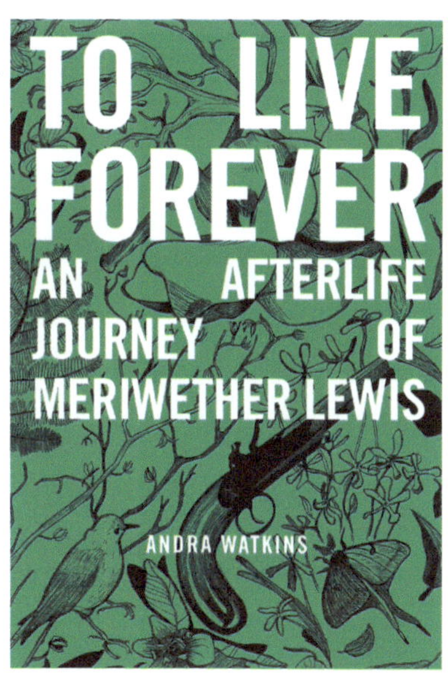

Explorer Meriwether Lewis has been stuck in Nowhere since his mysterious death nearly two centuries ago. His last hope for redemption is helping nine-year-old Emmaline Cagney flee her madame mother in New Orleans and find her father in Nashville. To get there, Merry must cross his own grave along the Natchez Trace, where he duels the corrupt Judge, an old foe who has his own despicable plans for Em.

A genre-bending novel that usually falls through the cracks as agents and publishers struggle to figure out 'what shelf does it go on?' *To Live Forever: An Afterlife Journey of Meriwether Lewis* is a rich palimpsest of history, suspense, paranormal and adventure. If you like *The Princess Bride*, you'll love this unique and original novel.

To Live Forever: An Afterlife Journey of Meriwether Lewis is available in paperback or e.book formats from: Ingram Book Company; Baker & Taylor; Barnes & Noble; Amazon; iTunes; Kobo; bookstores and libraries everywhere.

www.ingramcontent.com/pod-product-compliance
Lightning Source LLC
LaVergne TN
LVHW070125110826
845147LV00002B/190
9780990859321